D0425963

THE QUEST
FOR THE
TRUE CROSS

By the same authors:

The Jesus Papyrus

THE QUEST
FOR THE
TRUE CROSS

CARSTEN PETER THIEDE &
MATTHEW D'ANCONA

palgrave

THE QUEST FOR THE TRUE CROSS
Copyright © Carsten Peter Thiede and Matthew d'Ancona, 2000.
All rights reserved. No part of this book may be used or reproduced in any
manner whatsoever without written permission except in the case of brief
quotations embodied in critical articles or reviews.

First published 2002 by PALGRAVE™
175 Fifth Avenue, New York, N.Y. 10010
Companies and representatives throughout the world.

PALGRAVE is the new global publishing imprint of St. Martin's Press LLC
Scholarly and Reference Division and Palgrave Publishers Ltd.
(formerly Macmillan Press Ltd.).

ISBN 0-312-29424-7

Library of Congress Cataloging-in-Publication Data

Thiede, Carsten Peter.
    The quest for the true cross / Carsten Peter Thiede & Matthew
    d'Ancona.
        p. cm.
    Includes bibliographical references and index.
    ISBN 0-312-29424-7
Holy Cross. I. d'Ancona, Matthew, 1968- II. Title.

BT465.T48 2001
232.96′6—dc21   2001038757

First published in the United Kingdom in 2000 by Weidenfeld & Nicolson

First PALGRAVE edition: March 2002
10 9 8 7 6 5 4 3 2 1

Printed in the United States of America.

Dedicated to my godchildren in Britain, the United States, Switzerland and Germany – William Branton, Mark Schelbert, Laurent Schmidt, Jennifer Thiede and Michael Zopf, for their own quests in our global village.

Carsten Peter Thiede

For my parents, the hero and heroine of my life.

Matthew d'Ancona

CONTENTS

ILLUSTRATIONS

Gold medallion depicting Constantine[1]

Statue of Empress Helena at Santa Croce in Gerusalemme, Rome[2]

The crypt of St Helena, Jerusalem[2]

Pilgrims' prayers in the crypt[2]

The *Titulus* at Santa Croce in Gerusalemme, Rome[3]

Excavations behind the present church of Santa Croce in Gerusalemme[2]

The north-west façade of Santa Croce[2]

The present entrance to Santa Croce[2]

The Church of the Holy Sepulchre in Jerusalem[2]

The traditional but erroneous reconstruction of the *Titulus*[2]

The stone lid which covered the lead box of the *Titulus*[2]

The oldest, undisputed pictorial example of the Cross in a Christian context[2]

Memorial standard showing the Greek text of Constantine's vision, and the form of the Chi-Rho[2]

Silver medallion of Constantine's son Constans holding a standard with the Chi-Rho on the 'Labarum'[4]

Sources
[1] The Trustees of the British Museum
[2] C. P. Thiede
[3] Michael Hesemann
[4] Roman Museum Augst

ACKNOWLEDGEMENTS

Those who go in search of the Cross today do not face quite the same adversities as their medieval predecessors. Even so, our second collaboration as authors would have been much harder without the help and support of people all over the world.

In the scholarly community, we are indebted to Dr Leah Di Segni of the Institute of Archaeology at The Hebrew University, Jerusalem; Michael Hesemann in Düsseldorf; Professor Karl Jaros of the Institute for Oriental Studies, Vienna University; and Professor Martin Biddle of Hertford College, Oxford, who understands as well as any scholar the significance of holy sites to Christianity's beginnings. Dr Stephan Borgehammar of Uppsala University, an authority on Queen Helena, encouraged our own journey in her footsteps, as did P. Bargil Pixner, OSB, of the Theological Faculty of the Hagia Maria Sion Abbey, Jerusalem.

At the Vatican, Professor Walter Brandmueller, President of the Pontifical Committee of Historical Sciences, gave freely of his time, and unlocked many doors in Rome, physical and intellectual. We are greatly in his debt. The late Dr Timothy Potter, Keeper of the Department of Prehistoric and Romano-British Antiquities at the British Museum in London, stimulated our investigations time and again.

Several of the chapters of this book were written at All Souls College, Oxford, where the Warden and Fellows provided generous hospitality and a workplace of unrivalled tranquillity. In Edinburgh, Giles Gordon showed yet again why he is the best literary agent in Britain, while his colleague at Curtis Brown, Diana Mackay, offered energetic support. At Weidenfeld & Nicolson, Ion Trewin and Rachel Leyshon were more patient than we sometimes deserved, and made a host of intelligent suggestions.

Moral support was forthcoming from many quarters, not least

from John Patten, Alice Thomson and Simon Heffer. At the *Sunday Telegraph,* the Editor Dominic Lawson was supportive of his Deputy's quest for a 2,000-year-old scoop. Chris Anderson provided friendship and encouragement, as did Con Coughlin, himself an author of distinction on Jerusalem and its mysteries. It is no exaggeration to say that this book would not have appeared without the generosity and organisational genius of Jules Amis.

Matthew d'Ancona owes an immeasurable debt to Sarah Schaefer for her unfailing love and inspiration. Our families remain the foundation of all we do.

Carsten Peter Thiede
Matthew d'Ancona
Lent 2000

And when he had called the people unto him with his disciples also, he said unto them, Whosoever will come after me, let him deny himself, and take up his cross, and follow me.

St Mark 8:34

Not every relic that is above all doubt must be false.

Hippolyte Delehaye

INTRODUCTION

Listen! I want to tell the best of dreams,
That came to me in a vision in the middle of the night,
When other people were in bed,
It seemed to me that I saw the best tree,
Lifted into the air surrounded by light.

The Dream of the Rood, ninth-century Anglo-Saxon poem

This is a book about a symbol, perhaps the most powerful symbol in the history of the world. It is also a book about the sacred object which that symbol is said to represent and an exploration of the moment in history when one became the other. It is an argument about the threads which link history and belief, and the role of scholarship in making those threads visible and intelligible. It is an investigation of a period of fundamental change in the history of the West, when a Roman emperor and his mother grasped the uses of Christianity, its roots in recorded events, physical objects and visible sites. It is also a record of a voyage – and a discovery.

The idea came to us – as so many ideas have come to so many authors – in Jerusalem. Two years after the publication of our first book, *The Jesus Papyrus*, we found ourselves in the Holy City filming an American television documentary on the claims it advanced – claims which had already generated an extraordinary international debate. It was the bold, and in some eyes foolhardy, contention of our previous book that the earliest surviving New Testament papyri provided strong evidence that the Gospels had been written by contemporaries or near con-temporaries of Jesus, and that at least two fragments, one from St Mark and the other from St Matthew, could be dated, using

the most sophisticated forensic technology, to the early Sixties
AD and perhaps earlier.[1]

We argued that the so-called 'tunnel' separating the life of Jesus
from the work of the Evangelists was short, perhaps years rather
than decades, and that it was therefore wrong to assume that their
recollections were faulty or fabricated. We dared to suggest, on the
basis of forensic evidence rather than conjecture, that the first
readers of the Gospels could conceivably have heard the sermons
recorded in these ancient books. *The Jesus Papyrus* ended by
advancing the possibility of a 'new paradigm' in early Church
scholarship, which would question the seductions of liberal orthodoxy and look afresh at early Christian tradition, reassess archaeological and documentary evidence, and apply all available
forensic and scientific methods to it.

This book is not a sequel to *The Jesus Papyrus*, although it
aspires to similar goals. In Jerusalem on that blisteringly hot
afternoon, we took refuge in the cool of the Church of the Holy
Sepulchre, and there watched one of the most venerable and most
mysterious rituals of the Christian world. It was 5.30 p.m. and a
procession of Armenian monks followed the Franciscans with
whom, along with a community of Copts, they share this sacred
complex of buildings. The two orders sang their different chants,
each competing with the other until the vestibule of the Crusader
church was filled with a strange and haunting polyphony. The
monks proceeded down a flight of stairs to the Chapel of St Helena,
mother of the Emperor Constantine, to celebrate mass. Fabulously
ornate, the chapel was already packed with pilgrims from all over
the world, awaiting a service which had been heard on countless
days by countless of their predecessors. As the music curled
through the cool air of the Crusader church, towards the courtyard
where tourists milled with cameras, everything fell still for a
moment.

After the final benediction, some of the worshippers ventured
further into the bowels of the church to a much older crypt, carved
no more carefully than an ancient cistern, a place of silent prayer
almost completely unadorned by liturgical objects and decoration.
In the stillness of this little subterranean room it was hard to
believe we were in one of the most divided and violent cities in the

world. Here, according to tradition, the Empress Helena found – or rediscovered – the ancient wood of the True Cross: the *lignum crucis*, the surviving fragments of the Tree of Life, the wood grown from the seed cast on the soil of Eden. And here it was, as the pilgrims ascended the stairs towards daylight and the throng of Jerusalem's Arab quarter, that our own quest began. What, we wondered, had actually happened here more than 1600 years ago? Was there any respectable evidence for the legend of Helena's discovery? Were there any surviving fragments of what she is said to have found? And what might have been the significance of the Cross to the earliest Christians, not only as a sacred symbol but as a physical object worthy of their veneration?

Like Helena, we have travelled far in pursuit of answers. Our quest has taken us all over Europe, from Rome where the church of Santa Croce in Gerusalemme now stands on the site of the Empress's Palace, to Trier, her other headquarters, to sites all over the Holy Land where early evidence of the Cross as a symbol of ancient Christian veneration is to be found. No less than those fourth-century pilgrims who collected alleged fragments of the True Cross, our task has been not only to sift the real from the bogus but to make sense of the whole. Our purpose has been to construct a plausible history of the Cross, as well as to challenge the (astonishingly rigid) view that the entire Helena legend is, by definition, nonsense.

Edward Gibbon wrote that Helena 'appears to have united the credulity of age with the warm feelings of a recent conversion'.[2] We would argue that much contemporary scholarship on this subject is guilty of a different kind of credulity, a zealous readiness to dismiss ancient tradition as rubbish, as if the only purpose of legend were to distort and conceal the truth. As we shall suggest, the function of tradition in ancient societies was very much more subtle and bears little relation to the residual role played by folklore in the modern world. Just as the value of the Gospels as historical record has been gravely underestimated since the Enlightenment, so the reconstruction of the early Christian world from surviving legends and archaeological evidence has been hampered by a pathological scepticism verging on the unscholarly. It is true that the first Christian writers did not always mean exactly what they said; that does not mean that everything they said was untrue or ungrounded in some sort of reality.

This book is an unashamedly radical work of revisionism. It attacks the major premise of accepted thinking on its subject: that the Cross only became a significant Christian symbol *after* Constantine and Helena, and that the importance of this symbol in our civilization is an almost exclusively Constantinian achievement. We suggest that the centrality of the Cross to the life of the Church goes back to its earliest days and that its image was widely venerated by Christians in Palestine much earlier than has been acknowledged. We suggest that this cult had an unabashedly *physical* dimension and that the earliest worshippers flocked to the site of the crucifixion even when it was covered over by a pagan temple. When Helena came to Jerusalem in AD 326, she was responding to a local tradition, as well as founding an imperial one. She was not the first pilgrim to seek the True Cross, only the most important.

At the heart of our quest is one of the most extraordinary – and extraordinarily neglected – objects in Christian civilization: the *Titulus Crucis* now in the reliquary of Santa Croce in Gerusalemme, the alleged headboard from the True Cross bearing part of the inscription beneath which Jesus died. It has sometimes been remarked upon *en passant* that this remarkable object has never been the subject of a full scholarly study; oddly, however, none of those who have observed this deficiency have done anything about it.[3] Chapters 4 and 5 of this book constitutes the first comprehensive scholarly analysis of the *Titulus* – and draws startling conclusions about the possible origins of this forgotten artefact. It is our conviction that it is no less worthy of attention and debate than the Turin Shroud itself.

For almost two thousand years men and women have dreamt of the Cross, each putting his or her own construction on its apparently indelible image. Our quest in this book is to discover the historical origins of their dreams.

I

The Tree of Life:
A Brief History of the Cross

They took Jesus, and led him away and he bearing his cross
went forth into a place called the place of the skull, which
is called in the Hebrew Golgotha.

St John 19:16–17

The cross alone is our theology.

Martin Luther

Mythology is the study of whatever religious or heroic
legends are so foreign to a student's experience that he
cannot believe them to be true.

Robert Graves

In Western civilization the Cross has been, in every sense, the
stuff of legend. Even today, it is much the most recognizable
religious symbol in the world. Its spiritual significance continues
to attract scholarly attention. Its influence is visible in architecture, artistic iconography, church liturgy, religious decoration,
the insignia people wear and the signs they adopt to signify their
peaceful intentions. No symbol has ever exercised such power,
subtle and less subtle, over the human mind.[1]

Over the centuries, however, and particularly since the Enlightenment, interest in the physical object which that symbol
allegedly represents has dwindled. The fixation of the sixteenth-
century Protestant reformer Martin Luther with the profound
theological significance of the Cross – inspired by his ancestral
master St Paul – has ensured its prosperity as a religious sign in
the post-Reformation world. Thus did Luther explain his inter-

pretation of the meaning of the Cross in his *Heidelberg Disputation* (1518):

> The cross teaches us to believe in hope even when there is no hope.
> The wisdom of the cross is hidden deeply in a profound mystery. In
> fact, there is no other way to heaven than taking up the cross of Christ.
> On account of this we must beware that the active life with its good
> works, and the contemplative life with its speculations, do not lead us
> astray. Both are most attractive and give peace of mind, but for that
> very reason hide real dangers, unless they are tempered by the cross
> and disturbed by adversaries. The cross is the surest path of all. Blessed
> is the man who understands this truth.[2]

But Luther's implacably sceptical attitude to holy relics has proved
no less influential in the forming of the modern mind. As important
as the great Protestant reformer believed the Cross to be, he
despised the veneration of allegedly authentic relics almost as
much as he despised the credulity of those who traded in them
and trusted their talismanic power. Luther's contribution to the
history of the True Cross was to make it unrespectable for future
scholars to speculate about the origins and possible survival of
such artefacts.

In so doing, Luther effectively buried a rich tradition of legend,
myth-making and scholarly enquiry. His forebears had been in no
doubt that the physical remains of the Cross – or at least parts of
them – had survived the crucifixion of Jesus, and had plotted their
provenance and fate with all the obsessive energy that the pre-
Enlightenment mind could muster.

By Luther's time the whereabouts of the True Cross had been
unknown for almost four centuries. After Helena's great excavation, the main portion of the *Vera Crux* was held in the custody
of the Bishop of Jerusalem and displayed only at the most exalted
religious ceremonies. In 614, however, the Persian General
Shahrbaraz entered Palestine on behalf of King Chosroes II and
forced his way into the Holy City on 5 May of that year. In the
carnage that followed 60,000 were said to have perished and a
further 35,000 sold into bondage; the Holy Sepulchre was razed
and the True Cross sent as a gift to the Christian Queen of Persia,

Meryem. Its captivity was not to last long, however. In 627, the Emperor Heraclius I defeated the Persians at Nineveh and returned the Holy Cross to Jerusalem in triumph.

In the centuries which followed the physical reality of the Cross continued to exercise an unyielding grip on the imagination of Christendom. Fragments of the original – real or faked – were sought after by noblemen and religious houses alike as a means of enhancing their influence. In 569, for example, the arrival of one such relic at the monastery of Poitiers inspired Venantius Fortunatus to compose his celebrated hymns in honour of the Cross 'Vexilla regis prodeunt' and 'Pange, lingua, gloriosi cer-taminis', versions of which are still sung today. The composition of the great Anglo-Saxon poem The Dream of the Rood has been linked, likewise, to King Alfred's receipt of a fragment of the True Cross from Pope Marinus in 884. Few poems in any language communicate so forcefully the power of a single image to conquer hearts and minds across an entire continent. The writer of The Dream speaks of a profoundly mystical experience, but it is the apparent physical reality of his vision – its sensory side – which astonishes him most:

> It seemed to me that I saw the best tree,
> Lifted into the air surrounded by light,
> The brightest of trees. The whole symbol was
> Covered with gold; beautiful jewels stood
> At the surface of the earth, and also five were
> On the crossbeam.[3]

There is no evidence that this anonymous writer, any more than Cynewulf who wrote the great Anglo-Saxon poem on the Empress, Elene, had made the pilgrimage to see the True Cross.[4] What is clear, however, is that the mysticism of both writers was closely connected with an absolute conviction in the material reality of the Cross – which all educated men knew had been recovered by Helena and was kept in Jerusalem, the holiest of cities.

But in 1187 it was lost again, this time for good. The Crusader kings had made a practice of taking the Cross with them to the battlefield, both as an inspiration to their own armies but also as a talismanic weapon against the infidel foe. Baldwin I had carried it before his troops as he rode to defeat the army of the Egyptian vizier at Ramleh and thereafter it became as important to the Crusaders as the Ark of the Covenant had been to the Hebrews. As one historian of the Crusades has put it: 'It had been, for the soldiers and their leaders, the Holy of Holies to be defended to the bitter end, giving victory or comfort in defeat.'[5]

This made its capture an essential objective for the Sultan Saladin (1137/8–93) in his reconquest of Jerusalem after its eighty-eight-year occupation by the Franks. In July 1187 the Frankish army marched to Hattin on the plain of Galilee to meet the invaders, resembling, according to Saladin's private secretary al-Imad, 'a mountain on the move, a sea of tumbling, foaming waves'. At the heart of this iron-clad ocean was the Bishop of Acre, carrying the True Cross above the head of his horse. At dawn on 4 July battle was joined as, according to al-Imad, the Franks charged:

> The burning sky sharpened their fury; the cavalry charged in wave after wave among the floating mists of the mirage and the torments of thirst with fire in the wind and anxiety in their hearts. These dogs hung out their arched tongues and howled under the blows. They hoped to reach the water, but before them was hell with its flames and intolerable heat overcame them.[6]

The Franks were defeated by thirst, as well as their own internal divisions, and Saladin was victorious. Among the dead was the Bishop of Acre and with him the Cross had gone. Once again, the Christian world had lost its most precious relic.[7] Richard the Lionheart tried later to recover it in the 1190s, as did the Queen of Georgia who offered a 200,000 dinars ransom. But the Cross was not to be returned at any cost. Myths swirled around its eventual fate; it was said that the Templars had buried it somewhere, perhaps in the Holy Land, perhaps in France. Three centuries later the Christians of Constantinople claimed to have the wood in their possession, but to no avail. As far as Christendom was concerned, the *Vera Crux* had been lost for ever on the field of Hattin.

This did not, however, diminish fascination with the origin of the Cross and its history. Of the detectives who pursued this question, much the most celebrated was Jacobus da Voragine, the thirteenth-century religious encyclopaedist, whose compilation of miraculous events and saints' lives, *The Golden Legend*, was one of the most influential best-sellers of its time. According to Jacobus, the wood from which Jesus would one day hang had its origins in the earliest human history. An angel had given Seth, son of Adam, a branch from the tree under which his father had committed his sin and 'informed him that when that branch bore fruit, his father would be made whole'. Seth planted the branch over Adam's grave, where it grew – and still stood in Solomon's time. The great king so admired its beauty that he had it cut down and used it in the construction of a bridge across a pond. Its sacredness, however, was only properly grasped by the Queen of Sheba who, *The Golden Legend* reports, 'saw in spirit that the Saviour of the world would one day hang upon this very same wood'.

Later, Jacobus reports, the wood re-emerged to perform its terrible task in the history of men. 'When Christ's time to suffer was drawing near,' he wrote, 'the aforesaid wood floated up to the surface of the pond, and the Jews, seeing it, used it in making the Lord's cross. It is said that the cross was made out of four kinds of wood, namely, palmwood, cedar, cypress and olivewood.' The final phase of the legend was the rediscovery of the Cross by the Empress Helena (a story which we address in chapters 2 and 3), the moment when the story, which began with Adam's disobedience and ended with man's redemption, was revealed to the wider world – a story whose integrity was embodied in the continuous presence of the sacred wood. To this day, the skull of Golgotha is said to represent the skull of Adam in which the seed to the Tree of Eternal Life first took root.

Jacobus was a devotional writer and a fabulist rather than an historian. His account of the Emperor Constantine's battles is hopelessly confused and he is even unsure whether the Roman general he is writing about is the Emperor himself or 'Constantine's father, also named Constantine' (here Jacobus is wrong again – his father's name was Constantius, nicknamed 'Chlorus'). He also invents a 'Pope Eusebius' – presumably a muddled reference to Eusebius of Caesarea, the Emperor's biographer. The value of *The Golden Legend* in this context is not that it tells us much about the history of the True Cross; rather that it tells about the fascination of Jacobus's readers with the physical reality of the cruciform and their appetite for stories – however implausible and confected – about its physical ancestry. For them, the iconic significance of the Cross and the artefact itself were inextricable. Where this wood had come from and where it went were at the heart of their concerns and the essence of their curiosity. The purpose of this chapter is to ask what, exactly, they were curious about.

The first Christians were thought by the ancients to be mad because of their apparently demented belief that a crucified man should have divine status. As Justin Martyr put it in his Apology: 'They say that our madness consists in the fact that we put a crucified man in second place after the unchangeable and eternal. God, the creator of the world.' In his First Letter to the Corinthians, St Paul says that to some observers the 'message of the cross' was mere 'foolishness'. This sense of distaste was no doubt one reason why Suetonius, like so many of his contemporaries, considered the Christian teaching to be a 'new and pernicious superstition'.[8]

It is hard, indeed, to exaggerate the force of this paradox as it must have seemed to ancient eyes. Crucifixion was considered gruesome not only in the barbaric suffering it caused its victims but also in what it said about their lowly social and moral status. In his speech *In Verrem*, Cicero describes crucifixion as the '*summum supplicium*' – the 'worst punishment'. It was a penalty for slaves, murderers, traitors and heretics, an horrific act of public humiliation, as well as a slow means of execution. Quintilian, in the *Declamationes minores*, argues that crucifixions should be held in the busiest places because their deterrent value is so great. As the New Testament historian Martin Hengel has observed:

A crucified messiah, son of God or God must have seemed a contradiction in terms to anyone, Jew, Greek, Roman, or barbarian, asked to believe such a claim, and it will certainly have been thought offensive and foolish ... for Paul and his contemporaries the cross of Jesus was not a didactic, symbolic or speculative element but a very specific and highly offensive matter which imposed a burden on the earliest Christian missionary preaching.[9]

The first Christian writers are, naturally enough, a useful source of knowledge on this method of capital punishment.[10] The nailing of victims to the wood, for instance, is mentioned explicitly in Paul's Letter to the Colossians (2:14). St John refers to the breaking of victims' bones, apparently to end their torment – although by the time the soldiers came to Jesus 'they saw that he was dead already' (John 19:33). The writer of Acts describes Jesus as 'hanged on a tree' (5:30, 10:39). The Jewish historian Josephus supplies a much more detailed account of the practice, as applied to a group of fugitives during the great Jewish rebellion:

When they were going to be taken [by the Romans], they were forced to defend themselves, and after they had fought they thought it too late to make any supplications for mercy: so they were first whipped and then tormented with all sorts of torture, before they died and were then crucified before the wall of the city. Titus felt pity for them, but as their number – given as up to five hundred a day – was too great for him to risk either letting them go or putting them under guard, he allowed his soldiers to have their way, especially as he hoped that the gruesome sight of the countless crosses might move the besieged to surrender. So the soldiers out of the rage and hatred they bore the prisoners, nailed those they caught, in different postures, to the crosses, by way of jest, and their number was so great that there was not enough room for the crosses and not enough crosses for their bodies.[11]

From such grim recollections it is possible to speculate with reasonable confidence the means used to execute Jesus and others who were crucified in first-century Palestine. Knowledge of these practices has also been enhanced by archaeological finds – not least the discovery of the Dead Sea Scrolls at Qumran in 1947. The execution method is mentioned in one of the manuscripts found in Cave 4, while the so-called Temple scroll from Cave 11, dating back to the end of the second century BC, included the following injunction:

> If a man has informed against his people and has delivered his people up to a foreign nation and has done evil to his people, you shall hang him on the tree and he shall die. ... Their bodies shall not pass the night on the tree, but you shall indeed bury them that very day, for what is hanged upon the tree is accursed by God and men.[12]

The practice to which the Qumran writer refers was probably perfected by the Persians and is certainly mentioned often by Herodotus in the fifth century BC. There is, however, some evidence of its earlier use by other peoples, including the Indians, Assyrians, Scythians, Numidians and Carthaginians. Under the Roman Empire the execution procedure seems to have been as follows: the victim was first flogged, then forced to carry the beam to the place of execution, where he was nailed to the wood with outstretched arms, hoisted up and fixed to the vertical beam. The Roman writer Seneca (c.4 BC–AD 65) noted, however, the quest for ever more horrific variants on the theme: 'I see crosses there, not just of one kind but made in many different ways: some have their victims with head down on the ground; some impale their private parts; others stretch out their arms on the gibbet.'[13]

In some cases the victim was suspended from a crossbeam connecting them at the top – the *patibulum*. In others the beams more closely resembled the letter Y – the *furca*. It is also clear that crucifixion sometimes involved nailing the victim on to a tree still rooted to the ground, a practice which Tertullian says was used by the Emperor Tiberius against certain priests.

The full horror of crucifixion has been demonstrated graphically by a discovery of ossuary remains to the north-east of Jerusalem at Givat ha-Mivtar, first unearthed in 1968.[14] In one of the caskets were found the mortal remains of an adult male, aged between twenty-four and twenty-eight and about five foot five inches tall, and marked 'Yehohanan'. The lowest part of the leg had been broken and the heel bones had been pierced by an iron nail; the nail had itself first been driven through a small piece of pistaccia or acacia wood, and then, after it had passed through the heel bones of this particular unfortunate, into an upright beam constructed from olive. Since the remains of Yehohanan are datable to the first century AD, the crucifixion practice which they reveal could hardly be more relevant to our inquiry. This, it seems highly likely, is how Jesus himself died.

At the heart of this book is a new scholarly study of the Santa Croce *Titulus* and its possible relevance to the claims of all four Gospels that an inscription was affixed to the Cross of Jesus (Matthew 27:37, Mark 15:26, Luke 23:38, John 19:19). It needs to be asked at this stage, therefore, whether such an act of sadistically theatrical humiliation would have made any sense at all within the rituals of execution as they were understood in first-century Palestine.[15]

The very fact that all four Evangelists mention the inscription is itself suggestive, for there are many details of Jesus's life and death upon which they do not agree (Matthew 27:37; Mark 15:26; Luke 23:38; John 19:19). St Matthew tells us that 'they set up over his head his accusation written, THIS IS JESUS THE KING OF THE JEWS'; St Mark says that 'the superscription of his accusation was written over, THE KING OF THE JEWS'; some late manuscripts of St Luke's Gospel add that the inscription THIS IS THE KING OF THE JEWS was 'written over him in letters of Greek, and Latin, and Hebrew'. But it is St John who provides the most detailed account, claiming that Pontius Pilate himself 'wrote a title, and put it on the cross. And the writing was, JESUS OF NAZARETH THE KING OF THE JEWS. This title then read many of the Jews: for the place where Jesus was crucified was nigh to the city: and it was written in Hebrew, and Greek, and Latin.'

In spite of this unanimity among the four Evangelists, the story of the *Titulus* as it appears in the Gospels has long been cited by those who follow the great scholar Rudolf Bultmann (1884–1976) in doubting the value of these texts as historical narratives. Bultmann himself argued scathingly that the idea of an inscription was patently secondary 'editorial material'.[16] But it is not clear why he felt entitled to make such an assertion. Indeed, this seems to be a classic example of a Biblical critic wilfully ignoring external evidence to justify his ferocious scepticism of the Gospel's veracity.

There is, in fact, good reason to believe that such inscriptions were used quite regularly as instruments of deterrence in the Roman penal system. Dio Cassius, for instance, cites the punishment of a slave in 23 BC who was 'led through the midst of the Forum with an inscription declaring the reason why he was to be put to death' before his crucifixion.[17] The available evidence suggests that such messages were normally painted on to a board, possibly whitened with gypsum, or written on to parchment, then affixed to the wood.[18]

Suetonius gives later support to the idea that signs and inscriptions were used to justify severe penalties. At a public dinner in Rome, the historian relates, the deranged Emperor Caligula 'sent to his executioners a slave who had stolen a strip of silver from a couch; they were to chop off the man's hands, tie them around his neck so that they hung on his chest, and take him for a tour of the tables, displaying a placard in explanation of his punishment'.[19] The historian also tells us that Domitian threw an offender to the dogs wearing a placard round his neck which bore the words: 'A Thracian supporter who spoke evil of his Emperor'. The use of such inscriptions, in other words, was far from uncommon in the Roman world and there is no intrinsic reason to suppose *a priori* that such a placard was not used as an instrument of humiliation in the crucifixion of Jesus. If the wood of the Cross was preserved after his death, it is highly probable that the *Titulus* was too.

What happened to the Cross after the crucifixion of Jesus? Did the earliest worshippers of Jesus retrieve it, or at least try to? It is this book's contention that it survived both as symbol and as a venerated artefact among the earliest Christians, even when they were unable to see it with their own eyes. Its rediscovery by the Empress Helena in AD 326 is the subject of the next two chapters; later we provide new evidence that the Cross and the cryptograms which represent it were prevalent symbols among the very first Christians. At this stage, however, it is worth examining what evidence we have already.

One has only to read the impassioned outbursts of St Paul on the Cross and its centrality to Christian life to realise how important the image of crucifixion was to the earliest worshippers of Christ. 'Jews demand signs and Greeks seek wisdom,' he wrote in his first Letter to the Corinthians, 'but we preach Christ crucified, a stumbling block to Jesus and folly to Gentiles, but to those who are called, both Jews and Greeks, Christ the power of God and the wisdom of God.'[20] For Paul, the Cross was the very heart of the new religion: 'Far be it from me to glory except in the cross of our Lord Jesus Christ, by which the world has been crucified to me, and I to the world.'[21] Later writers emulated Paul's priorities, although sometimes in more prosaic form. Tertullian, writing c. AD 200, tells us that the Cross was used as an antidote to injury, such as the sting of a scorpion: 'We have faith for a defence, if we are not smitten with distrust itself also, in immediately making the sign [of the Cross].'[22] This, he argued, was not the same as the pagan worship of carved wooden images: 'A cross is, in its material, a sign of wood; amongst yourselves also the object of worship is a wooden figure.'[23]

Today, St Paul is widely regarded as the founder of modern Christianity. But his obsession with the Cross – and, more important, the evident obsession of his less learned readers with it – has been explored only in theological terms. It is constantly asserted as a matter of unassailable fact that the Cross was only an important symbol in the Christian world *after* Helena's excavations and her son's political and religious exploitation of what she found. The author of the most recent academic monograph on the Empress, Jan Willem Drijvers, asserts as a matter of uncontestable fact that 'in the first three centuries of the Christian era the Cross had been a symbol of minor importance'.[24] A recent biographer of Constantine has written that the sign was 'almost unknown as a Christian emblem'.[25] One standard text on the history of the Cross as an image claims that 'there is no known depiction of the Crucifixion until after the time of Constantine the Great'.[26]

This is simply not the case. It may be true that there is no sophisticated representation of the crucifixion which has survived older than the mid-fourth-century marble sarcophagus now in the Lateran Museum, which bears five panels depicting the Passion of Christ.[27] But there is strong prima-facie evidence to suggest that the simple, unadorned image of the Cross was in use as a mainstream Christian symbol long before Constantine's long reign. The two signs used were ✝ and ✶. The origins and meanings of these symbols have been disputed for centuries, some scholars even claiming that they have no religious content whatsoever.[28] They have been linked to the Egyptian ankh symbol ✝, a hieroglyph often depicted in the hand of Osiris and believed to signify the key to the River Nile. Most agree, however, that the so-called 'Chi-Rho' is, at one level, a cryptogram signifying the first and last Greek letters of the name of Christ, X (*Chi*) and P (*Rho*). In another sense – and, as we shall see, for the Emperor Constantine in particular – it was also a symbol representing the physical shape of the Cross itself. It resembled, in other words, not only the name of Christ but the instrument of his death – an instrument which, as St Paul's writings indicate, was of the gravest importance to the first Christians. The ingenuity of this double meaning would also have pleased the earliest Christians who, following the persecutions of Nero, became master cryptographers in order to pursue their beliefs as discreetly as possible.[29] In 165, the Latin apologist Minucius Felix quotes a non-Christian as saying that Christians recognize each other by 'secret symbols and signs [*occultis se notis et insignibus noscunt*]'.[30]

An underrated discovery in this context was Papyrus Bodmer 14 in the Bodmer collection, Cologny-Geneva, a copy of the Gospel according to St Luke, which could be as old as AD 225 and may be much older. In this manuscript the scribe uses the ✝ image quite unmistakably on three separate occasions, suggesting that it was in use in the Mediterranean world from the second half of the second century at the latest.[31] This manuscript has been edited for almost forty years, but it seems to have done almost nothing to alter scholarly orthodoxy on the history of the Cross.

No less intriguing are the graffiti symbols that have been discovered beneath the basilica of St Peter's in Rome. These complicated cryptograms, according to their greatest analyst, Margherita Guarducci, had two purposes: 'Not only to give the Christians freedom to express their feeling during times of persecution, but also that of bringing by its own power, comfort to the faithful.'[32] Under this system – the so-called *disciplina arcani* – certain letters were given special significance. 'E', for example, represented Eden; 'N' stood for Victory; 'R' for Resurrection; 'S' for Health; and 'A' for 'Beginning' or 'Life'. In this way a single letter could be transformed into 'a small treasure chest of precious thoughts'.[33] And no treasure was so great as the symbol of Christ's Cross and his name, the Chi-Rho, which appears often on Wall G of the Vatican necropolis. The writing on this wall can be dated from 290 to 315 – a further hint that the symbol was already in common use before Constantine's adoption of it as the official imperial insignia.[34]

There is, therefore, more evidence than generally has been acknowledged to suggest that the Cross was an important Christian symbol long before its exploitation by Helena's son as the most exalted image of imperial power. In subsequent chapters we shall argue that this was not merely a spiritual tradition but that the physical reality of Christ's crucifixion – its site and the wood used by his executioners – was of the utmost significance from the earliest time. The Empress and Constantine were exploiting a well-established tradition which, as we shall see, was particularly strong in the Holy Land itself, and were turning it to universal-imperial uses. They were building on existing foundations rather than laying them down. And that, as the next two chapters will show, was their genius.

2

Queen Helena and
the Birth of Christian Europe

As the news spread everywhere in Christendom, from
every altar a great wind of prayer gathered and mounted,
lifted the whole squat smoky dome of the Ancient World,
swept it off and up like the thatch of a stable, and threw
open the calm and brilliant prospect of measureless space.

Evelyn Waugh, *Helena*

The Christian religion is an intendedly political revolution
which, having failed, has turned moral.

Goethe

In the Vatican Museum's Sala a Croce Greca, designed by the
architect Michelangelo Simonetti, there stands a mighty porphyry
sarcophagus, adorned with powerful images of war and imperial
triumph. The martial character of the reliefs, it is thought, indicates that it was originally intended for the Emperor Constantine
himself. In the event, the mortal remains of his mother Helena
were buried in this imposing casket and interred in the mausoleum
known as the 'Tor Pignattara' on the Via Labicana, just outside
the Aurelian wall.[1] In the twelfth century the remains of her
skeleton were transferred to the church of S. Maria in Aracoeli
and the sarcophagus itself reused for the burial of Pope Anastasius
IV (1153–4). Today the casket attracts little attention among the
tourists at the Vatican Museum who flock past it on their way to
see the Sistine Chapel.

There is injustice in this, for the Empress Helena – Flavia Iulia
Helena Augusta – is surely one of the most remarkable women
ever to have lived. She rose, as we shall see, from humble origins

to found an imperial dynasty, transformed the fortunes of Christianity as a world religion by an extraordinary adventure in the 320s and, in alliance with her son, invented the idea of European Christendom. She was a pitiless court politician, an extravagant patron of art and architecture and, even in great old age, a pilgrim and Biblical detective of uncompromising ambition. It is no exaggeration to say that the idea of Christian Europe, of a continent bound together, however loosely, by a faith, would not have been the same without this cantankerous dynastic genius. The Helena of Christian legend is a pious, chaste and other-wordly figure. The Helena of history was altogether more robust, determined that the empire her son had inherited should hold together and that nothing should stand in the way of that goal.[2] Her role in the history of the True Cross is remarkable enough, but Helena would still be a figure of world historical importance even if she had never made her perilous pilgrimage to Jerusalem.

One of this book's inspirations was our discovery that so little has been written in recent times about the Empress,[3] if one discounts Evelyn Waugh's devotional novel *Helena*. First published in 1950, Waugh's book opens with this droll prefatory anecdote:

> It is reported (and I for one believe it) that some few years ago a lady prominent for her hostility to the Church returned from a visit to Palestine in a state of exultation. 'I got the real low down at last,' she told her friends. 'The whole story of the crucifixion was made up by a British woman named Ellen. Why, the guide showed me the very place where it happened. Even the priests admit it. They call their chapel "the Invention of the Cross".'[4]

Waugh's objective was to address this state of ignorance and his book, though an unashamed work of Roman Catholic apologetic, is well researched and has ensured the survival of Helena as a figure of literary interest. Nonetheless, it is not a biography. New books on the Emperor Constantine appear every year, but practically nothing on his mother is published outside the pages of academic journals and doctoral dissertations.[5]

Any attempt to correct this deficiency must begin with the legend of Helena itself, the *Inventio Crucis*, or discovery of the

Cross, to which Waugh's American woman confusedly referred. This Christian story is best known for its appearance in *The Golden Legend* of the thirteenth century and in Cynewulf's poem in Anglo-Saxon, *Elene*. But the legend first attested much earlier, in the funeral oration written by Ambrose, Bishop of Milan, for the Emperor Theodosius the Great. The *De Obitu Theodosii*, our oldest surviving source for the history of the True Cross, was composed in 395 – although it seems to have been based on a slightly earlier work, the *Historia Ecclesiastica* of Gelasius of Caesarea, probably written during the 390s.[6]

Ambrose, who was bishop from 374 to 397, was one of the most prominent churchmen of his time, a fierce defender of doctrinal orthodoxy and the cult of the martyrs, whose many achievements included the conversion of St Augustine. In this instance, however, his purpose was narrowly dynastic. He wanted to demonstrate that the discovery of the Cross by Helena had legitimized hereditary Christian rule in the Empire, the so-called *hereditas fidei*. He depicts her as a second Mary who defeats Satan in her quest to unearth the most precious relics of the faith. His intention is to remind the successors of Theodosius that they must prove worthy of this awesome act of dynastic foundation. He was also the first chronicler explicitly to connect the discovery of the Cross and the nails with the Old Testament prophecy of Zechariah 14:20: the Empress has a bridle made for her son of the holy nail, thus fulfilling Zechariah's prediction: 'In that day, there will be written on the bit of the horse, "Sacred to Almighty God"'.

A slightly later account of the legend appears in the *Church History* of Rufinus, a monk and scholar born in Aquileia *c.*345, who composed this work around 402 after spending nearly twenty years on the Mount of Olives. His is generally reckoned to be the purest literary version of the inherited Helena tradition – apparently a tradition born in Jerusalem – and is therefore worth quoting at length:

> At about the same time, Helena, the mother of Constantine, a woman of outstanding faith and deep piety, and also of exceptional munificence, whose offspring indeed one would expect to be such a man as Constantine, was advised by divinely-sent visions to go to Jerusalem.

There she was to make an enquiry among the inhabitants to find out the place where the sacred body of Christ had hung on the Cross. The spot was difficult to find, because the persecutors of old had set a statue of Venus over it, so that if any Christian wanted to worship Christ in that place, he seemed to be worshipping Venus. For this reason, the place was not much frequented and had all but been forgotten.

Here Rufinus is referring to Aelia Capitolina, the pagan temple built on the site of the Holy Sepulchre by the Emperor Hadrian after the Second Jewish War. As we shall discuss in a later chapter, this structure had prevented Christians from visiting the most sacred location of their faith.

But when, as we related above, the pious lady hastened to the spot pointed out to her by a heavenly sign, she tore down all that was profane and polluted there. Deep beneath the rubble she found three crosses lying in disorder. But the joy of finding this treasure was marred by the difficulty of distinguishing to whom each cross belonged. The board was there, it is true, on which Pilate had placed an inscription written in Greek, Latin and Hebrew characters. But not even this provided sufficient evidence to identify the Lord's Cross. In such an ambiguous case uncertainty requires divine proof. It happened that in that same city, a certain prominent lady of that place lay mortally ill with a serious disease. Macarius was at that time bishop of the Church there. When he saw the doubts of the queen and all present, he said: 'Bring all three crosses which have been found and God will now reveal to us which is the cross which bore Christ.'

Bishop Macarius says a prayer and the woman is miraculously cured when the 'wood of salvation' is brought near to her.

When the queen saw that her wish had been answered by such a clear sign, she built a marvellous church of royal magnificence over the place where she had discovered the Cross. The nails, too, which had attached the Lord's body to the Cross, she sent to her son. From some of these he had a horse's bridle made, for use in battle, while he used the others to add strength to a helmet, equally with a view to using it in battle. Part of the redeeming wood she sent to her son, but she also

left part of it there preserved in silver chests. This part is com-
memorated by regular veneration to this very day.[7]

Rufinus concludes by recording that, as an additional sign of her
piety, the Empress held a banquet for the consecrated virgins of
Jerusalem to whom she herself acted as handservant, bringing
them food, pouring their cups and washing their hands.

The story told by Ambrose and Rufinus spawned many variants,
having in common the core narrative which the two ecclesiastics
had established. In 403, Paulinus of Nola wrote a letter to his
friend Sulpicius Severus in Primuliacum in reply to a request for
a holy relic; Paulinus promises to send a fragment of the cross
given to him by Melania the Elder who had herself received it
from John, Bishop of Jerusalem. He structures his version of the
Helena legend quite differently from his predecessors, although
the essential elements are the same. Sozomen, a scholar from
Constantinople, included a version of the story in his *Church
Histories* of the 440s which claims that Helena discovered the
place where the Cross was buried through divine signs and dreams
rather than, as others claimed, the guidance of a Jew called Judas.
He also introduced the notion that the Roman Sybil had prophesied the discovery of the Cross and its subsequent veneration.
Theodoret (393–c.466), the Bishop of Cyrrhus, added the unhis-
torical claim that Helena had raised Constantine as a Christian
and also alleges that she gave her son instruction on her deathbed
on how best to run his dominions. The *Church History* of Socrates,
written some time after 439, draws an explicit connection between
the discovery of the Cross and the construction of the Holy Sepulchre.

These, then, are the texts which gave birth to the legend of
Helena as it passed down the centuries in literature and art. In the
next chapter we examine the historical reality lurking beneath
the surface of the *Inventio Crucis* tradition. But it must first be
asked who this extraordinary woman was and what led her to
Jerusalem and her awesome discovery.

Waugh embraced the romantic tradition that Helena was a British princess, the daughter of King Coel of Colchester – a chieftain of the Trinovants tribe on the east coast of Britain who is himself memorialized in the nursery rhyme 'Old King Cole'.[8] This myth gained currency among English chroniclers during the twelfth century and became more prominent in the fourteenth and fifteenth centuries when the propagandists of the Hundred Years War grasped its usefulness in their development of a distinctively British notion of empire.

In 1125, William of Malmesbury included Constantine in his *Gesta Regum Anglorum* and even observed that the supposedly cool climate of Constantinople suited him well because he had been born in Britain and therefore disliked the sun. Four years later, Henry of Huntingdon drew up an elaborate genealogy for Constantine giving him claim to the throne of Britain as well as the Roman Empire. Henry's *Historia Anglorum* described the arrival of Constantine's father, Constantius Chlorus, in Britain after conquests in Gaul and Spain, whereupon he came to terms with Coel of Colchester. Constantius married Coel's 'beautiful daughter, Helena, later called "saint"' and became king when Coel died. Their son, Constantine, Henry related, succeeded Constantius when he died at York.

Geoffrey of Monmouth's *Historia regum Britanniae* (1137–9) offers yet another version of this implausible story. According to Geoffrey, Coel, Duke of Colchester, rebelled against a certain King Asclepiodotus and seized the throne. His daughter, Helena, later wed Constantius, who had come to British shores to collect tribute. Their son Constantine brought peace to Britain and a group of Roman nobles called upon him to avenge the wrongs done them by Maxentius the Tyrant. Crucial to Geoffrey's account, moreover, was the claim that Constantine was an ancestor of King Arthur, thus establishing a genealogical link between the late Roman Empire and the once and future king.

By 1295, the notion that Constantine's mother was a Briton was sufficiently current in Europe to warrant inclusion in *The Golden Legend*: 'Others declare that she was the only daughter of Coel, the king of the Britons, and that Constantine's father took her to wife when he went to Britain, and thus became the master of the island at the death of Coel. This is also maintained by the Britons.'[9]

Later, during the Hundred Years War, it suited English propagandists to expand the myth still further. In the 1430s, for instance, John Lydgate's translation of Boccaccio's *De casibus illustrium virorum* included a long hymn in praise of the British Constantine, 'cheef monarche, prince and president, / Over al the world, from est til occident'.[10] At the Council of Constance (1414–18) the English delegation claimed Constantine as a precedent, pointing out that he had summoned the first ecumenical council, and 'first gave permission to Christians to assemble freely in general councils for the extirpation of schism and heresies'.

Henry VIII found the idea that Constantine's mother was British particularly appealing and exploited the myth in his struggle with the Papacy over his divorce, wearing the imperial diadem as a signal of his defiance. The Tudor historian Polydore Vergil described Constantine as 'being begott of a Britishe mother, born and made Emperour in Brittaine'.[11] The myth continued to surface in later writings such as Spenser's *Faerie Queene* and Milton's history of Britain. But it lost its prominence after the sixteenth century and was treated as a matter for scorn alone by Edward Gibbon.

In this respect, if not in all others, Gibbon's scorn seems to have been justified. It was natural for English myth-makers to seek association between later dynasties and the imperial genes which had spawned Constantine. And the British were by no means the only European people to claim Helena as one of their own: Orderic Vitalis, the twelfth-century Anglo-Norman chronicler, reports the French tradition that Constantius Chlorus had met Helena in Neustria. The British tradition is, in any case, hopelessly muddled and in many cases the chroniclers seem to have confused the Empress – wilfully or otherwise – with an entirely different namesake of the fourth century, Elen of Carnarvon.[12]

What is not disputed is that Constantine's father was indeed associated with Britain, having gone there to subdue the usurper Allectus in 296. Constantius Chlorus was an ambitious Danubian, born in Illyricum, the present Dalmatia, in March 250. His rise through the ranks was exceptional, capped by his appointment by Maximian as Prefect of the Praetorian Guard. The crushing of Allectus was certainly a significant demonstration of his military ability, as well as of the loyalty of his troops far from home. But Constantius seems, in fact, to have spent less than a year restoring order to Britain and strengthening its currency after the rebellion had been quelled. When Maximian made him Caesar of Gaul and Britain, he took up residence in Trier. Constantius returned to the scene of his triumph only much later, in 306. It was chance, therefore, rather than patriotic affinity, that brought Constantine to York (Eburacum) in that year, to be at his father's side when he died and to be proclaimed Augustus by his father's troops. The young pretender seems to have wasted no time in leaving for Gaul.

As arresting as the idea of Helena as a British aristocrat is, it is much more probable that she was from the near East and of low birth.[13] Many possible birthplaces have been proposed for the Empress: Naissus, Caphar, Edessa and Trier, as well, of course, as Colchester. But the likeliest site was Drepanum, modern Herkes, in Bithynia or Asia Minor, and the likeliest date about 248. In the sixth century – not, admittedly, a particularly early source – Procopius reports that Constantine changed the name of Drepanum to Helenopolis because his mother was born here. Eusebius (Bishop of Caesarea in Palestine c.313–39) says in his *Life of Constantine* that, towards the end of his life, Constantine fell ill in the city of Helenopolis, which was named after his mother.

As to Helena's background, the evidence is clearer. The mid-fourth century writer Eutropius says that Constantine was born '*ex obscuriore matrimonio*'; in his funeral oration for Theodosius in 395, Ambrose refers to Helena as a '*stabularia*' – literally, an innkeeper's daughter, definitely of low birth and perhaps even a concubine. For Ambrose, Helena's humble origins are an essential aspect of her inspirational achievement and her rise from poverty through the operation of divine Grace. 'Christ', he says somewhat brutally, 'raised her from dung to power.' In a slightly later text, the *Origo Constantini*, Helena is called '*vilissima*'. Philostorgius writing in the mid-fifth century, says she was 'a common woman not different from strumpets'.

Although pagan writers had a vested interest in presenting the great Christian matriarch as low-born and therefore morally suspect, the near unanimity of the sources on this point would seem to point to a kernel of fact. Constantius, Constantine's father, was an ambitious provincial whose family would never have allowed him to marry a *stabularia* like Helena – whom he is likely to have taken up with when serving the Empire in the Balkan provinces. She would have been recognized not as his wife, but in some quasi-marital role, probably simply as the general's *concubina*, his mistress-in-residence. Constantine himself was born Flavius Valerius Constantinus in 272 or 273 in Naissus, a military city on the Nisava. But his mother was later moved aside for political reasons in 289 when Constantius married Flavia Maximiana Theodora, the stepdaughter of Maximian, who gave him six children.

As heartless as this act of renunciation doubtless seemed, it was essential to Constantius's prospects in Diocletian's newly established tetrarchy, which divided control of the Empire after March 293 between two Augusti and two Caesars: Diocletian's Caesar was Galerius, while Constantius performed the same role for Maximian. The Empire was threatened from the north by the Germans and by the Persians in the east; its internal politics were intrinsically unstable. It was essential to the young Constantine that his father do what was judged expedient to hold together this dynastically fissile political arrangement, even if, in the short term, this involved the humiliation of his mother. His immediate reward was to stay at court in Nicomedia, in Bithynia – the second capital of the Empire – where his education was supervised by Diocletian himself; in time he would more than make up for his mother's sacrifice.

Constantine's apprenticeship for power was that of a soldier rather than the philosopher-king he would later aspire to be (although it was while he was with the Emperor that he first encountered Lactantius, the Christian orator and philosopher). He accompanied Diocletian against the usurper Domitius Domitianus in Egypt and fought alongside Galerius against the Persians in 297 and 298. The original tetrarchy fell apart in 305 with Diocletian's abdication, but Constantine's ambitions were by now evidently much greater than to preserve this fourway division of authority or some variant upon it. In March 307 he was declared Augustus, claiming descent from the Emperor Claudius II Gothicus (268–70) and thus basing his claim to absolute power not in the tetrarchic system but in heredity. His first rival for absolute power was Maxentius, whom he defeated at the Battle of the Milvian Bridge in 312. Twelve years later, on 18 September 324, he vanquished his rebellious fellow Emperor Licinius at Chrysopolis.

Thus did Constantine become the first sole ruler of the Empire since the earliest years of Diocletian's reign (284–6). His panegyrists celebrated him as the *Rector Totius Orbis*, the ruler of the whole world, a second Alexander. This book is not the place for a full appraisal of his reign and its character, except insofar as the events of that reign and Constantine's personal ambitions help explain what brought his mother to Jerusalem, probably in 326. It is important, certainly, that Constantine combined the martial ruthlessness of his father with the dreams of a state builder. He was a zealous church builder and a more active religious publicist than any other ruler in antiquity. He created Constantinople, a city which was to be the capital of the eastern Empire and, in time, of the Byzantine world. He constructed a vast bureaucratic machine for the Empire, built cities and minted a new coin for his realms – the *solidus* – which maintained its purity and weight for seven hundred years. For all his Balkan asperity, Constantine was the first European idealist: he designed his own single currency and in his adoption of Christianity bequeathed to Europe the cement which would hold it together until the Enlightenment.

In all this, Helena's role seems to have been central, although one has sometimes to look hard for the footprints of the stealthy politician she could evidently be. After his acclamation in York in 306, Constantine inherited his father's base at Trier, which remained his own headquarters for ten years, a rival to Galerius's base in Thessalonica. His mother, by now in her late fifties, seems to have resided with her son at the family's complex of buildings in Trier, the showpiece of which was the magnificent basilica, 74 metres long, and 32.5 metres wide. As a consequence the Helena tradition has always been strong in Trier (including the legend that she bequeathed the robe of Jesus to the cathedral). A life of the Queen, composed in the ninth century by Altmann of Hautvillers, went as far as to allege that she had been born there, but this appears to have been a unilateral claim no more reliable than the British chroniclers' enthusiasm to give her an English ancestry.

The most interesting legacy of Helena's time in Trier are the remains of buildings dating from the first quarter of the fourth century, which were excavated beneath the cathedral in 1945–6 and again in 1965–8. These digs revealed a room which had been constructed after 316 but then torn down after 330. This suggests there may be truth in the medieval tradition that this was the original site of the Queen's palace, which she donated to Bishop Agritius of Trier. Force has been added to this theory by the discovery of the remains of ornate ceiling frescos from a similar period. The fifteen panels, which have been painstakingly reconstructed and are now exhibited in Trier's diocesan museum, show human figures and dancing putti; the lavish use of the colour purple has led some scholars to conclude that the figures represented are members of the Constantinian dynasty, including Helena herself, Constantine's wife Fausta, his half-sister Constantia and the wife of his son Crispus – although an alternative explanation is that they are allegories of the seasons or personifications of Wisdom, Beauty, Youth and Health.[14]

If the images are, indeed, those of the Emperor's family, it is all the more intriguing that the ceiling painting seems to have been knocked down only a few years after its creation. The likeliest explanation for this apparent act of vandalism is that the frescos fell victim to the most dramatic crisis of Constantine's reign, one which erupted at the very heart of his family. The Emperor's chief lieutenant at Trier was his son Crispus, whose mother was Minervina, another of Constantine's female companions. A glittering future appeared to lie ahead of him as a Christian emperor, a task for which he was prepared by Lactantius; he held the consulship in 318, 321 and 324.[15] But in 326 Constantine had Crispus abruptly tried and executed – probably for committing adultery with Fausta, the wife of the Emperor. Shortly afterwards, Fausta herself was suffocated in her bath. Constantine issued an edict, declaring that the names of the two miscreants should never again be mentioned – the so-called *damnatio memoriae* – and it is significant that Eusebius avoids the whole bloody episode altogether. With this in mind, it seems probable that the Trier frescos were destroyed as part of the eradication of Crispus and Fausta from history.

Helena herself may have played a critical role in the unfolding of this crisis, for she was fond of her grandson and was doubtless grooming him to succeed his father. According to the fourth-century *Epitome* of Aurelius Victor, it was the wrathful influence of the Empress which sealed Fausta's fate: 'At the instigation of his wife Fausta, it is believed, Constantine ordered that his son Crispus be killed. Then, when his mother Helena, deeply grieving for her grandson, rebuked him, he killed his wife Fausta by placing her in a hot bath.'

A later version of the same story is reported by Zosimus, the early sixth-century pagan historian:

> When all the power devolved on Constantine alone he no longer hid the evil nature that was within him, but allowed himself to do all things as he pleased. ... His son Crispus, who had been honoured with the rank of Caesar, as previously mentioned, came under suspicion of being involved with his stepmother Fausta; Constantine destroyed him without any regard to the laws of nature. When Constantine's mother Helena was disturbed by these events and was taking the loss of the young man very hard, Constantine, as if to console her, corrected one evil by an even greater evil; he ordered an unbearably hot bath to be prepared, had Fausta placed in it, and had her taken out only when she was dead.[16]

It is certainly probable that a rivalry had arisen between Helena and Fausta. The Emperor's mother was promoting the interests of Crispus, while Fausta was presumably doing the same for her own sons. Helena may also have disliked Fausta because she was the half-sister of Theodora, who had ousted Helena as Constantius's consort. This accusation that the Dowager was directly responsible for Fausta's death has been rejected by many historians and the evidence of these two authors is far from conclusive. Even so, the fact that the story was considered plausible is in itself revealing. She was, and remained, a formidable force in Constantine's court.

Helena is also known to have had a considerable estate in Rome, the Fundus Laurentus, and a magnificent dwelling place in the Sessorian Palace. It is on this site that the church of Santa Croce in Gerusalemme – the home of the *Titulus* – now stands: indeed, the modest chapel, which lies beneath the reliquary built by Mussolini, is thought to have been the Empress's living quarters.[17] Whether or not this particular identification is correct, there is evidence everywhere in the church (which was originally known simply as the Basilica Heleniana) and its locale of fourth-century foundations. There seems to have been a villa on the site from the end of the second century but Helena added a circus, amphitheatre and public baths, to make her palace the political and social focus of the south-east of Rome. An inscription near the church includes reference to the repair of the public baths – Thermae Helenae – after they had been destroyed by fire, and two of the other seven inscriptions dedicated to Helena have been discovered in this part of the city. Evidently, Constantine was happy to regard this part of Rome as a maternal barony. He may even have involved her in the construction of St Peter's: according to the *Liber Pontificalis*, a mighty gold cross once covered the grave of St Peter, bearing an inscription of black enamelled letters with the name of Helena Augusta.

To mark her importance to him personally, and to the Empire institutionally, the Emperor honoured his mother in late 324 by granting her the title of Augusta. There were, of course, many precedents for this, the most recent being the award of the title to the wife of Galerius, Galeria Valeria (305–11). In Helena's case, however, the elevation had an instant and politically significant effect. The number of coins bearing her portrait and inscriptions dedicated to her increased considerably, and in some cases, indeed, were linked explicitly to Constantine's defeat of Licinius at Chrysopolis.[18] Helena, then, was much more than an honoured dowager: she was a governing personality of the Constantinian Empire, identified in its coinage with the *securitas rei publicae* – the well-being and safety of the Republic. In inscriptions, she was called *procreatrix*, *mater* or *genetrix*: the low-born *stabularia*, in other words, had become the foundress of an imperial dynasty. There was personal advantage for Constantine in this, of course, since such claims helped entrench his own and diminish those of his father's children by Theodora, and their descendants. But it is hard to believe that the Emperor's elevation of his mother in this way – in effect, his personal establishment of the Helena cult – did not reflect much more: namely, the potent influence the Dowager Empress, now in her seventies, had clawed to herself over the management of the whole Empire.[19]

Our final purpose in this chapter is to consider the Christianity that Constantine and his mother shared, in both cases, although perhaps in different ways, with the zeal of the convert. The Christianization of the Empire over which they presided was far from complete, as is often argued; but to look for its deficiencies (which is easy) is to miss the point of how extraordinary a development it was in the history of the West.

This is a book about the Cross and it was under the Cross – at least in the account of his biographers – that Constantine embraced the new faith. At some time prior to his conquest of Maxentius the battle of the Milvian Bridge – perhaps even the night before – the Emperor saw a vision, in which he was instructed to put the sign of Christ on the shields of his soldiers. This, at any rate, is the account of Lactantius (c.240–c.320), the tutor of Constantine's eldest son, Crispus, in his treatise *On the Death of the Persecutors*, which was probably published in 314: 'Constantine was advised in a dream to mark the heavenly sign of God on the shields of his soldiers and then to engage in battle. He did as he was commanded and by means of a slanted "X" [*transversa X littera*] with the top of its head bent round, he marked Christ on their shields. Armed with this sign, the army took up its weapons.'[20]

According to Eusebius, Bishop of Caesarea and author of the later *Vita Constantini*, the Emperor and 'all his troops' saw a cross of light in the sky one afternoon and the words 'in this conquer [*en touto nika*]'; Christ later appeared to Constantine in a dream and commanded him to make standards for his troops in the form of the sacred sign, 'using its likeness in his engagements with the enemy'.

Eusebius's account has generally been regarded as less credible, although some scholars have tried to explain the luminous vision that appeared to the Emperor and his armies as a solar flare.[21] Whatever the precise timing and nature of this alleged divine intervention, Constantine's response was to replace the pagan insignia of his troops with a new Christian sign – a sign which soon came to be known by the name *labarum*. In this interpretation he was doubtless spurred on by his chief ecclesiastical adviser, Ossius, Bishop of Cordoba (c.257–c.357), who performed this function at Constantine's court from 312 to 326; certainly, Ossius's influence was critical in the Emperor's decision to adopt the faith of the crucified man. But it is Eusebius who has left the best account of the new symbol. The Emperor's biographer relates that the standard was constructed from a long spear, covered with gold, joined by a transverse bar which gave it the shape of a cross; at its apex was a wreath made of gold and precious stones, denoting the Chi-Rho (the initial letters of *Christos* in Greek, written X and P). The Emperor also inscribed the Chi-Rho upon the shields of his soldiers, replacing the traditional devices of war such as thunderbolts, animals and images of Mars.[22] When he entered Rome after defeating Maxentius, the vast new basilica that his rival had built was dedicated to Constantine and a vast statue of the conqueror holding the Christian *labarum* raised in its main hall.

One of the attractions of this ingenious symbol, which signified both the name of Christ and the means by which he was put to death, was that it bore resemblance to the Roman trophy or *tropaeum*, the symbol used to reflect Roman victory, which had first appeared on Roman coins at the end of the third century BC. Early Christian writers, doubtless with an eye to potential advantage, had already noted this similarity. Justin Martyr, for example, had demonstrated in the course of his argument that the Cross was not an evil but that it was the very core of the *tropaeum* carried in all processions as a sign of Roman omnipotence. Tertullian had written of Jesus triumphing *'per tropaeum crucis'*, an image Eusebius picked up when he described Constantine's heavenly sign as the 'trophy of the cross of light'. Indeed, it was the achievement of this churchman and biographer to transform the Cross from a symbol of Christian memory into the pre-eminent insignia of the Empire – which it became, officially, in the reign of Theodosius II (408–50).[23] What Eusebius had grasped was the extraordinary versatility of this sign and the web of resonances that those who adopted it could exploit. It recalled the Roman symbol of triumph, but it was also an inspirational sign of the name of Christ and his death. It acted as a magic totem on the battlefield and a focus of contemplation in the chapel. And it enabled his master Constantine to posture as the thirteenth apostle.[24]

By the time of his final battle against Maxentius, therefore, the Emperor seems to have clearly associated his armies with the hand of the Christian God, their victory on the field of war decisive evidence of the part the Emperor had to play in the unfolding of divine providence. By aiding Constantine in his hour of need, the God of the Gospels had shown himself a stronger ally than the competitors who crowded the religious market place of the early fourth century. His embrace of monotheism was not, in itself, remarkable: Eusebius claims that Constantius Chlorus had dabbled with such beliefs. In early life, Constantine had been happy to depict himself as protected by Apollo, who also came to him in a vision – this time when he was on his way south from the Rhine to defeat Maximian in Marseilles. Apollo, it was claimed, had appeared to Constantine, in the company of Victory, and presented him with laurel crowns, promising him a long and prosperous reign. This was said to be the fulfilment of the 'divine songs of poets', a reference to Virgil's prophecy of a divinely inspired world ruler.

In 311, Constantine hailed the sun as his tutelary, portraying the deity on his coins as his unconquerable ally, *Sol Invictus*. This cosmic arrangement between Emperor and solar god survived on Constantine's coinage long after the Battle of Milvian Bridge, in contrast to the classical pagan gods who had largely disappeared by 317. It has been argued that solar religion offered an attractive staging post to the Roman aristocracy on the road between paganism and Christianity, and it is certainly true that Jesus was often called *Sol Justitiae* or depicted in statuary in a form closely resembling the god Sol.

Such theological promiscuity was not regarded as fickle, but prudent – evidence of a ruler's quest for the God who would bring his people prosperity at home and triumph in war.[25] The emperors no longer claimed to be gods, but behaved instead as the servants of a providential purpose, acting under its direction and protected by its divine influence. There were, as one historian of Constantine's reign has observed, 'bridges of thought touching both paganism and Christianity by which men like Constantine could pass from one to the other without need violently to repudiate their earlier worships and without need of any miraculous or magical act from on high'.[26] It was not a huge leap for a bellicose, opportunistic warrior-king to move from worship of Sol to worship of the Christian God. And such a leap was even more straightforward when providence seemed to be intervening on his side. The battle of Milvian Bridge was presented by Constantine's propagandists as the triumph over the old by the new, the defeat of charlatanism by purity, and the conquest of sullied paganism by robust imperial Christianity.[27]

The Emperor, then, had aligned himself with a religion the central symbol of which was a recognizable and evidently powerful talisman, which had brought him almost immediate triumph in battle. He may also, with his mother, have been attracted to the potential of Christianity as a cohesive force, the breadth of its potential appeal across the Empire and its proponents' evident talent for social organization. It would seem, at least, that he had grasped its potential as a prop to imperial authority, where his immediate predecessors had seen it as a threat. But Constantine's decision to become Christian remains an extraordinary one, a choice that ultimately defies sure analysis. At some level, however primitive, it seems to have been a true leap of faith rather than merely the act of an astute politician, weighing up the political advantage he could gain from professing a particular faith. As any observer of modern politics can attest, sincerity and ruthlessness often march together.

The faith to which he turned was enduring a ferociously schismatic period in its history, torn apart by the breakaway of the African Donatists and by open heresy in Alexandria. There, the Presbyter Arius taught that Christ was not co-eternal with and not equal to God (a theological position for which he was condemned by a local synod in 318 or 319 and by the Council of

Nicaea in 325).[28] More to the point, the Church had been persecuted recently by the tetrarchs Diocletian and Galerius, who evidently regarded its impressive cellular organization and the powerful cohesion of Christian communities as a threat to the integrity of the Empire and the *genius populi Romani*.

In one sense early Christianity, for all its internal divisions, was the only organized force in the Empire apart from the army. This made it, notionally at least, a threat; more important, it made the Church a good enemy and a useful scapegoat in politically unstable times. It is also possible that Constantine and Maxentius had already indicated some sympathy towards Christianity and that Galerius and Diocletian undertook this new assault on the faith partly to embarrass the two princes.[29] In February 303, the Christian church in Nicomedia was torn down on Diocletian's orders and an edict of persecution issued on the next day, instructing the Christians to hand over their holy texts to be burnt and all churches to be destroyed. Further edicts followed, including demands that Christians make sacrifice or face execution. It was not until April 311 that Galerius issued an edict from his deathbed, ending the persecutions over which he had previously presided, a recantation which Eusebius considered a 'manifest visitation of divine providence'. But it would not have escaped Constantine's attention that the persecutions had themselves been a fiasco, patchily imposed and failing completely to impose religious conformity upon the Empire. It must have struck him that a religious movement which cannot be destroyed must instead be harnessed.

Edward Gibbon claimed that 'the nicest accuracy is required in tracing the slow and almost imperceptible gradations by which the monarch declared himself the protector, and at length the proselyte, of the church'.[30] He still held the pagan office of *Pontifex Maximus*. His coinage became Christian only slowly and the triumphal arch erected in his honour in 315 included no Christian symbols of any kind. Constantine evidently appreciated the value of evolution in the context of religious change. But a proselyte for Christianity he most certainly did become, however slowly he made this transition. In 313, he and his fellow Emperor Licinius jointly issued the so-called Edict of Milan, building on the foun-

dation of Galerius's Edict of Toleration and granting positive privileges to Christians. During his reign, those who owned
confiscated Christian property were ordered to restore it, church
lands gained exemption from taxes, clergymen were excused from
public municipal duties and provincial officials were instructed
to organize the construction of churches.

Constantine himself took an extraordinarily detailed interest in
the appointment of bishops, of whom there were 1800 in his
provinces. He abolished crucifixion and, in 321, made Sunday a
public holiday. He became personally involved in the battles
against Donatism and Arianism, and in 325 convened the Council
of Nicaea, attended by 2000 senior churchmen, at which he
declared – contrary to the heretic Arius – that God was *homoousios*
with God, or 'of one substance'. It would be optimistic to describe
this most rough-hewn and martial of rulers as a theologian, but
Constantine was enough of a conceptualist to grasp that theological rifts were a grave threat to the doctrine of Christian unity
he was seeking to impose upon his dominions.

What part did Helena play in these extraordinary events? It has
often been speculated that she and Constantius had both flirted
with the new faith; it is certainly true that Constantius and his
second consort, Theodora, chose a conspicuously Christian name,
Anastasia (meaning resurrection), for their daughter. Theodoret,
the fifth-century church historian, claims that Constantine
himself was raised a Christian by his parents and some historians
have judged there to be some truth in this myth.[31] But Theodoret's
claim seems to be mere assertion. Another theory that has been
advanced by modern scholars is that Helena was of Jewish descent,
on the particular grounds that her finding of the Cross could
have been seen as an act of atonement for the Jews' part in the
crucifixion of Christ.[32] But the only evidence for Helena's Jewishness is the *Actus Silvestri*, a prolifically copied text of the late
half of the fifth century, in which the Queen, an adherent of
Judaism, expresses initial opposition to her son's conversion to
Christianity. She is herself converted to the faith, after the
Emperor organises a debate in Rome between Jewish and Christian
learned men. It is highly unlikely that such a disputation would
have taken place in Constantine's time and there are few scholars

who regard the *Actus Silvestri* as an historically reliable source, for all its zest and colour.

It is possible, as the *Vita Constantini* claims, that she was converted by her son, rather than vice versa. It is also possible that Helena was converted by Lucian, the head of the theological school at Antioch, who taught Arius and Arius's defender Eusebius of Nicomedia (not to be confused with Constantine's biographer, Eusebius of Caesarea).

Certainly Lucian, who was martyred in January 312, was a favourite of the Queen – a sympathy that may have inspired her conflict with Eustathius of Antioch, an outspoken anti-Arian, whose deposition in 327 has been attributed to the hostility of the Empress.[33] Athanasius, Bishop of Alexandria 328–73, records the allegation thus in his *Historia Arianorum*:

> A certain Eustathius was bishop of Antioch; he was a confessor and held the orthodox faith. Because he was very zealous for the truth, and detested the Arian heresy, and would not receive those who held Arian opinions, an attack on him was made to the emperor Constantine, and the pretext was invented that he had insulted the emperor's mother.

Helena may even have had Arian leanings herself, although one should not conclude from this that she was any more an instinctive theologian than her son. Her talents, like his, lay in a genius for religious propaganda, a jackdawish ability to see what aspects of Christianity – notably the Cross – could be turned to imperial-dynastic ends. On her own estate, the fundus Laurentus, she constructed the basilica of Ss Marcellino e Pietro during the second decade of the fourth century. There is some evidence that she was also involved in the building of the basilica of St Peter, arguably the most remarkable architectural achievement of the Constantinian age. But her greatest contribution to the new age of imperial Christianity was not architectural, doctrinal or scriptural. It was a journey.

3

The Discovery of the True Cross

'But how do you know He *doesn't* want us to have it – the cross I mean? I bet He's just waiting for one of us to go and find it – just at this moment when it's most needed.'

Evelyn Waugh, *Helena*

She may be said to have been the most successful archaeologist in all history.

Amos Elon, *Jerusalem – City of Mirrors*

[She] united the credulity of age with the warm feelings of a recent conversion.

Edward Gibbon

In the mid-AD 320s, a low-born woman in her late seventies undertook a journey of great arduousness and uncertain prospects. Her quest would take her across vast distances and into many provinces of the Roman Empire. She would pass through countless towns and settlements, and encounter many adversities along the way. But by the time she returned to her son, after a voyage of two years, she would have made one of the great discoveries in the history of European culture and belief, one that has inspired art, poetry, literature and pilgrimage ever since.

At this distance it is impossible to know exactly why the Empress Helena chose this moment in her life to embark upon her odyssey to the Near East. But the tumultuous events of the mid-320s must have played a part in determining her course. In September 324 Constantine had vanquished his last rival, Licinius, on the Asian shore of the Bosphorus at Chrysopolis. At Nicaea in

325 he had held a great council to settle the divisions within Christianity, which threatened its usefulness as a binding force in the Empire. And in 326 the Emperor had executed his son Crispus and wife Fausta – the latter perhaps at Helena's instigation.

This has prompted some historians to speculate that the purpose of her pilgrimage was to do penance and to atone for her sins in the last years of her life. Yet the image of an empress burdened by guilt is hard to reconcile with what we can construe of Helena's ruthless behaviour in the Constantinian court. It is much more likely that she felt liberated rather than weighed down by Fausta's death, free at last to assist her son in their campaign to Christianize the Empire – a campaign that seems to have accelerated noticeably after 324. There was church building to supervise in the Holy Land. There was also political and religious turbulence in the eastern provinces, probably caused by the sudden change of religious policy after the defeat of Licinius, which required the imperial presence – of the mother if not the son.

Above all, there was the mystical allure of the holy places. The faith that Constantine and Helena embraced had many attractions, but one which had evidently been impressed upon them was its strikingly *historical* character. The events described in the Gospels had taken place only three centuries before; they had happened, moreover, in a land under Roman dominion. It was possible, therefore, to offer the pilgrim a sense of unbroken contact with Jesus.[1] The places where he had lived, preached and suffered could be identified with relative ease. There was every prospect that precious artefacts associated with his life and ministry might be unearthed. In this physicalism, or 'historicity', lay the prospect of great power for those who would associate themselves with it. If a faith could be appropriated by an imperial dynasty, then so could the place of its origin and the relics left by its founders. In this endeavour, no site could be holier than the place where Jesus died and rose from the dead; no artefact as sacred as the cross on which he died. Fourteen years had passed since the Emperor's adoption of this Christian sign and the possibility that he might conceivably recover the remains of the wood – the *lignum crucis* – which it symbolized must have had a special poignancy for Constantine and his mother.[2]

This extravagant project was almost certainly the inspiration of Macarius, Bishop of Jerusalem. His influence at the Council of Nicaea (325) is evident from his achievement in winning from his fellow bishops the recognition that his see was of 'ancient' and 'customary' standing. This, as we shall see, was a victory in his battle to rival the metropolitan status of the bishop of the provincial capital, Caesarea. It may also have been at Nicaea that Macarius first approached the Emperor – who had visited Palestine as a young prince with Diocletian – with the idea of reclaiming the great sites of Christianity for its greater glory and, by implication, the greater glory of the Empire.

The first and most important task was the destruction of Aelia Capitolina, the pagan temple to the west of Hadrian's forum, raised by the Emperor in 135 on the alleged site of Jesus's death and resurrection. His intention had been to build a 'colonia civium Romanorum', to raise a second Rome from the ashes of the Jewish city in the wake of Bar Kokhba's great rebellion. The eastern hill had become a new Capitoline Mount and the temple of Venus built over the Holy Sepulchre. It was Eusebius's belief that Hadrian had done this to obliterate all memory of Christ's Passion and to thwart the spread of the Gospel. In fact, the effect was probably the opposite: to advertise, rather than to obscure, Christianity's holiest site, now covered by a lavish pagan structure.[3]

It was here that Macarius's architects, masons and excavators set about their task. And in the course of the work, as the bishop had no doubt fervently hoped, the alleged tomb of Jesus was discovered – in Eusebius's words, an 'image of the Saviour's return to life'. This archaeological triumph prompted Constantine to plan a New Jerusalem, with the Holy Sepulchre at its heart. In a letter to Macarius, recorded by Eusebius, he instructed the bishop to build on the site 'a basilica more beautiful than any on earth'. And it was apparently to help supervise this task – and much more – that Constantine despatched his elderly mother to the East on her last and greatest mission for the Empire.

Eusebius devotes paragraphs 42 to 47 of Book III of the *Vita Constantini* to the details of Helena's journey, beginning his story thus:

For she, having resolved to discharge the duties of pious devotion to the God, the King of Kings, and feeling it incumbent on her to render thanksgivings with prayers on behalf both of her own son, now so mighty an emperor, and of his sons, her own grandchildren, the divinely favoured Caesars, though now advanced in years, yet gifted with no common degree of wisdom, had hastened with youthful alacrity to survey this venerable land; and at the same time to visit the eastern provinces, cities, and people, with a truly imperial solicitude.[4]

Without delay, Eusebius explains, Helena dedicated two churches to 'the God whom she adored', one in Bethlehem and the other on the Mount of Olives: 'Thus did Helena Augusta, the pious mother of a pious emperor, erect over the two mystic caverns these two noble and beautiful monuments of devotion, worthy of ever-lasting remembrance, to the honour of God her Saviour, and as proofs of her holy zeal, receiving from her son the aid of his imperial power.'[5]

According to her son's biographer, the Empress's journey was also a triumph of pious munificence:

In the splendour of imperial authority, she bestowed abundant proofs of her liberality as well on the inhabitants of the several cities collectively, as on individuals who approached her, at the same time that she scattered largesses among the soldiery with a liberal hand. But especially abundant were the gifts she bestowed upon the naked and unprotected poor. To some she gave money, to others an ample supply of clothing; she liberated some from imprisonment, or from the bitter servitude of the mines; others she delivered from unjust oppression, and others again, she restored from exile.

In many respects her journey had the character of a pilgrimage. Eusebius tells us, quoting Psalm 132:7, that she wished to pray at the places where Christ's feet had touched the ground; she did not overlook the churches 'even in the smallest towns'. He compared Helena, as the mother of the Emperor, with the Virgin herself, the mother of Jesus. When describing her deeds in Bethlehem, Eusebius pointedly wrote that 'the most pious empress honoured the scene of her travail who bore this heavenly child'. But Helena also used her itineration to publicize the benevolence of her son's rule, giving money to those army units who may have been becoming mutinous and making other gifts along the way. Money and shelter, as we have seen, was offered to the poor, prisoners were released and freedom offered to those condemned to the mines or exiled. Her trip, it is clear, was as much a spectacular public event as a private pilgrimage; it dramatized the Constantinian ideal of religious monarchy as much as it reflected the inner conviction of a single Christian convert.[6] She had merged the rituals of an imperial progress with the itinerant humility of the Christian pilgrim.

It has been observed that 'in making the transition from empress to pilgrim, Helena smoothed the way for her successors; the journeys of those who sought out the holy places became a natural element in a Christian Roman Empire'.[7] This is so, but it would be quite wrong to suggest that hers was the first serious pilgrimage to Jerusalem. There is sporadic, but conclusive, evidence that many before her had undertaken the *peregrinatio ad loca sancta*. Bishop Melito of Sardis had made such a journey in about 170, recalling in the sermon 'On Pascha' that he 'came to the place where these things were proclaimed and done'. Eusebius recorded in his *Church History* that Alexander, a Cappadocian bishop, came to Jerusalem in about 210 'for the purpose of prayer and investigation of the [holy] places'. Firmilian, bishop of Cappadocian Caesarea, and Origen, the great biblical scholar, both made recorded visits during the third century. Well before Helena's pilgrimage, Eusebius referred to Bethlehem as 'so famous that men hasten from the ends of the earth to see it'; he also published his own biblical gazetteer, the *Onomasticon*, years in advance of her voyage,[8] evidence of a market among pilgrims for such information long before of the Constantinian excavations of the 320s.

This early wave of pilgrimages is all the more remarkable given that the sites which the pilgrims most wanted to see had been covered over by Hadrian who had built a temple to Venus alongside his Forum.[9] It suggests that the magnetic force of the Jerusalem church and the site of Christ's crucifixion in particular was felt not only by those Christians living in the locale but by worshippers much further afield. They came, even in the knowledge that a pagan edifice dedicated to Aphrodite would prevent them from seeing the holiest site of the Gospel story. The aura of Jerusalem did not die with Hadrian's triumph over Bar Kokhba's Jewish rebels in 134, therefore, but remained strong in the hearts of Christians. And this is what Constantine and Helena had evidently grasped in their sleepless quest for new sources of numinous power.[10]

Travel in late antiquity was both sophisticated and arduous. It provided great opportunities for the restless élite of the Roman world, but it also imposed great demands. On the high seas, piracy was common; overland, brigandry was no less a danger; the carriage used by the wealthy, the two-wheeled *carpentum*, offered a rough ride to its passengers. For a woman in her late seventies, even with all the advantages her imperial position conferred, the journey to Jerusalem was undoubtedly an ambitious undertaking and potentially a foolhardy one. Eusebius does not provide a detailed account of the Empress's itinerary, but it is possible to reconstruct the routes she would almost certainly have taken.[11] If Helena had chosen to travel by land, she would have set off from Bithynia and, passing through the Cilician Gates, made her way to Antioch. Thence, she would have gone to Tyre, Caesarea and finally Jerusalem, a journey of about 1200 miles. The alternative route, by sea, would have got her to the ports of Caesarea Maritima or Yafo, north-west or west of Jerusalem in about a fortnight, assuming a fair wind for her galley.

The Empress's journey itself would have been a mighty carnival of activity, involving armies of servants, cooks, soldiers offering protection and scouts running ahead to make sure no traffic obstructed the way.[12] As an imperial envoy of the most honoured kind, Helena would have enjoyed the most lavish hospitality offered by the *cursus publicus*, the system created by Augustus, enabling those travelling on official business to claim special privileges en route. By the fourth century the routes were dotted with staging posts – *mansiones* for imperial parties and *stationes* for others – at which travellers could replenish their supplies, change their animals, carriages and drivers, rest and be fed. Each of these inns was separated by twenty-five to thirty-five miles, the distance a traveller could expect to cover on a good day; all were expected to offer these services to any holder of an official *diploma*.[13] This system was naturally open to abuse and abused it most certainly was. An ecumenical council held at Sophia in 343 decreed that no bishop was to appear at the emperor's court unless in answer to a summons. In 362, Julian the Apostate declared that 'the *cursus publicus* has been prostrated by the immodest presumption of certain people'.

Although Eusebius emphasizes Helena's generosity to those she met on her way, a traveller of her exceptional status would have imposed acute burdens wherever she stayed. The well-born pilgrim Melania the Younger lived in the palace of Lausus, chamberlain to Theodosius II, during her stay in Constantinople, and Paula, a wealthy widow who made her pilgrimage in 385, was invited by the governor of Palestine to stay at his mansion in Jerusalem (she declined in favour of a cell in Bethlehem). How much greater, then, would have been the demands made by the mother of the Emperor, a woman in her seventies used to the Sessorian Palace and the imperial complex at Trier. It has been speculated, quite plausibly, that these demands, rather than the nuances of Arian theology, may have been the true cause of her disagreement with Bishop Eustathius in Antioch. At any rate, it is not hard to imagine the mood of the Empress as she finally arrived in the Holy City for her rendezvous with Bishop Macarius.

The scale of the Constantinian scheme for the Holy Land that Helena had been sent to supervise was breathtaking. It was at this moment, definitively, that Christianity ceased to be a faith practised in discreet shrines and private rooms, and became a faith of public splendour, one whose magnificence was greatest in its homeland. At Bethlehem, the Church of the Nativity was constructed over the grotto where Jesus was said to have been born, although it is Justinian's larger structure of the sixth century that now stands on the site. On the Mount of Olives, the Church of the Ascension, the so-called Eleona Church, a three-aisled basilica, was raised, below which was a crypt in which Jesus was said to have taught his disciples. Later histories record that Helena founded as many as forty-eight churches during her pilgrimage, and Eusebius certainly associated her with those at Bethlehem and the Mount of Olives. Egeria, the late-fourth-century pilgrim, speaks of Constantine's building *'sub praesentia matris suae'*, which suggests that Helena was closely associated with all the Emperor's construction in the Holy Land.[14]

Helena was not the only imperial envoy sent by Constantine to the Holy Land. Constantine also despatched Eutropia, the mother of Fausta, to assist in his various undertakings there, and it seems to have been at her urgings that he ordered the building of a church on the site of Mamre, where Abraham encountered the three angels. But the Empress was his true plenipotentiary in this great plan. At its heart was the Holy Sepulchre itself, the basilica intended to mark Golgotha and the tomb of Christ, which was finally dedicated long after the Empress's journey, on 13 September 335. There were two construction sites enclosed in a single precinct – the first for a five-aisled basilica, also known as the Martyrium, which was greatly admired by the so-called Bordeaux Pilgrim in 333: 'There was recently constructed, on the orders of the Emperor Constantine, a basilica, a church of admirable loveliness, with reservoirs alongside it from which one draws water and, behind, a baptistry where children are purified.'

Adjoining this was a court enclosing the rock of Calvary or Golgotha, and the tomb itself, which was later covered over by a rotunda known as the 'Anastasis'. This was never seen by Eusebius, who died in 340, but the pilgrim Egeria records the liturgical services which were celebrated within it in later years.

As many visitors have commented, the present-day church, a smaller Crusader structure built in the first half of the twelfth century, is hard to connect with the exquisitely beautiful basilica which fourth-century writers celebrated. Today, the Holy Sepulchre is almost hidden, accessible only through a small forecourt off an Arab street; it is, as Charles Couasnon remarked in his lectures on the Sepulchre, 'engulfed by the City; one approaches without seeing it' and, upon entering, the visitor has, in the words of another great Jerusalem scholar, L. H. Vincent, 'an oppressive feeling of being in a labyrinth, a sensation of chaos'.[15] Within the church the tomb itself is now enclosed by what David Roberts, the great Scottish engraver, memorably called a 'hideous kiosk'.

But the basilica described by Eusebius was anything but hideous.

In his eyes it was a 'divine monument of immortality'. Its nave was flanked by aisles on either side, surmounted by galleries supported on high columns; the walls of the aisles were adorned with marble; the nave ended with a structure covered by a half-dome, itself enveloped by twelve columns, bearing silver vessels. Egeria, who visited the East between 382 and 384, wrote of the Martyrium: 'It was built by Constantine, and under the supervision of his mother it was decorated with gold, mosaic, and precious marble, as much as his empire could provide.'[16] Constantine had not sent his mother simply to supervise the construction of a church; he wanted a visible manifestation of his majesty as a lawgiver and representative of God on earth, as awe-inspiring a declaration of divinely ordained power as the mason could muster.[17] He wanted to build a *Nova Roma*.

Part of Helena's purpose in Jerusalem was to oversee this project. But that was not her only objective – not, at least, if Ambrose, Rufinus and the other founders of the written *Inventio Crucis* tradition are to be trusted. These writers believed without equivocation that the Empress made her journey because she had been persuaded that the wood of the Cross might be recovered. As explained in the last chapter, this tradition can be traced in surviving writings to AD 395, although it is clear that an earlier text relating the story, by Gelasius of Caesarea, was in circulation at the time. We have already discussed the rudiments of this tradition. But what must be faced at this stage of our argument is that the tradition, for all its richness and rhetorical force, has been completely dismissed by modern scholars. Jan Willem Drijvers, one of the most thoughtful academics to have addressed the question in recent times, puts the argument thus:

> A legend is ... the product of imagination. It is generally held that the function of a legend is to explain things and to give a meaning to things. Although the legend of the discovery of the Cross contains historical elements and is perhaps based on a historical event, i.e. the finding in Jerusalem of a piece of wood considered to be the Cross of Christ, the main outlines of the legendary account are pure fiction.[18]

Drijvers goes further than many of his more sceptical colleagues in accepting that there may be a grain of truth in the *Inventio Crucis* tradition, but agrees with them in denying Helena any possible role in it.[19] It is one of this book's principal contentions that this position is wrong and that the tradition, for all its embellishments, deserves to be taken seriously. It almost certainly has a kernel of truth at its core. In later chapters we look at the archaeological finds that have been made at the Holy Sepulchre and new evidence that the Cross was an object of veneration in the surrounding area from the earliest times. Most important, we offer the first full analysis of the *Titulus Crucis* at Santa Croce in Gerusalemme, Rome. First, however, we must examine the case – widely assumed to be conclusive – which has been mounted against the Helena legend.

Eusebius of Caesarea (c.260–339) is generally acknowledged to be the father of ecclesiastical history. His *History of the Church* appeared in its final form some time after the defeat of Licinius in 324 and before the execution of Crispus two years later. In 336, he delivered his oration *In Praise of Constantine* and published a more comprehensive biography of the Emperor after his death in 337.[20]

In modern times Eusebius has continued to inspire strong emotions. A recent biographer of Constantine described him as 'not only a mediocre stylist but a depressingly unobjective historian ... he falsified the emperor into a mere sanctimonious devotee'.[21] Jacob Burckhardt considered him 'the first thoroughly dishonest historian of antiquity'. But in one respect, if not in others, contemporary scholars are very happy to take Eusebius at his word – or rather the absence of his words. For the chronicler, in his description of Helena's journey to Jerusalem, makes no mention of her discovery of the Cross.

Edward Gibbon, considering the legend of the *Inventio*, referred to 'the silence of Eusebius ... which satisfies those who think, perplexes those who believe'. This position has certainly satisfied most modern academics, who find Eusebius's omission, to quote one, 'impressively convincing'.[22] Constantine's biographer is, after all, effusive about the discovery of the Holy Sepulchre and the church built there, but says nothing of the discovery of the *lignum crucis* by the Empress, which so animated Ambrose and subsequent writers. The conclusion generally drawn is that the silence of Eusebius enables us to dismiss completely the Helena tradition as a tissue of lies.

It is intriguing that those who most readily condemn 'literalism' among scholars keen to explore the historical value and reliability of ancient Christian sources are most ready to embrace it themselves when it suits their scholarly purposes. For the silence of Eusebius is not in itself a sufficient reason to reject the *Inventio Crucis* story, even though it is treated as such by the vast majority of those writing on this subject.[23]

The *argumentum e silentio* is always perilous when analysing ancient texts. It is wrong to assume that writers such as Eusebius intended, or were expected, to be comprehensive when undertaking a subject. We have already seen, indeed, that he was quite willing to avoid all mention of Crispus and Fausta after their deaths, even though the familial crisis of 326 was self-evidently one of the most compelling events of the Emperor's reign.[29] Eusebius is universally acknowledged to have been a partial, self-interested and often devious writer: what he does not say is often as interesting as what he does. The question is whether there was any plausible reason for him to make such an egregious (and potentially offensive) omission as to ignore the discovery of the Cross by the Empress.[25]

There are several possibilities. Eusebius, as an historian rather than a theologian, might have had some doubts about the authenticity of such an object. As a theologian, rather than a historian, he tended to emphasize Christ's resurrection rather than his death. He was also a spiritual sophisticate by nature, who, like Origen, saw Christian worship as a metaphysical experience and might, therefore, have felt distaste for a discovery which so vividly symbolized the physical origins of the faith and much worse, its potentially idolatrous future. It may be that Eusebius was trying to educate Constantine and other worshippers out of what he would have seen as a primitive piety based upon relics and holy places.[26] It has even been suggested that he feared the discovery of the Cross would grant Constantine too much power and that

Christianity would become, as a consequence, merely a branch of imperial ideology. According to this explanation, Eusebius paid greater attention in his account to the tomb, the site of Christ's resurrection, than to Golgotha, the site of his death, because he did not want the Cross to become little more than an imperial standard. It is hard, however, to see how this suggestion can be reconciled with Eusebius's celebration of the Cross as the 'trophy of the empire'.[27] It could be argued, indeed, that he was the imperial ideologist of the Cross par excellence.

There is a more straightforward reason why the proud, vainglorious courtier and historian might have preferred to remain silent about Helena's discovery, while lauding her in every other respect. Eusebius was Metropolitan Bishop of Caesarea and, as such, tremendously threatened by the Jerusalem Church and its apparently unstoppable rise. Jerusalem's claim to be the very 'centre of the world' would have been given overwhelming force by the discovery of the True Cross: the presence in the Church of the Holy Sepulchre of the wood itself and the bishop's consequent power to distribute portions of this awesome relic posed a great threat to the institutional authority of Caesarea and to Eusebius personally. It had been decided at the council of Nicaea that Jerusalem should enjoy a special place of honour alongside the bishoprics of Rome, Alexandria and Antioch, even though, in theory, it remained subordinate to the metropolitan bishopric of Caesarea. Eusebius's failure to mention the discovery of the Cross is certainly striking, but no less striking are the lengths to which he goes to avoid mentioning Macarius, except when he is quoting directly from Constantine's correspondence. It is not hard to imagine the petulant Bishop of Caesarea omitting all mention of the *Inventio Crucis* as a deliberate snub to the increasingly powerful see of Jerusalem (although Jerusalem was to prevail in this battle, when the bishopric became a patriarchate in the fifth century).[28]

This is, of course, hypothesis, but it is a hypothesis strengthened, inadvertently, by Eusebius himself. In the *Vita Constantini* he includes a letter from Constantine in which the Emperor refers to a 'token of that holiest Passion'. Cardinal Newman, in his *Two Essays on Biblical and Ecclesiastical Miracles*, observed that this phrase would seem to admit of only one interpretation: 'Did we read it without knowing the fact of the historian's silence when writing in his own person,' Newman noted, 'we certainly should have the impression that it is of the Cross that Constantine was speaking.'[29] This is surely correct. It is also significant that in his earlier work, *In Praise of Constantine*, delivered in 336 to celebrate the Emperor's thirtieth jubilee, Eusebius refers to the Basilica of the Holy Sepulchre as a 'temple to the saving sign' and a 'memorial full of eternal significance and the Great Saviour's own trophies over death' – which can only be a reference to the Cross. Speaking before Constantine, rather than writing after his death, the churchman felt compelled to refer to the basilica as a monument, above all else, to the crucifixion.

There are good reasons, therefore, not to accept Eusebius's silence at face value. But this only takes the argument so far. What matters much more is the evidence to suggest that a beam of wood was, indeed, discovered in Jerusalem by Helena and the reasons why the location she chose to excavate was almost certainly the authentic site of the crucifixion and tomb of Jesus.

Tradition plays a different role in different cultures. In our own highly technologized society tradition is seen as a sea wall against the tidal wave of change. Its function is to preserve that which is best, and protect future generations against degeneracy and arbitrary social practice. But in ancient societies such as that of first-to fourth-century Palestine, the function of tradition was more fundamental. Its purpose was not only to safeguard particular modes of behaviour: it was also a means of *handing on information* from generation to generation. In this sense tradition was a matter of the deadliest seriousness.[30] Diligent memorialization of important sayings and locations was a sacred task, as well as a social duty.

The sites of tombs were considered particularly significant and are often referred to in the Bible.[31] The Jewish saying 'whose sepulchre is with us to this day' is still used. In Jesus's day, we are told, people could point out the burial sites of notables such as Alexander Jannaeus, John Hyrcanus, and Helen Adiabene and her sons. Hegesippus reported that the tomb of James, brother of Jesus, who was killed in AD 62, was still in existence in 175. Before the second Jewish rebellion the sites of the sepulchre of David and Solomon were known and Josephus reports that Herod the Great had restored the edifice.

It would have been unthinkable for the earliest Christians to forget where their Saviour had been executed, buried and discovered risen from the dead. At the beginning of the Jewish insurrection of AD 66–73, most of them fled to Pella, a town in Peraea beyond the River Jordan, but they returned and continued to exist as a community in Jerusalem until the second revolt in AD 131–5. Even after this epochal event and its aftermath, a community of Gentile Christians remained in Aelia Capitolina, enough for the topographical tradition to survive. As we have seen, the tradition was evidently sufficiently strong to attract pilgrims from far afield, even though Golgotha and the tomb were covered over by a pagan monument. It is striking, too, that no alternative and more accessible site seems to have been proposed by the ancients. Evidently the tradition was so strong that nobody dared so to do. Long before Eusebius became involved in the excavations of the late 320s, he affirmed the association of place and event in his *Onomasticon* guidebook, describing Golgotha as 'the place of the skull, where Jesus was crucified; it is to be seen at Aelia, north of the hill of Sion'.[32]

It is true that the Evangelists agree that the events of the Passion took place outside the city, which would seem to make a nonsense of the site that Christian pilgrims have chosen to visit.[33] The Epistle to the Hebrews says that Jesus, 'might sanctify the people with his own blood, suffered without the gate'.[34] It is also true that no tombs were permitted within the city fortifications. But the walls of the city of Jerusalem underwent considerable changes in the years after the crucifixion. To the first Iron Age wall, and the second outer northern defence of the city, Herod Agrippa added a third wall between AD 41 and 44, and it seems that this new construction enclosed the site of Golgotha.[35] The new circuit was intended to protect the new suburb, known as the 'New City', which had grown up outside the northern wall, and would have encompassed both the site of the crucifixion and the garden of

Joseph of Arimathea. Again, what is striking is that Macarius and others felt so confident to identify intramural sites as those of Golgotha and the Sepulchre, given the explicit record in the Gospels that they were originally outside the walls. They can only have done so on the basis of very strong – indeed, unquestioned – local tradition.

This tradition enshrined both belief and expectation. It was believed by the earliest Christians that their Messiah had died and risen again on the site of the pagan temple. But they also believed that this place would be the venue of the Second Coming, an event which they heralded in their ceremonies at the church on Mount Sion, outside the perimeter of Aelia Capitolina. The tradition Helena tapped was not, therefore, merely antiquarian, a matter of pedantic scholarly debate for the greybeards of Jerusalem and elsewhere. It was a matter of the greatest urgency to the Christians living in the vicinity of the holy place and those who came to visit it. To err in this question would be to err about the very place to which the Son of God would, imminently, be returning.

It is very likely, therefore, that Helena was excavating on the correct site. The question then arises: what, if anything, did she find? In the following chapters, we examine the Santa Croce *Titulus* and ask whether this might, conceivably, have been a fragment of the wood she is said to have discovered. But first it must be asked whether she found anything at all, since this itself is disputed by most modern scholars, taking their (silent) cue from Eusebius.

Our contention is that – in this debate at least – Eusebius has enjoyed disproportionate attention at the expense of another great churchman.[36] Cyril, Bishop of Jerusalem (c.315–86), was appointed to his see by Eusebius's successor in Caesarea, Acacius, in about 349. Cyril's career was one of great turbulence, marked by his repeated banishment from his own see; he inspired suspicion on all sides, among Arians and non-Arians alike, and so alarmed the Council of Antioch in 379 that it sent St Gregory of Nyssa to Palestine to report on his conduct in Jerusalem (Gregory's mordant conclusion was that the Church in the holy city was morally corrupt but theologically sound). Cyril was not an ecclesiastical historian of Eusebius's distinction nor, perhaps, quite as successful an imperial courtier. No less than Eusebius, he had an axe to grind: in this case, the axe of the Church of Jerusalem, for which he was a relentless propagandist, and for which he declared independence from the metropolitan see of Caesarea. But his writings are underrated as a source in this context. While Eusebius is too often given the benefit of the doubt, Cyril is too often treated with suspicion – or ignored altogether.[37]

At the end of the 340s, while still only a priest, Cyril wrote in a series of lectures delivered in Lent and Eastertide and known as the *Catecheses* that 'already the whole world is filled with fragments of the wood of the Cross'. He added: 'The holy wood of the Cross gives witness: it is here to be seen in this very day, and through those who take [pieces] from it in faith, it has from here already filled almost all the world.' A third time, he referred to 'the wood of the Cross which from this place is spread piecemeal all over the world'.[38] In 351 the Bishop elaborated in a letter to the Emperor Constantius II, referring to a cross of light seen above Golgotha:

> For if in the days of your imperial father, Constantine of blessed memory, the saving wood of the Cross was found in Jerusalem (divine grace granting the finding of the long-hidden holy places to one who nobly aspired to sanctity), now, sire, in the reign of your most godly majesty, as if to mark how far your zeal excels your forebear's piety, not from the earth but from the skies marvels appear, the trophy of victory over death of our Lord Jesus Christ, the only-begotten Son of God, even the holy Cross, flashing and sparkling with brilliant light, has been seen at Jerusalem.[39]

Leaving aside Cyril's bombastic flattery of his imperial master, the import of these four passages is very considerable. The Bishop attests without equivocation that a great devotion to the physical remains of the Cross has already developed; he says that fragments of the *lignum crucis* have dispersed widely; and he says that the wood was discovered during Constantine's reign. He could not, in fact, be more explicit.

Like Helena and her son, Cyril understood the power of the holy places and the holy relics they had yielded, and the demand for a version of Christianity based on popular needs rather than esoteric spiritualism. 'Should you be disposed to doubt it [the crucifixion],' he told his pupils, 'the very place which everyone can see proves you wrong, this blessed Golgotha ... on which we are now assembled.'[40] Cyril spoke to the needs of Christians such as the Bordeaux Pilgrim (who visited the Holy Land in 333 and clearly associated each of the places he visited with a precise scriptural reference).[41] In the *Catecheses*, the Bishop draws attention no less explicitly to the historical evidence of Galilee, the Mount of Olives, Gethsemane, Golgotha, Bethlehem, the house of Caiaphas, Pilate's deserted *praetorium* and other such sites. He understood that the faith would in future be constructed around relics, places, the memorialization of events and their assimilation to the liturgy of the Church.

In particular, he grasped that the *lignum crucis* had a unique talismanic power which was capable of convincing the faithless to embrace the true religion and persuading the faithful that the Church of the Holy Sepulchre was 'the very centre of the world'. The distribution of fragments of the Cross, furthermore, was a means of communicating this message almost instantaneously to those unable or disinclined to make an arduous pilgrimage to Jerusalem. Small wonder, then, that Eusebius, fearing the eclipse of Caesarea by the junior see, had declined to promote the discovery in his *Life of Constantine*.

There is corroboration for Cyril's claim that fragments of the Cross were spreading 'around the world'. As early as 359, a 'martyrium' near Tixter in Mauretania boasted the deposit of a piece: a '*memoria sa[n]cta de ligno crucis*'.[42] According to Gregory of Nyssa, St Macrina, who died in 379, used to wear a relic of the Cross in his locket.[43] Towards the end of the fourth century, John Chrysostom noted that everyone was 'fighting over' fragments of the wood.[44] By the beginning of the fifth, there is evidence of such relics reaching Gaul, Africa, Asia Minor, Syria, Italy and elsewhere.[45] In a letter to Sulpicius Severus in 403, sent with such a fragment, Paulinus of Nola explained that the purpose of these relics was to animate inner vision of the crucifixion: 'With his interior eyesight he will see the whole meaning of the cross in this tiny fragment.'[46]

The proliferation of these pieces made the high-minded suspicious. Jerome used the occasion of an annual veneration of the Cross to argue that there was no special spiritual merit to be had from seeing or owning wooden relics: 'By the cross I mean not the wood, but the Passion. That cross is in Britain, in India, in the whole world ... Happy is he who carries in his own heart the cross, the resurrection, the place of the Nativity of Christ and of his Ascension.'[47]

Ambrose himself, although obviously in awe of Helena's discovery, was evidently nervous of any suggestion that the wood itself should be venerated, 'for that is the error of pagans and the folly of the unrighteous'.[48]

But such scholarly nuances were lost on the thousands who flocked to Jerusalem to see the wood of which Cyril spoke so rapturously. For this phenomenon an extraordinary source survives in the account left by the pilgrim Egeria, who visited the Near East between 382 and 384. It is pure chance that her story survives at all, since it was lost for 700 years and recovered in manuscript copy only in the late nineteenth century. The fact that it does, however, is of immense value to the historian of the Cross, since Egeria's sometimes breathless account is a magnificently detailed description of the Jerusalem liturgy, which had emerged under Cyril's command and developed subsequently.

We shall encounter her again at the beginning of the next chapter, meeting a woman who leaves her reader in no doubt of the passion which the experience of touching the Cross and the *Titulus* inspired in the pilgrims who, like her, had travelled far to see the alleged physical remains of the Cross on which Jesus died. After kissing the fragments, the worshippers went into the courtyard of the church – so crammed that there was not 'even room to open a door'. There they listened for three hours to homiletic readings about the sufferings of Christ and related prophecies foretelling his Passion:

It is impressive to see the way all the people are moved by these readings, and how they mourn. You could hardly believe how every single one of them weeps during the three hours, old and young alike, because of the manner in which the Lord suffered for it. Then, when three o'clock comes, they have the reading from St John's Gospel about Jesus giving up the ghost, and, when that has been read, there is a prayer and the dismissal.[49]

No less interesting is Egeria's account of the festival of Encaenia, a dedicatory celebration held on the alleged day of the discovery of the Cross (3 May). On the second day of this feast the Cross was displayed in the same way as on Good Friday:

> At the time of Encaenia, they keep festival for eight days, and for many days beforehand the crowds begin to assemble. Monks and apotactites come not only from the provinces having large numbers of them, such as Mesopotamia, Syria, Egypt and Thebaid, but from every region and province. Not one of them fails to make for Jerusalem to share the celebrations of this solemn feast. There are also lay men and women from every province gathering in Jerusalem at this time for the holy day. And although bishops are few and far between, they never have less than forty or fifty in Jerusalem at this time, accompanied by many of their clergy. In fact I should say that people regard it as a grave sin to miss taking part in this solemn feast, unless anyone had been prevented from coming by an emergency.[50]

Egeria's rhapsodic account provides a unique insight into the mind of the fourth-century pilgrim. 'Journeys', she says, 'are not hard when they are the fulfilment of hopes.'[51] The very tone she adopts speaks of the lengths to which men and women were prepared to go to see the holy places and their relics.[52] She, and other pilgrims like her, had joyously embraced the potential offered by the Constantinian Church to link belief with place, to experience through the senses the physical world described in the Gospels. This in itself was a quite fundamental development in the history of popular Christianity. But Egeria's story is important for another more particular reason, simply because it demonstrates beyond reasonable doubt that *something* had been found in Jerusalem before her pilgrimage, that news of the discovery had reached the most distant shores of the emerging Christian world and that to be in the presence of this great find was already regarded as one of the most profound experiences the new faith had to offer.

Who had found this something? It is usually suggested that the Helena legend was grafted on to the Jerusalem tradition by Ambrose and his successors.[53] On this basis, the rhetoricians and historians from whom we have inherited the story of the Empress's discovery were propagandists pure and simple, linking the name of Constantine's mother to the excavation of this most holy relic for exclusively political reasons. Again, this interpretation exaggerates the role of pure invention in tradition in late antiquity: it was not open to Ambrose, discoursing over the coffin of Theodosius, simply to pluck from the air such a contention and present it as fact to his gilded listeners. Indeed, this occasion would have been a quite inappropriate moment to venture such a claim if, as modern scholars argue, it was completely groundless. Ambrose must have been drawing on a deeper well than his own imagination. There is no intrinsic reason to suppose that he did not believe what he said. Others before must have believed it too. The real question is why the possible authenticity of his claim has never been taken remotely seriously.

Helena, mother of Constantine, died in 328 or early 329, not long after her return from the Holy Land. Her work was incomplete, but she had set in train a series of momentous projects, religious, dynastic and cultural. She had risen from the lowly station of *stabularia* to a position of near cosmic significance in the firmament of the late Roman world. Almost as much as her son, she had accrued to herself the awesome power of the founder of a civic faith, the architect of a belief system which synthesized the power of the State and the power of a jealous God. In Rome, she had acted ruthlessly to destroy the enemies of her dynasty; in the Holy Land she had led the transformation of Christianity from an essentially private faith to a monumental public religion.

Her great journey became a model for the high-born anxious to prove their zeal for the faith, or *eusebia*.[54] The Empress Eudocia, wife of Theodosius II, made a pilgrimage to the Holy Land in 438, which was effectively an explicit homage to her illustrious predecessor. Eudocia assisted at the consecration of churches and prayed at the empty tomb of Christ, kneeling 'like a penant girl'.

Humility had its limits, of course: the Empress arrived in Jeru-salem in a carriage adorned with gold and precious stones, escorted by a contingent of the imperial guard. But the sight of an Augusta on her knees before the holy sites must have been a startling one. Later, when the Emperor Marcian was acclaimed by the bishops at Chalcedon in 451 as a 'new Constantine, new Paul, new David', his consort Pulcheria was hailed as a 'new Helena'. By this stage the cult of the great Empress was evidently well established.

Emulation was the first of posterity's rewards. But Helena had done much more than establish a cult of herself. She had helped to found a Christian empire and, by her alleged discovery of the Cross, to give visible form to the new alliance between God and emperor. This discovery was to have a momentous impact upon the destiny of the human race. As one forgotten clerical writer of the late nineteenth century put it: 'We might follow various small fragments of the wood which were taken from Jerusalem and thus show the streams of its influence flowing here and there and permeating European life, action, and history.'[55]

The fate of the main Jerusalem fragment is unknown, except that it was lost on the scorched field of Hattin in 1187, thence to become the stuff of mythology, secret cults and arcane knowledge. But Helena, wise investor that she was, did not leave all of her sacred find behind. She had sent a crucial portion of it ahead to Rome, to her great Sessorian Palace. Today, her home has become a church, watched over by Cistercian monks who pad quietly through its dark halls and corridors. Behind a locked door, in a reliquary built by Mussolini, is kept the *Titulus Crucis*, the sup-posed headboard discovered by the Empress seventeen centuries ago. It is to that cold, stone-clad room, and the mysteries within it, that our quest now takes us.

4

A Kiss of Life – Jerusalem and Rome, or: How a Piece of Walnut Wood Made History

Thanne longen folk to goon on pilgrimages,
And palmeres for to seken straunge strondes.
To ferne halwes, kowthe in sondre londes.

Chaucer, The Canterbury Tales

The Patriarch rearranged himself on his throne and
clutched a miniature icon in a gold setting, suspended on
a chain around his neck. 'Even a small oil lamp', he said,
'can give light to a big room.'

William Dalrymple, From the Holy Mountain

Collectors' Items

It is Good Friday in Jerusalem and the year is AD 383. A holy
ceremony is enacted and observed:

A table covered with a linen cloth is placed before the bishop. The
deacons are forming a circle around the table. A small, gold-plated
silver box is brought in. It contains the wood of the Cross. It is opened,
and the wood of the Cross is placed on the table together with the
Titulus. The Bishop still sitting, seizes the ends of the holy wood. The
deacons guard it, standing, for now the *Catechumens* and the faithful
come up to the table, one by one. And so the whole people goes past
the table, everyone bows and touches the wood and the inscription
first with the forehead, then with the eyes, and kissing the Cross, they
move on. But no one touches it with their hands. On one occasion,
however – I do not know when – one of them bit off a piece of the Holy

Wood and took it away by theft. And for this reason the deacons stand round and keep watch so that no one dares to do the same again.

This is our earliest surviving account of the veneration of the Cross and of Pilate's inscription, the *Titulus*, in Jerusalem. It is an invaluable, tantalizing eyewitness account of a liturgical event aflame with mystical significance. And we owe this account to Egeria, the fourth-century pilgrim introduced in chapter 3.

As we have seen, the Empress Helena's invention of Christian archaeology – for that is what her discoveries amounted to – inspired believers all over the Roman Empire. Her journey became a model, too, for other women, seeking to prove their piety by visiting the churches Helena had built in Jerusalem and Bethlehem. While in the Holy Land, they would also seek traces of other venerated sites – the house of Peter in Capernaum, the village of Nazareth, the hamlet of Emmaus. Most of these early post-Constantinian pilgrims did not write about their adventures, or if they did, composed only diaries never meant for publication.

Only two such accounts have survived from the fourth century, the century of Helena. The first was written just a few years after the Empress's visit, in 333, by an anonymous pilgrim from Bordeaux and is essentially a detailed itinerary rather than a personal record. But the second account is of a quite different character: a series of letters sent home to a group of pious women, not by a seasoned merchant or valiant knight, nor a bishop with his entourage, but by a lady from Spain who visited the holy sites between AD 382 and 384. Her name was Egeria, or perhaps Atheria: all we know about her must be gleaned from the surviving parts of her book.[1] But since its beginning and end (which would undoubtedly have identified her) have not survived, her name has only been preserved in a letter of a Spanish abbot, Valerius of Bierzo, who died in AD 695, some three hundred years after her death.[2] Different manuscript copies of his letter about this intriguing woman call her Egeria, Atheria or Etheria. So who was she?

In Roman mythology her name means the etherial one, or the nymph of the fountains. She may have come from southern France (Aquitaine), or, as most scholars assume, from northern Spain

(Galicia). Wealthy enough to afford a pilgrimage via Constantinople (Byzantium) to Jerusalem, she stayed in the region and
travelled widely through Galilee and Samaria, visited Egypt twice,
saw Edessa – modern Urfa – and finally, after three years, returned
home. She knew Greek but wrote in Latin, the language of the
West: not the classical Latin of Cicero or Seneca, but a rough,
everyday idiom which already suggests the origins of Spanish.

Egeria's ambitions were not literary but practical. As a devotional scout, it was her aim to tell her friends at home what the
holy places looked like and, above all, how the great feast days of
the Christian year were celebrated. To her, the liturgy of Jerusalem
should be the model for the Church at large, at a time when Rome
was already establishing its supremacy in Christendom. Here,
only here, in Jerusalem, could Christians understand and celebrate
the unity of time and place; only here was it possible to connect
Salvation past and present in the heart of the faithful. To her, the
Cross and the *Titulus* were the visible, tangible signs of this unity,
not merely talismans or relics but physical testament to universal
truths.

As a result, Egeria strives to record what she sees as richly and
with as much vivid detail as possible: even those who cannot go
to the holy sites themselves shall see what she saw in her mind's
eye. And those who do want to make such a pilgrimage shall find
in her letters an indispensable guide.

To appreciate her ambition, it is important to remember how
important the concept of *witness* was to the early Church; how
important it was *to see* and *to touch*. St Paul had made it clear to
the Corinthians that they could go to Jerusalem, see the places
and interview witnesses. This was the force of his reference to the
'more than five hundred' who had seen the risen Christ and most
of whom were still alive.[3] In similar spirit John, the Evangelist,
and with him the author of the Letter to the Hebrews, had insisted
that Golgotha and the empty tomb were real sites, known to
contemporaries, not far from the city wall.[4]

And there was an injunction still more ancient to pilgrims to
go and see God's holiest city, the ancestral call of Psalm 122: 'I
rejoiced that they said to me, "Let us go to the house of the
LORD." At last our feet are standing at your gates, Jerusalem!'

Remarkable evidence has survived at the Holy Sepulchre to suggest that some of the very first Christian visitors from abroad believed, and claimed explicitly, that they were answering the challenge of this psalm. Into the rock of Golgotha slope they incised the simple shape of a boat, just underneath the Temple of Venus, which Emperor Hadrian had erected above the hillock in AD 135. *'Domine ivimus'*, says the Latin inscription beneath the boat: 'Lord, we have arrived!'[5] This extraordinary graffito – a passionate declaration resonant through the centuries – can still be seen today. We shall return to its significance in the following chapter.

Like Helena before her, Egeria knew what she was doing. Then as now, there were many reasons to embark on a pilgrimage, personal, political, or monastic. But for a devout Christian the overriding purpose was an empirical one: to see and touch the stones and holy relics which gave physical form to a spiritual message. For the first time in the religious history of the Mediterranean world, a faith had emerged that did not simply refer its adherents to a pantheon of mostly absent deities, nor to the myths of invisible godheads whose marble statues populated the cities and the countryside. In the Christian faith, the one and only God had become Man in Jesus, a man of normal appetites and vulnerabilities who had been seen by many people. These witnesses – Paul's 'five hundred' and many more – claimed to know where he was born in Bethlehem and brought up in Nazareth, where he lived in Capernaum, where he celebrated his last meal with his disciples, where he was sentenced by Pilate, where he was crucified, where he was buried, where he met his followers after his resurrection and even where he ascended to heaven. To know such things was not to explain or understand them, of course. It is interesting, though, that this tradition of holy sites had survived so strongly in the area where the events of the Gospels take place between the death of Jesus and the fourth century.[6]

So embedded are the basic concepts of Christianity in our culture that it is easy to forget how revolutionary they must have seemed in the first centuries of the faith. What was being proposed, after all, was unique, quite unheard of in human history: a God who had taken on human form, while remaining God and a spiritual presence at the same time. Paul tried to find words for this when he ended his second Letter to the Corinthians with a formula which all Christians know by heart: 'The grace of the Lord Jesus Christ, the love of God, and the fellowship of the Holy Spirit be with you all.'[7] At the end of Matthew's Gospel, Jesus himself tells his followers to go and baptize 'all nations', and to baptize them 'in the name of the Father, and of the Son, and of the Holy Spirit.'[8] The Son, the Lord Jesus Christ, had lived among people: he had been made flesh in a world where deities proliferated, claimed sacrifice but did not deign to walk among mortals.

This is why, as we noted in the last chapter, Hadrian's building project was so important to early Christians, for it inadvertently marked out quite clearly where the darkest and greatest events of Christ's life had taken place. And they came, and reached the rock outside the temple precinct: '*Domine ivimus* [Lord, we have arrived].'

But was their zeal rooted in any sort of historical reality? What was this object which Egeria saw and touched, and which so many others had kissed before her? A forgery? An ingeniously crafted artefact? Or an authentic relic, plausibly linked to the suffering and death of Jesus? As we noted in the last chapter, thousands of alleged fragments of the True Cross have been preserved worldwide (although too few, in fact, to account, as some critics have claimed, for whole forests of trees, or even, in fact, the stem of a single Roman Cross[9]). As we have seen, many places of worship still claim possession of an authentic fragment, a portion of the *Vera Crux* to signify their supposed connection with the divine.

But the *Titulus* survives, if it has survived at all, in only one place. Today, only one church or archive claims to own the inscription on the Cross of Jesus, or a part of it: Santa Croce in Gerusalemme, a church on the outskirts of ancient Rome, one of the seven official pilgrimage churches in the Eternal City.

The name of this church is in itself interesting – Jerusalem, but in Rome – for what Helena was trying to do was to bring the history of her faith full circle. In the first century, Peter and Paul had arrived from Jerusalem to establish the Church in the imperial city.[10] And here they were martyred, St Peter – according to tradition – in Nero's Vatican Gardens, St Paul, the Roman citizen, at a place now called Tre Fontane. Their burial sites – archaeologically well attested – are still to be seen, in the Vatican Scavi (the excavation area of a Neronian graveyard) and underneath the church of San Paolo fuori le Mura. Helena followed their lead. After her great discoveries she could have joined her son in Byzantium – his new capital, soon to be called Constantinople – and she could have returned to her previous residence in Trier or to one of her old homes in Naissus or perhaps even York. But she made a typically independent-minded decision. Having sent some of the relics discovered at Golgotha to the Emperor, she journeyed back to Rome, the city of Peter's and Paul's glory in martyrdom, the city which at her time had begun to claim supremacy over all other bishoprics in the Empire, and took up residence once more in the Sessorian Palace, a sumptuous imperial villa built by Septimius Severus and finished by Elagabalus, an adherent of orgiastic Syrian sun god cults who was murdered in AD 222. It was an ideal location, next to a major road linking the city with the countryside, within walking distance of an amphitheatre, a circus and public baths which she restored and embellished after a fire.

Her palace is today's church of Santa Croce in Gerusalemme. Not quite, of course: the church as one sees it from the road is baroque, while the side chapel with the reliquary is a typical example of Mussolini's early fascist architecture; but the lower parts of the north-west façade are fourth century and the remains of the Sessorian Palace have been excavated in the grounds next to the church. Even some walls of the amphitheatre are still there and have been incorporated into a museum of the Italian army.

At her Roman palace Helena collected the items she had brought with her from Jerusalem.[11] It is unlikely that she built a chapel for them, given the more idiosyncratic uses to which she put the crucifixion nails. According to Ambrose[12] – the bishop of Milan whom we met in a previous chapter – Helena had one nail made into a bridle, another into a diadem and sent both to her son – who duly used the bridle for his favourite horse.[13] We may doubt whether the Christian community of Rome had access to the relics in her palace; there is, at any rate, no contemporary account describing liturgical scenes in Rome like the one so vividly recalled by Egeria in Jerusalem.

Those finds, therefore, seem to have been Helena's private property, jealously guarded evidence of her stature and status as the mighty Dowager Empress. Only in the second half of the fourth century, after the deaths of both Helena and Constantine, was permission given to convert the largest hall of the palace into a church: a spacious but unspectacular room, 36.46 metres long, 21.80 metres wide and no less than 22.15 metres high. An apsis was added facing south-east – that is towards Jerusalem – a neighbouring passage of the palace was turned into an aisle and direct access to the palace was closed. A further room was made accessible by a circular passage around the apsis. That room, today called the Chapel of St Helena, was the ancient home for the relics from Jerusalem and it is the one place within the church of Santa Croce in Gerusalemme where fourth-century stonework can still be seen today.

The only alleged archaeological discovery from the Holy Lane which was immediately given to the Church of Rome and was publicly accessible was the famous 'Scala Santa' (or Holy Staircase) opposite the Church of St John Lateran. This is associated with the Empress only by the most tenuous of late legends and can hardly claim to be authentic. In Helena's times the whole area was covered by a vast palatial precinct, given to the Bishop of Rome by Constantine himself. To this day the Lateran Church, rather than St Peter's in the Vatican, is the official residence of the Bishop of Rome. Here, this staircase was installed at an unknown date, to be venerated as the steps that Jesus had climbed on his way to Pilate's courtroom in Jerusalem. It soon became an obligatory destination for pilgrims to Rome. Even Martin Luther, not yet a rebel, ascended them on his knees when he visited Rome in 1510. In the late sixteenth century, Pope Sixtus V ordered his architect, Domenico Fontana, to build a new chapel opposite the Lateran basilica and the twenty-eight marble steps were taken across the road, where they still are. It is not the kind of relic uniquely related to Jesus in which Helena would have been interested. In any case the Jerusalem Praetorium of the Roman governor was not a permanent building: the administrative seat was in

Caesarea and Pilate, his predecessors and successors only went to Jerusalem on special occasions, staying at one of the Herodian residences. This means it is much less likely that Macarius and his team of excavators would have been certain where to look for the 'authentic' steps – if they ever existed. In fact, modern archaeological research has shown that the provisional Praetorium of Pilate was not where the Via Dolorosa followed by contemporary pilgrims supposes it to be, at the Antonia Fortress (now an Arab boys school). In fact, it is much more likely to have been at the southern Hasmonean Palace. This palace, partly re-excavated and visible in the modern Wohl Museum built above it, is in the Jewish Quarter of the Old Town, and there are no traces of ancient stairs, removed or otherwise. But what of the other relics?

The church built on the site of the Sessorian Palace may house the *Titulus* – but it is still called Santa Croce in Gerusalemme rather than, as one might initially expect, Santo Titolo in Gerusalemme. This is because the inscription had always been treated as an integral part of the Cross. Some accounts, indeed, do not even identify it as a separate object in its own right, while others refer to it distinctly only because of its role in the identification of the True Cross. Not surprisingly, therefore, the Church of the Holy Cross in Jerusalem also houses supposed particles of the True Cross, the very relics that gave it its name. As we noted before, Cyril of Jerusalem recorded the distribution of such alleged fragments as early as the Eighties of the fourth century,[14] and Helena herself was always associated in legend with the ownership and dissemination of parts of the True Cross. Alas, the fragments preserved at Santa Croce are too small to be analysed by any reliable method.

More can be said about the nail which is displayed alongside the *Titulus*. Although Ambrose of Milan concentrates on the two nails which Helena had sent to Constantine, it is historically quite plausible that there once were four – two for the feet, and two for the arms. Thanks to the discovery of the nailed heel bone in the ossuary of Yehohanan – the first-century crucified Jew from Givat ha-Mivtar in Jerusalem – we know that those medieval artists who depicted the feet of the victim one above the other, pierced by one nail, painted misleadingly and that early Christian images were more accurate. The feet were nailed to the cross separately, to the left and right of the vertical beam.[15] As for the arms, they could be tied to the cross with ropes or nailed through the wrists, rather than through the palms. In Jesus's case, the Gospel accounts specify that the arms were nailed, not tied (John 20:25–8; Luke 24:38–9).[16] Whatever may have happened to the nails – including the possibility that all of them were found by Helena and her excavators – we may assume that once there were indeed four (later legendary stories added a fifth nail).

The single nail on display at Santa Croce has a new head. It is easy to be thrown off course by decorative additions, but an error nonetheless. It is quite possible, in the first place, that the nail allegedly found at the Holy Sepulchre had lost its head. The one discovered in the Givat ha-Mivtar ossuary had certainly done so, the top of the nail apparently broken off under the force of the hammer blow. More interesting, however, is the fact that the nail found in Yehohanan's heel bone and the one preserved at Santa Croce look almost identical: Yehohanan's is 12 centimetres long, squared with four sides of 0.9 centimetres each. The Santa Croce nail, without the new head, measures 11.5 centimetres – and is squared with four sides of 0.9 centimetres. Since the ossuary of Yehohanan was only found in 1968, the nail in Rome cannot be an artful facsimile of it. And yet it fits the type almost to perfection. If the Santa Croce nail is a forgery, it must have been based on the model of other Roman crucifixions or, by sheer coincidence, closely resemble a common form of Roman nail which happened to have been used to crucify Yehohanan.[17] It seems at least possible, and perhaps even plausible, that one of the nails excavated in Jerusalem could have reached the Sessorian Palace of Helena in Rome and survived to this day. All sources which do mention the nails agree that Helena retrieved at least some of them and that only parts of two were sent to Byzantium. Again, the absence of absolutely conclusive evidence should not exclude constructive debate about this intriguing object.

Three further relics are kept in the church's Cappella delle Reliquie, of varying degrees of interest: two supposed thorns from Jesus's crown of thorns, a bone from the finger with which Doubting

Thomas touched the wounds of the risen Christ and the horizontal bar of the cross of the penitent thief crucified with Jesus who was identified, according to tradition, as Dismas. This piece of wood has been part of the church's collection since 1570, when it was discovered in the altar steps of the chapel dedicated to Helena. Although there is enough wood left for a dendrochronological analysis this has not yet been attempted. In theory, it is no less likely that a piece of wood of this size could have survived as long as tiny fragments – not least if it had been protected by the climate of Jerusalem for three centuries in an old cistern underneath Hadrian's temple. But even if we accept, for the sake of the argument and with no reason in our written sources to do so, that crosses or parts of crosses other than that of Jesus were preserved and sent abroad, there is still no way to find out whether it belonged to Dismas, to the other thief or even to any other crucified man among the hundreds put to death by the Romans in those years on a hill like Golgotha. Some observers have noticed that there are no nail marks in the Dismas bar and that this conforms to the iconography of many early paintings where the two thieves were tied to the cross (and may have survived longer than Jesus for that reason: see John 19:31–3). But the ends of that beam, which today measures 1.78 metres in length, are clearly and cleanly cut off, perilously close to the points where nails would have been made for a man of average size. Accident or design? It is surely impossible to say. Confident study of this relic must await dendrochronological analysis and a biological survey of the remains of flora found in the crevices of the wood.

As to the crown of thorns at Santa Croce, not even Helena's most ardent admirers connect her with this relic. There are numerous stories about the Crusaders who gave thorns to churches all over Europe, after the conquest of Byzantium-Constantinople in 1204 where the crown had been venerated since the days of Emperor Justinian in the sixth century. But there is no pedigree for any of the pieces, nor for the two in Rome, nor for the more substantial fragments in Paris. The trade in Byzantine objects was, in any case, often ludicrous in its extent and liquidity. Around 1237 King Baldwin II sold the French King Louis IX a medieval weed headband with a few thorns, and later spoilt the insatiable French-

man with the 'regal' purple robe with which the soldiers mockingly clad Jesus (John 19:2), the sponge with which his lips had
been wetted on the cross (John 19:29), a fragment of the lance used
to pierce his side (John 19:34), and even a piece from the linen
shrouds (John 20:5–7). It is hard to take such ready availability
seriously.

At Santa Croce, the relic which comes closest to such obviously
bespoke artefacts is the forefinger of St Thomas. Skeletal remains
of this apostle suddenly appear on the stage of Church history at
the time of Emperor Severus Alexander (222–35). According to
legend, this emperor, scarcely known for his pro-Christian leanings, acted on behalf of the Christians at Edessa – a city Chris-
tianized by Thomas – who wanted to bury his relics. According to
the early third century 'Acts of Thomas', Thomas had died in
north-west India, at Mylapore near Madras, where his tomb was
seen by the first Portuguese explorers in 1522. Severus Alexander,
however, dutifully wrote to the Kings of India[18] and, according to
one version, the bones of Thomas were solemnly translated – to
use the ecclesiastical term for such actions – in AD 232.[19] When
the Muslim armies approached Edessa in the thirteenth century
the relics were taken to safety, to the island of Chios, where Greek
tradition locates the birth of Homer, and finally to Ortona, a town
in the Abruzzi. And there they remain – unless, of course, one
prefers the version of the Indian Christians themselves who insist
that he is still buried in India at San Tome. At some stage a finger
bone may or may not have reached Santa Croce in Rome, for
whatever reason. Whose finger it was we shall never know.

The Cistercian monks and scholars, who act as guardians of
Santa Croce and its treasures, rightly discourage credulity when
discussing these artefacts. They acknowledge that the market in
relics spun out of control in the Middle Ages and that it was
possible to procure supposedly holy objects more or less on
demand. So much so, in fact, that the Fourth Lateran Council of
1215 prohibited the selling and buying of relics without proof of
authenticity and episcopal permission. As ever, however, it proved
hard to buck the market: certificates of authenticity could be
manufactured easily or bought at a price, and the acquisition of
relics remained too important a symbol of status and authority

for bishops, kings and abbeys to submit to such stringent regu-
lation. As we saw, only some twenty years after that council, the
French King Louis IX was the happy and credulous recipient of
the sponge mentioned in John 19:29. A man like the Saxonian
Elector Frederick, who protected Martin Luther and hid him at
Wartburg Castle (where he translated the New Testament), owned
one of the most valuable collections of relics in Europe – not-
withstanding Luther's savage criticism of the proliferation of such
relics and the cults they inspired. In the great reformer's time, and
long after, ordinary Christians continued to believe in the allegedly
miraculous healing power of such objects and sought contact with,
if not ownership of, them. And there was some Biblical authority
for this primal urge: the Acts of the Apostles record that people in
Ephesus were healed when they touched the handkerchiefs and
scarves once worn by St Paul (Acts 19:12).[20] It followed that objects
connected with an apostle, let alone Jesus himself, had powerful
healing properties and potentially awesome numinous power.

That primal urge has not abated. At the Cathedral of San Nicola
in Bari, the place where St Nicholas of Myra, the progenitor of
Santa Claus, is buried, we saw people selling small bottles of
what looked like water but turned out to be a liquid purportedly
trickling from the marble sarcophagus of the saint. Collected
and sold as a miraculous gift, the 'Santa Manna di San Nicola', it
has been used as an ointment, or even a drink, as a remedy for all
sorts of ailments since the Middle Ages. And, no less than in
Ephesus nineteen centuries ago, there is still a market for such
things.

As one might expect, items linked to Jesus himself were at an
even higher premium than those associated with lesser figures
such as the saints and apostles. Here, supply was always struggling
to keep pace with demand. There were two ways of dealing with
this: one was to subdivide alleged holy objects into the tiniest of
slivers, as Cyril records was done with the Cross. The other, less
reputable, approach was to produce obviously fanciful relics like
the prepuce of Jesus, which was apparently so much in demand
that more than one has been preserved. Milk from the breast-
feeding Mary, a milk tooth of Jesus and hair from his beard, jars
from the wedding at Cana, leftover bread from the feeding of the

five thousand and, most impressively, a tear shed by Jesus when he wept over the fate of Jerusalem: all could be (and were) obtained in the medieval era. If the forefinger of St Thomas at Santa Croce seems preposterous, then what is one to make of the two heads of St John the Baptist or feathers from the wings of the Archangel Michael once venerated elsewhere?

Such health warnings are essential in any exploration of relics and what they mean. At Santa Croce in Gerusalemme, only three of the relics in the Cappella delle Reliquie can be connected with Helena with any degree of plausibility: the nail, the fragments of the Cross, and the so-called *Titulus*. Of these three, the *Titulus* is much the most striking, not least because it bears an inscription. Egeria, who kissed part of it – or something like it – in Jerusalem on that Good Friday in AD 383, had no doubt that it came from the True Cross of Jesus. But does modern research give any reason to support the certainty she felt?

The Case of the 'Triumphal Superscription'

All over Christendom there are churches with medieval or modern works of art on, above or behind the altar, depicting the crucified Christ. Above his head there is often a piece of stylized wood or cloth with the four capital letters 'INRI: Jesus of Nazareth, King of the Jews', or in Latin, the language of the abbreviation, *Iesus Nazarenus Rex Iudaeorum*. This is sometimes referred to as the sacred monogram and it is certainly a scriptural text drawn from John 19:19 – or rather Jerome's late-fourth–early-fifth-century Latin translation of the original Greek.

The INRI monogram excites little attention today, but there was a time when it played a major role in church ritual.[21] The medieval Salisbury or 'Sarum' prayer against thunder and storms has this to say: 'The triumphal superscription: Jesus of Nazareth, King of the Jews – Christ conquers, may Christ reign, may Christ vindicate us, and from all thunder, tempest and every evil free and defend us. Amen. Behold the Cross of the Lord, flee you enemies: the lion of the tribe of Judah, the root of David, conquers.' That such a belief should have arisen in England is not in itself surprising. Many fragments of the Cross found their way across the Channel, among them the piece of the *Vera Crux* given to King Alfred by Pope Marinus in 884. That pope, a man from Tuscany, liked the Saxons and exempted their quarter in Rome, the Schola Saxonum, from tax; his gift was doubtless a sincere reflection of his Anglophilia. References abound to the importance of such precious objects to the development of English devotion. Henry VIII's great Protestant minister, Thomas Cromwell, received reports from the royal commissioners that 'peces of the olie crosse able to make a hole crosse of' were in use at Bury St Edmunds.

The 'Triumphal Superscription' referred to in the Sarum *Horae* – that is, the *Titulus* mentioned in the four Gospels – is very likely to have existed in some form. The fact that all four Evangelists refer to such an inscription is in itself persuasive; and, as we have seen, the practice was commonplace at executions in the Roman world.[22] St John records that the title was taken down from the Cross with Jesus after Joseph of Arimathea had obtained Pilate's permission (John 19:38).[23] Joseph and his helpers had to act quickly, since a special sabbath was approaching (John 19:31) and all work, including the burial, had to be finished before sunset. It is highly probable that the vertical beam was left standing. Crosses were used more than once, so that there would before long have been another condemned man languishing in agony on the same beam, with his own *titulus* describing the crime for which he had been crucified.

The Gospels tell us nothing specifically about the fate of Jesus's inscription. It would have made no sense to leave it on the abandoned cross. Was it discarded by the Roman executioners? Was it taken down to be buried with Jesus, or to be preserved for posterity by Joseph or another follower? All we can say with certainty is that it is not mentioned in the inventory of objects observed by Peter (Luke 24:12) and the 'beloved disciple' (John 20:2–8) when they looked into the empty tomb. This does not, of course, mean it had been destroyed. The shrouds, the only specific items mentioned, are singled out to make a particular point: Jesus had left his earthly existence behind, casting off even his burial shrouds. Other objects, in other words, may have been present in the tomb but were not remarked upon by the Gospel writers. In any case the literary sources do not tell us what happened to the 'title'. There is no reference to it of any sort between the description in the Gospels of the crucifixion and Egeria's travelogue some three and a half centuries later. Meanwhile, at about the same time as Egeria was writing, the accounts of Helena's archaeological work started to make explicit mention of the *Titulus*. But is it remotely plausible that what the diggers of Constantine's age found was the same headboard that had mockingly adorned the Cross of Christ?

As we saw in the last chapter, several of the first historians of the early Church, beginning with the circumspect Ambrose of Milan, emphasized that the excavators found three separate beams. Their number and proximity to one another caused predictable excitement: Bishop Macarius must have felt, with some relief, that he had at last satisfied the expectations of the Empress and won glory for the see of Jerusalem. But why were only three crosses discovered, rather than dozens of beams in varying states of decrepitude?

A possible explanation is that wood was extremely scarce in the Jerusalem area: here, more than anywhere else in the Roman world, the vertical beam would be used time and again in crucifixions. In such a climate, furthermore, solid beams of wood could easily survive for decades, if not centuries. The wooden writing tablets from first-century Vindolanda found with perfectly readable texts (see below), and the centuries-old 'stave churches' in Norway are pertinent examples. There would have been many crucified on that particular cross before Jesus – who, it should be remembered, carried only the horizontal bar from Pilate's Praetorium to the place of his death – and there may have been many after him. As can be seen today, within the Holy Sepulchre, there is only limited space on the hill of Golgotha. It is quite possible, in other words, that three vertical beams, including the one used to crucify Jesus, remained in place on the rock for many years, a grim reminder of the State's pitiless authority, in much the same way as the gallows were to be in centuries to come.

But the crucifixions at Golgotha did not continue for long. It has been suggested that the Romans, unnerved by the sudden disappearance of a crucified man from his tomb two days after his execution, abandoned this execution site out of superstition. This

is pure speculation. In fact, the real reason for the change seems
to have been much more practical. In AD 41–2, as we have seen,
the course of the city wall was changed, as Herod Agrippa I
extended the perimeter of Jerusalem.[24] Suddenly, Golgotha was no
longer just outside the walls, but just inside. Custom dictated that
public executions did not take place within a city's boundaries,
but at a conveniently accessible site *extra muros*. Some eleven
years after the death of Jesus, therefore, crucifixions on Golgotha
came to an end and the weathered, bloodied beams which rose
from its peak were suddenly redundant. They were presumably
pulled down and thrown into an old cistern – where, allegedly,
Helena's men found them.

This does not, however, explain the likely fate of the *Titulus*
itself. Two of the chroniclers who mention its discovery say explicitly that it was found with the True Cross and indeed that it was
the proof of the wood's authenticity.[25] A third account, composed
at Constantinople, confirms the discovery of the *Titulus* with the
crosses but seems to imply that it was not firmly attached to any
of them:[26] Hence the need for additional miraculous identification
which was recorded by Theodoret of Cyrrhus and Rufinus of
Aquileia.[27] As we have seen, however, the *Titulus* must have been
removed after Jesus's crucifixion. To have left it on the beam
would have been nonsensical.

The only early historian who was, it seems, aware of this contradiction, and interested in its solution, was John Chrysostom
('Goldmouth'), a man with many influential enemies who reached
the pinnacle of his career as bishop of the Empire's eastern capital,
Constantinople. In one of his great works of interpretation, the
eighty-fifth of eighty-eight homilies on the Gospel according to St
John, written in *c*.398, he has this to say:

> The wood [of the Cross] might have been lost from sight: no one made
> an effort to preserve it, mainly under the influence of fear, but also
> because at that time they were concerned with other, more pressing
> matters. But at a later stage they looked for it and, to all probability,
> the three crosses were in one place. Therefore they had to take pre-
> cautions so that the one which belonged to the Lord would not remain
> unidentifiable – first, because it was the middle one, but second, it

would be obvious to everyone because of the *Titulus*, since the crosses of the thieves had no superscriptions.[28]

This is an odd and astonishing series of assertions, worthy of some analysis.

First there is John's statement that the followers of Jesus had made no effort to preserve the Cross and had better things to do. This may appear ludicrous but, in fact, the assertion is worth taking seriously. Since the crosses were probably not taken down until AD 41–2 or thereabouts, there was neither need nor occasion for Jesus's followers to do anything about them until that year. They stood on the hill, visible to all. Then, as we have seen, the perimeter of the city wall was altered and the use of Golgotha for public executions discontinued. And John Chrysostom is quite right to record that the local Christians were at this time 'concerned with other, more pressing matters'.

This was a dark and turbulent hour for the fledgling Christian community in Jerusalem. The vassal king Herod Agrippa I decided to please the Jewish hierarchy in Jerusalem by executing James, the brother of John and, since this proved popular, took the further step of imprisoning Peter, the leader of the Christians.[29] Peter managed to escape from jail, handing over the reins of power to his colleague James, the brother of Jesus, and to flee Jerusalem, probably for Rome.[30] James was an able and strict administrator – even those who later preferred St Paul's strategy to that of 'the brother of the Lord' (as Paul himself called him, Galatians 1:19) admitted as much. But the whole structure of authority and organization had changed, literally overnight. Some might have felt that the very future of the community in Jerusalem was threatened by the departure of the apostle whom Jesus had called his 'rock'. And was James himself safe from Herod Agrippa's persecution? These, surely, were the pressing diversions to which John Chrysostom was referring three centuries later.

But however distracted they were, the Jerusalem Christians would have been well aware of, and concerned by, the architectural alterations to the city wall. They would have watched the work of the builders and the removal of the crosses. And perhaps, as John Chrysostom claimed, they formed a plan to preserve the most sacred artefact of their faith and to mark it for posterity. Later, when their community was more settled, they looked for the crosses, discovered them in the area where they had seen the Romans discard them and marked one of them, the middle one, with the surviving *Titulus*.

Again, we can suggest a precise date: the life of the Christian community – which in Jerusalem consisted almost exclusively of Jews – continued to be difficult for some years after the flight of Peter. In AD 62 James, the brother of Jesus, was illegally executed by the Sanhedrin. In AD 66 Jewish nationalists began their revolt against the Romans in which the Jewish Christians refused to participate. To avoid reprisals, as we saw in the last chapter, the Christians escaped to Pella in Transjordan. After the crushing of the revolt, Jews were not allowed to live in Jerusalem – but an exception was made for the Jewish Christians who had not joined the rebellion. They were permitted to return to the city, to their former quarter on what today is called Mount Zion, and began to rebuild their houses, to construct a synagogue-church and to reorganize their community. Most scholars would date these events to the mid- and late seventies of the first century.[31] This, then, was the moment when the crosses might have been recovered by a community which had survived, drawn breath and begun to look to its future. The Romans, who had allowed them back, had no particular reason to hinder the Jewish Christians; the Jewish authorities, who might have tried, were no longer there to do so.

What had happened to the *Titulus* between the death of Jesus and the alleged reclaiming of the crosses? John Chrysostom clearly – and logically – implies that it was no longer on the vertical cross beam when the Romans discarded it in AD 41-2. He notes, furthermore, that 'the crosses of the thieves had no superscriptions'. This, as we have seen, was to be expected: the superscriptions, informing bystanders about the crime of the crucified men, were removed with each corpse to make way for the next condemned man and his admonitory 'title'. This adds lustre to the suggestion that Jesus's *Titulus* would have been removed immediately after his death and claimed by Joseph of Arimathea or another close follower. It would then have been buried with the body of Jesus and, in keeping with custom, would have been given to one of his relatives, most likely his mother, after the discovery of the empty tomb.

It is easily forgotten that Jesus's family survived identifiably in the Jerusalem community for very many years after his death, a proud dynasty which would have treasured such precious heirlooms as the *Titulus*: some even referred to it as a kind of caliphate, jealously guarding the legacy of the founder of the faith. The second leader of the Jerusalem church, after Peter, was James, who had not distinguished himself as a follower of the first hour. But he was a brother of Jesus: argument enough, it seems, to prefer him to any of the ten original apostles left after the suicide of Judas and the departure of Peter.[32] Similar favour fell to the family of Cl[e]opas, whom Hegesippus calls an uncle of Jesus.[33] His son Symeon, 'a cousin of the Redeemer', became the third leader of the community in Jerusalem, as successor to his relative James.[34] In other words, it was Symeon Bar Cleopas who continued the family tradition during the dangerous years after the death of James and in exile at Pella. Hegesippus – and Eusebius who quotes him – seems to imply that Symeon Bar Cleopas was confirmed or re-elected in his position after the community's return to Jerusalem. It would have fallen to him, therefore, to orchestrate the location and identification of the True Cross. As the leading member of Jesus's bloodline, it seems most probable that the *Titulus* would have been handed down to him not only as a sacred object but as a precious family heirloom. Symeon, in short, would have had the authority – dynastic, religious and proprietorial – to place the headboard next to the True Cross when the site became accessible after AD 73–4.

It seems that pilgrims began to flock there. This, at least, can be surmised from the Emperor Hadrian's remarkable effort to bar access to this otherwise uninteresting place at the north-western edge of the city. A splendid temple to Venus – or, in Greek, Aphrodite[35] – was built over the old execution ground. The crosses and the *Titulus* were no longer accessible to worshippers. But, as we have seen, local Christians knew precisely where they were, passing the tradition on from generation to generation, waiting for a more clement time. That time was to come with Constantine and Helena, less than two hundred years later.

It is possible, therefore, to establish a plausible if unprovable chronology which could account for the survival of the *Titulus* after AD 30, the removal of the Cross from Golgotha in the 40s, its retrieval after the Christian exile, its burial in a cistern by Hadrian after 135 and its final excavation by the Empress in the 320s. But – to concentrate upon the *Titulus* – is it possible that such a board could have lasted so long, in such frequently hazardous conditions?

The evidence that it could is surprisingly strong. The most remarkable examples of such survival are the Vindolanda Tablets, more than 1900 writing tablets, purpose-made slivers of wood, discovered since 1973 at the Roman fort of Vindolanda, south of Hadrian's Wall, near Bardon Mill in Northumberland. Dating from the period c.AD 85–125, they were written by members of this Roman garrison and their dependants or by correspondents from other garrisons: private letters, recommendations, orders, invitations to parties, shopping lists. It seems that the archive was meant to be burnt by a Roman unit posted to the Danube, during a final clear-out – a plan thwarted by rain, which extinguished the fire. The mud and later layers of earth conserved these astonishing documents for almost 2000 years. Other, smaller discoveries of tablets, for example at Carlisle, have suggested to archaeologists that rain after fire – and human urine, also found with the tablets at Vindolanda – is helpful, but not essential. 'It seems likely that the damp, anaerobic environment is sufficient to account for the preservation [of wood with writing on it], as it seems to be elsewhere,' is the verdict of those who have analysed the Vindolanda find.[36] This describes precisely the conditions in which the Cross and *Titulus* appear to have been found by Helena: in an old cistern which, presumably, remained slightly damp and muddy beneath Hadrian's foundations.

What can be said about the likely physical attributes of the headboard used in Jesus's crucifixion? We know that wood – rather than, say, papyrus – was generally used for this type of public sign.[37] Sources for the imperial period mainly refer to whitened wood panels bearing laws or names, so-called *alba* (hence the modern use of the word album to refer to collected information). Such an album, or *tabula dealbata* (whitened tablet), would be used to publicize urgent, topical information, in contrast to inscriptions carved into stone or bronze, which were intended for posterity's consideration. The message was incised into the wood, then the wood was whitewashed or, as some scholars have described the procedure, stuccoed.[38] The letters were coloured, usually red or black. When Vespasian, the emperor who gave permission for the Jewish Christian community to return to Jerusalem in AD 73–4, published an edict confirming certain privileges granted to doctors, it was displayed to the general public in Rome on such a *tabula dealbata*.[39]

According to one scholar who has investigated the extant material, 'Edicts which usually contained short-term orders, were, it seems, commonly published on *tabulae dealbatae*.'[40] It was in precisely such circumstances that Pontius Pilate dictated and made public the *Titulus* for Jesus, or indeed for any of his other crucified victims. As we have already seen, the use of a *Titulus* to publicize the crime of a condemned person can be demonstrated from literary sources after the time of Emperor Augustus at the latest. One account (of a slave paraded through the Forum in Rome, then led to his crucifixion) is in Greek and it is compelling that the author, the historian Cassius Dio, uses the same juridical term to express 'cause for punishment' and 'crime' as Mark and Matthew in their description of Jesus's inscription.[41] No less notably John, in his account, describes the inscription with its Latin technical term *titulus* rendered, of course, in Greek spelling.[42]

This practice went beyond ritual humiliation, although it naturally assisted that purpose. The use of titles was meant to alert others to the severity of the crime committed and serve as an explicit deterrent. The Roman rhetorician Quintilian (c.AD 35–c.95), a contemporary of the New Testament generation, even recommended that crucifixions should be as public as possible for this very reason; and St John tells us that this is exactly what happened with Jesus.[43] A *titulus* could not be as large as a court notice board or protocol. It had to be big enough to be legible to bystanders, but small enough to be attached to a crossbeam. It could have been nailed to the cross, or tied to it, above the head of the crucified person. Some accounts of Roman *tituli* note that they were carried by someone else walking ahead of the condemned person[44] or were tied around his neck.[45] In the case of Jesus it seems likely that the headboard was either hung from his neck or carried by Simon of Cyrene on the walk to Golgotha and finally attached to the cross itself.[46] Nothing in the written sources indicates the size of the *tituli* and, while numerous texts on wood have survived from this period, none of them appears to have performed this particular function. The fragment at Santa Croce in Rome is therefore *sui generis*: it is 25.3 centimetres wide and 14 centimetres high, which means that the reconstructed piece with the complete text would have been approximately 60 centimetres by 21 centimetres.

On the *Titulus* of Jesus we would expect to read his alleged crime, succinctly and unequivocally expressed. Three of the four Gospel accounts report precisely such an inscription. The fourth, St John's, adds the name of the crucified man. Let us pick up the thread from the previous chapter to look at the four versions and compare then with the fragment preserved in Rome. Is it a copy of one of them, or – intriguingly – an independent fifth version?

As a starting point, all four Gospel accounts give us a text in Greek, without actually saying that this was the language in which the inscription was originally written. The Evangelists merely record the contents of Pilate's dictated message and, since they wrote their Gospels in Greek, this is the language used to convey the text of the inscription. One of the four, however, insists that the inscription was trilingual – etched into the wood in Hebrew, Latin and Greek (John 19:20). The one language we would expect as a matter of course is Latin: the crucifixion of Jesus was inescapably the act of the Roman administration and the language of Rome, even in that distant province, was Latin. That the imperial language was invariably used by Pilate in his inscriptions is clear from his dedication of a temple in Caesarea Maritima to the Emperor Tiberius.[47] A large fragment of the dedicatory inscription was discovered in 1961, reused as a stone in the steps of the late Roman theatre. Famous as the only surviving inscription with Pilate's name – and with his rank of 'praefectus' not 'procurator', as Tacitus erroneously styles him[48] – it is, indeed, written in his mother tongue.

But, from the Romans' point of view at least, Jesus was crucified as a dangerous Jew, a royal pretender whom the Jewish authorities wanted eliminated too. Hence it makes sense that the inscription would also have been written out in Hebrew, the formal language of the Jews: this would be Pilate's way of making his message comprehensible to more people, but also a signal that the problem was not one of Rome's making.[49] Nor is it any surprise, finally, that he should have had it translated into Greek to complete the trio of languages. To an extent which is greatly underestimated, Judaea was a multilingual, multicultural country, in which, as elsewhere in the Roman world, Greek was the esperanto or lingua franca, understood and spoken by people across the tribal and religious boundaries. One remembers the stones erected in the Temple, prohibiting non-Jews, on pain of death, to continue further into the sanctuary of the Temple: two copies have been found and both are in Greek. It would have been quite illogical to translate Jesus's inscription into Hebrew but not into the Hellenic tongue.[50]

Thus St John's account of a trilingual *Titulus* is perfectly plausible. In parenthesis, it is worth noting the evidence that the writer of St Luke may have made precisely the same assertion about the three languages. The orthodox scholarly position, reflected in the standard editions of the Greek New Testament and our modern translations, is that this passage in St Luke is a late interpolation, which should be relegated to the critical apparatus or to the footnotes. But is this right? St John, as we saw, mentions three languages in the order: Hebrew, Latin, Greek. The *longer* reading in Luke 23:38 has Greek, Latin, Hebrew. We find it in the original, uncorrected text of the Codex Sinaiticus, which was written during the second quarter of the fourth century. Another important text, the Codex Alexandrinus of the fifth century – like the Sinaiticus on display in the British Library at St Pancras – also has the longer version. Other very early books and the two most important families of minuscule manuscripts – known as f^1 and f^{13} – confirm the reading, as does the so-called Majority Text, the group of New Testament manuscripts which was shaped in the Byzantine era as the result of scholarly efforts to edit an empire-wide version of the Greek New Testament.[51] The manuscripts used by Erasmus for the first printed edition of the Greek New Testament in 1516 belonged to that group of minuscules and the Majority Text. In turn, William Tyndale, and the Authorized Version which followed him, mainly relied on the text provided by Erasmus; consequently they incorporated the longer text of Luke 23:38 into their translations. They did not do so blindly: Tyndale was an excellent philologist and was happy not to follow Erasmus whenever he thought that the Dutchman's editorial decisions were wrong. In the case of Luke's longer description of the *Titulus*, however, he accepted the Greek text as he found it. Readers of the Authorized Version will therefore still find it in their texts unchanged. And anyone familiar with the Book of Common Prayer will know the longer version as part of the Gospel for the Thursday before Easter (Maundy Thursday): 'And a superscription also was written over him in letters of Greek, and Latin, and Hebrew, THIS IS THE KING OF THE JEWS.'

Today, trust in minuscules and in the Majority Text has given way to scepticism. Furthermore, the reference to the three languages in Luke 23:38 makes the text longer – and this is considered by contemporary scholars to be very bad indeed, on the dubious basis that, in cases of doubt, the shorter text must be better (that is, less embellished) than the longer one. The shorter text of Luke 23: 38, it is true, has been preserved in one papyrus, the P75, by a corrector's hand in the Codex Sinaiticus, in the Codex Vaticanus and a small number of further manuscripts. But unless one assumes – which one must not – that a papyrus always offers the best possible version of a text as opposed to other carriers of information, the manuscript evidence is at the very least inconclusive. And, as we have seen, there is plenty of strong evidence in favour of the longer reading.

Whatever the outcome of further philological studies may be, one thing is certain: at a very early stage, before the mid-fourth century at the latest, a version of St Luke's text had been widely circulated in the Church, relating that there was a *Titulus* in three languages, appearing in the order Greek, Latin, Hebrew. This differed starkly from the sequence recorded by St John: Hebrew, Latin, Greek. It follows, therefore, that the longer text in Luke's Gospel cannot have been copied from John's Gospel. Nor indeed, if we assume for a moment that the original manuscript of St Luke's contained these words, could St John have copied them from his colleague's scroll. Whatever else one says about these two accounts, they are clearly independent. And to the philologist this is perhaps one of the strongest arguments in favour of the authenticity, in St Luke, of the longer text with the three languages: anyone seeking, on a whim, to add to St Luke what St John had already written would not have risked such a remarkable variation in the order of the languages on the *Titulus*.[52]

In the case of St John's Gospel, the account of the three languages is included in all papyri, codices and minuscules that include the relevant passage. But, even in this case, there is a challenging, if minor, problem which is often overlooked since it is hidden in the 'critical apparatus' of the Greek New Testament's standard editions and has not, therefore, found its way into modern translations. As mentioned above, St John's order for the languages on the *Titulus* inscription is Hebrew, Latin, Greek. Not so, however, in the Authorized Version or the Book of Common Prayer, where this passage is part of the Gospel for Good Friday. In *that* context the passage reads: 'This title then read many of the Jews: for the place where Jesus was crucified was nigh to the city: and it was written in Hebrew, and Greek, and Latin.' It is an order which is extant in a couple of old codices, among them the aforementioned Alexandrinus. The minuscule family *f¹* and the Majority Text, known to us from the longer Lucan version, also have this order: Hebrew, Greek, Latin. Hence its appearance in the Greek New Testament of Erasmus and, thanks to him, in the Authorized Version and the Book of Common Prayer. To put it differently: by comparison, the textual evidence for the authenticity of this order of languages is considerably weaker than that for the inclusion of the three languages in St Luke; but it exists and must be mentioned.[53]

To add to the uncertainty, there is a peculiar reading of the early fifth-century Codex W, now at the Freer Gallery of Art in Washington, which presents the following sequence: Hebrew, Latin, Hebrew. This is clearly a scribal error. But if we assume that it was due, like so many scribal errors, to the optical deflection caused by the identical first and equally identical last four letters in Greek (*Hebraisti* = in Hebrew; *Hellenisti* = in Greek), we might tentatively use it as additional evidence for the order Hebrew, Latin, Greek. And what is more: the manuscripts with either of the two variants are late. The oldest of them are the Codex Alexandrinus and the Codex Washingtoniensis, and both are fifth century. In other words, they were written about one hundred years after the discovery of the Cross and *Titulus* by Helena. Conversely, for St Luke's longer text in 23:38, with Greek, Latin, Hebrew, we have at least one relatively early codex – the Sinai-ticus – which is contemporary to Helena's discoveries and certainly precedes the first references to the *Titulus* by Egeria and Ambrose. The question remains why a few late manuscripts eventually got so much backing throughout the empire that they shaped the textual tradition of the Majority Text in John 19:20. There may be a surprising answer. But first, after this rather technical excursus, let us summarize the position thus far:

– We have four Gospel accounts. Two of them, Mark and Matthew, do not mention different languages, but merely present us with a Greek version. In other words, they simply tell us what the inscription contained and say it in the language of their books, that is, in Greek.

– Luke, according to most contemporary scholars, says exactly the same. But there is strong, probably persuasive external and internal evidence for the traditional text of Luke 23:38, which lists three languages, in the order Greek, Latin, Hebrew.

– John definitely refers to three languages. There is virtually no doubt that the original version had the sequence Hebrew, Latin, Greek, but there are some late, and surprisingly influential, manuscripts of his Gospel with the order Hebrew, Greek, Latin.

– None of the versions of John 19:20 is identical with the longer text of Luke 23:38. The two Gospels are independent witnesses.

– Mark's and Matthew's passages are written in a way which does not necessitate a reference to the language used. Luke's passage either follows the scheme of the other two, or, more probably, actually lists three languages. There is no reason to doubt the manuscript evidence of John 19:20, that there were indeed three languages on the *Titulus*.

– Even so, we cannot be certain of the sequence. It may have been Hebrew, Latin, Greek. But alternatives cannot be ruled out: Greek, Latin, Hebrew (St Luke); Hebrew, Greek, Latin (late St John manuscripts).

So much for the sequence of languages on the original *Titulus*. The actual wording of the inscription in the Gospels is not identical in the various Gospels either – as we saw briefly in chapter 3. But this should not be seen as evidence of inauthenticity; rather, the contrary. It is the nuanced differences between the various Gospels which suggest they reflect the real, if sometimes inexact, memories of eyewitnesses or those their authors had spoken to. None of the four Gospels was written in Jerusalem and, in the case of St Luke's and St John's accounts, may have been written a very long way indeed from the Holy Land. Their purpose was to record with reasonable accuracy the contents of the *Titulus*, not to offer a word-perfect rendering. In fact, no Jewish or Graeco-Roman reader would have expected such pristine congruence. True command of an existing text was illustrated by nuanced changes, by subtle shifts of perspective. The Dead Sea Scrolls are full of biblical quotes which have undergone such minor variations. Later in the history of Jewish exegesis, St Peter performs a similar trick in which he quotes Joel 3:1–5 in his speech at Pentecost (Acts 2: 14–36); St Paul does it with Psalm 68:19 in his Letter to the Ephesians 4:8; and there are many other examples. The minor differences between the four Gospel accounts of the *Titulus*, in other words, are not an argument against their authenticity.

Different as they are, the four versions do agree on the following key respect:

THE KING OF THE JEWS (*ho basileus tôn Ioudaiôn*; Mark 15:26)

THIS IS JESUS, **THE KING OF THE JEWS** (*houtos estin Iêsous **ho basileus tôn Ioudaiôn**; Matthew 27:37)

THIS IS **THE KING OF THE JEWS (*ho basileus tôn Ioudaiôn* houtos; Luke 23:38)**

JESUS THE NAZOREAN (= OF NAZARETH) **THE KING OF THE**

JEWS (*Iêsous ho Nazôraios **ho basileus tôn Ioudaiôn***; John 19:19)

To this may be added a fifth version, the earliest account by a post-biblical author who not only refers to the rediscovery of the *Titulus* but actually says what he knew about the inscription itself – Ambrose of Milan.[54] Writing in Latin, he gives the version: IESUS NAZARENUS REX IUDAEORUM. This sounds like a literal rendering of the Greek in John 19:19 and is the version of the Latin Bible, and of all abbreviated or written-out 'INRI' superscriptions on crosses in later Christian art.

It is surely no accident that this element is common to all four – or five – accounts, since the law did indeed require that the inscription borne by a crucified man explained the *aitia* (Greek) or *causa poenae* (Latin) – that is 'the reason for the penalty'. From the legal perspective, Jesus was crucified as an insurgent who had treasonably claimed to be 'King of the Jews': a rival to the emperor and a usurper of his inalienable right to decide who would be king anywhere in his empire. No *Titulus* above the head of Jesus would have made sense without these words.

Let us reconsider the background. It is unlikely that Pilate continued to believe, after his cross-examination, that Jesus was a true enemy of Rome, at least in any meaningful political sense (John 18:36–8). But he was under immense pressure, not least a subtle threat made by the Jewish authorities: Pilate knew that if news of his leniency against a royal pretender were to reach Rome, he might lose his prestigious honorary title of *amicus Caesaris*, 'Caesar's friend' (John 19:12). Suetonius, the Roman historian, reports a precedent horrible enough to frighten a man like Pilate. The prefect C. Cornelius Gallus, an *amicus Caesaris*, had provoked the emperor's displeasure for disloyalty, ingratitude and 'crimes against the crown'. Gallus was subjected to the *renuntiatio amicitiae*, the revocation of the emperor's friendship. He was sacked from the civil service, and barred from the court and from residence in the imperial provinces. His many enemies fell upon him until, desperate and without hope, he committed suicide.[55] So the high priests and their followers knew they had Pilate in a tight corner. Whatever the prefect may have thought after his interrogation of Jesus, the claim to be 'King of the Jews' could, and some would say had to, be interpreted as *lèse-majesté*. Indeed, the power of this allegation against Jesus was made apparent once again in a conflict at Thessalonica a few years later, where Paul, Silas and a local Christian called Jason proclaimed Jesus at the synagogue. Some Jews were sufficiently incensed by this to cause a riot in front of Jason's house, but shouted a political rather than a theological accusation: 'They act against the laws of the emperor and claim that someone else is King, namely Jesus' (Acts 17:7). To these supposedly loyal Jewish subjects the Roman emperor, and he alone, was king of the Jews. Only one other person could legitimately claim to be the King of Israel: the true Messiah. And they, like many of those at the Cross, simply refused to accept that Jesus was this man.[56]

Another charge was made against Jesus with far-reaching implications. 'We have a law,' the high priests told him, 'and according to this law he has to die, since he called himself "Son of God".' As Pilate knew – and as the Jewish leaders knew when they told him this – 'Son of God' was not only a Jewish term. It also was a formal title of the Roman emperor. Augustus had initiated the custom when he had his adoptive father Julius Caesar pronounced divine by the Senate. By definition, he himself was therefore a 'Son of God'. Other emperors followed the practice, among them Tiberius, who was emperor at the time of Jesus's crucifixion. Inscriptions and coins provide ample evidence that this title, in Greek and in Latin, was widely used as part of the imperial cult. If the high priests told Pilate that Jesus called himself 'Son of God' and that this claim – which they deplored – compelled the death sentence, they did so in the knowledge that the Roman prefect, the *amicus Caesaris*, would not be unimpressed. The authority of Tiberius had been belittled in more senses than one by a religious leader trying to usurp two titles sacred to the emperor.

It is quite plausible that Pilate tried to negotiate his way out of this dilemma. Although the Jewish authorities were noisily claiming to be on the side of the emperor and the imperial authorities, the prefect probably did not trust them. In fact, his deep distrust of the Jews, amply documented in non-Biblical accounts,[57] would have been one of the reasons why he hesitated to yield to their leaders and crucify a single, seemingly harmless individual –

harmless to the Roman authorities, that is. Yet the safest course, politically, was undoubtedly for him to have Jesus crucified. This, in any case, is what we can glean from St John's account. The other three Gospels confirm this interpretation, in spite and even because of the nuances they add. St Mark and St Luke do not go into details, St Matthew adds a couple of narrative elements, but it is left to St John to give the fullest description. And this is hardly surprising, as the author claims explicitly to have been there himself: 'This is vouched for by an eyewitness, whose evidence is to be trusted. He knows that he speaks the truth, so that you too may believe' (St John 19:35).

How far can we judge which of the four Gospel versions comes closest to Pilate's original text? St Mark's, the shortest, was technically sufficient. Jesus's claim to be 'The King of the Jews' was the legal cause for the death penalty. It was either the gist of what the *Titulus* said, or its whole text. No inscription could have appeared without this clear *aitia*. Matthew adds three introductory words: 'This is Jesus ...' (*houtos estin Iêsous ...*). This may be an example of Matthew's well-known habit of padding out his material, apparently a device to introduce more fluency and elegance to his prose. But it is also quite possible that the words 'This is' appeared as part of the original inscription. This much is clear from Eusebius's account of the martyrdom of Attalus, one of the victims of the local persecution at Vienne and Lyon in AD 177. He was paraded, we are told, through the arena, and a placard carried before him bore the Latin text: 'This is Attalus, the Christian' – or, in Greek: '*houtos estin Attalos ho Christianos*'.[58]

St Luke's record is different. He begins with the *aitia* or *causa poenae*, 'The King of the Jews'. And then, almost as an afterthought, he adds the Greek word *houtos*: that is, 'The King of the Jews – *this one*'. The way St Luke puts it, without changing the legally decisive core of the charge, amounts to a subtle shift of emphasis: Pilate's attitude towards the Jews is underlined. Look at this man, he seems to imply scornfully, flogged, crowned with a garland of thorns, crucified, utterly abject, *this* one is your king.

St John's version of the inscription is by far the longest. Like St Matthew's, it has the name of Jesus, but instead of preceding it with 'This is ...', he adds the byname which distinguished him from hundreds of other bearers of the same first name in the Jewish community:[59] This Jesus was 'the Nazorean (*ho Nazôraios*)'. This is not the place to enter the debate about the etymological meaning of *Nazôraios* or the literary and archaeological evidence for the town of Nazareth at the time of Jesus. Suffice it to say that the three Gospels of Mark, Matthew and Luke occasionally use another form of the attribute, *Nazarenos* (the Nazarene), but that whenever one of them occurs it is always linked to the name of Jesus. In later centuries some Christian groups and sects called themselves 'Nazarenes' or 'Nazoreans', rather than *Christianoi*, Christians. They followed the precedent of a passage in the book of Acts, where Tertullus, a Jewish advocate, accused St Paul at the Roman procurator's Praetorium in Caesarea Maritima, on behalf of the High Priest Ananias: 'Your excellency,' Tertullus said to Felix, 'we have found this man [Paul] to be a pest, a fomenter of discord among the Jews all over the world, a ringleader of the sect of the Nazoreans' (Acts 24:5). Whatever Jewish and Jewish-Christian interpreters may have seen in the Hebrew roots of '*Nazô-raios*',[60] at the time of Jesus it undoubtedly referred to the place where he was brought up, his home town in Galilee. None of our earliest sources leaves any room for doubt about this link and recent archaeology has established the existence of the village at this time.[61] If Pilate intended to name the crucified man, it made sense to identify him clearly as Jesus from Nazareth.

He would certainly have had to be this precise, when he submitted his *Acta*, the annual reports which every regional governor was required to send to the imperial court in Rome.[62] This custom was well known, it seems, even in Christian circles: it is mentioned explicitly by Justin, who died in Rome in c.160.[63] And in these reports the name of a crucified man had to be given in a clear and unambiguous form. Jewish nomenclature did not accord with the tripartite Roman procedure of *praenomen* (first name), *nomen* ('surname' or name of 'clan') and *cognomen* (family name or characteristic byname). The normal practice, therefore, was for the Roman prefect to use the place of origin after the Jewish name: Jesus, *of Nazareth*. It seems likely that Pilate would have used the same formulation on the *Titulus* as he was bound to use, after Jesus's execution, in his *Acta*.

To sum up, one may tend to prefer St John's version of the *Titulus* as the one which corresponds best to the likely practice of a Roman prefect acting in such circumstances. It is only St John who mentions expressly that Pilate had personally ordered a *Titulus* to be written and that he backed it with the full authority of his office: when some of the priests protested against the unqualified *causa poenae* and wanted him to write that Jesus himself alone had claimed 'I am the King of the Jews', Pilate rejected this legally unsatisfactory form with the pique of an aggrieved bureaucrat: 'What I have written, I have written' (St John 19:21–2).

A Fragment in Rome

Egeria, the fourth-century pilgrim and authoress, tells us that the Bishop of Jerusalem produced the wood of the cross and the *Titulus* from a small box. This seems to indicate that by *c.*383, they were no longer complete and could be stored in a small container. Helena had distributed the spoils of her excavations with a strategy in mind: to the Empress, keen to entrench the prospects of her dynasty, Constantinople and Rome were of equal if not greater geopolitical importance than Jerusalem. Bethlehem and Jerusalem were given their splendid new churches; the holy sites had been excavated and Christianity given back its rootedness in history. In return, the capital cities of the Constantinian Empire were to have the relics, or in any case most of them.

None of the nails was left to the locals. The True Cross was divided up. And the *Titulus*? Helena, it seems, was more generous than may be supposed. She took only a part from the bottom right, with one complete word in Greek and Latin: the one which describes Jesus as the Nazarene. Everything else, the whole Hebrew line (bar a few lower elongations of some letters) and most of the Greek and Latin lines, were left in Jerusalem. This was a typically elegant act of division. The *aitia* or *causa poenae*, the legal reason for the death sentence – THE KING OF THE JEWS – was more or less intact on the piece which remained in Jerusalem. But a smaller fragment, with a word that clearly identified the *Titulus*, could go to Rome.

It is clear that Egeria saw the *Titulus* in Jerusalem and Ambrose knew that it was in Rome at the same time. Both were right. But only the Roman fragment has (allegedly) survived.[64] What does it say? What does it tell us about its past and its claim to authenticity? As we saw at the beginning of this chapter, it seems that the Roman *Titulus* was not placed on public display by Helena. This is not in itself surprising. Even the Jerusalemites did not place their fragment of the *Titulus* in a display cabinet; it was shown to the locals and pilgrims only twice a year, on Good Friday and on 14 September, the feast of the Exaltation of the Cross, also known as 'Holy Cross Day', with the strictest security precautions. As for the Roman fragment, at some stage in the mid-twelfth century, the titular cardinal at the church of Santa Croce in Gerusalemme decided to put it in a new box, one of his own, distinguished by his seal. On the stone that covered it there is a Latin inscription in capital letters: TITVLVS CRVCIS. The seal identifies its owner as Gerardus Cardinalis S. Crucis: that is, Gerardo Caccianemici, Archbishop of Bologna and titular cardinal of Santa Croce, who ruled as Pope Lucius II from 1144 to 1145. It follows that his choice of a special box for the *Titulus* and its marking with his cardinal's seal must have taken place before 1144.

This was about half a century before the great explosion in fake relics which followed the Crusaders' conquest of Byzantium, when such artefacts, as we have seen, became the increasingly devalued currency of religious and political ambition. There is no reason to suppose that the cardinal's box fell into this category. Indeed, there is no evidence that the *Titulus* was any more publicly accessible than it had been before. It remained, in effect, a secret treasure until it was found, yet again, three hundred years later during restoration work on a mosaic in 1492, when a part of the ceiling was taken away. How had it found its way there? The most probable reason may be connected with the artwork itself: Emperor Valentinian III, who ruled from 425 to 455, had decorated St Helena's chapel with sumptuous mosaics in the tradition of those sponsored by his mother, Galla Placidia, in Ravenna. They showed scenes from Helena's voyage to the Holy Land and in particular from her discovery of the True Cross. Since the authorities had decided not to display the fragment, the worthiest, symbolically most meaningful – and also the safest – place for it was behind the mosaic which showed the moment of its discovery. Cardinal Caccianemici may even have thought that from on high, it could exercise a beatific influence upon the chapel and on the whole church.

Some three hundred and fifty years after the cardinal's action, and more than one thousand years after Emperor Valentine's generosity, a thorough restoration was urgently needed. On 1 February 1492, when a layer of damaged stucco had been taken off, a brick appeared with an inscription: TITVLVS CRVCIS. The restorers took it away and discovered a niche behind it. And there it was, the leaden box, with a further inscription identifying the contents. The rediscovery of the box may well have stirred the uglier emotions of the time. This was to be the year of the discovery of a new continent by an explorer of Jewish origins, one Christopher Columbus, the year also of the expulsion of all Jews from Spain, many of whom fled or emigrated to Italy. Anti-Semitism surged once more. Again, Jews were vilified as Christ killers and mementoes of the crucifixion brandished not only as spiritual artefacts but alleged evidence of the Jewish people's crime. It would doubtless have made sense to the ecclesiastical authorities to display at last the *Titulus* and other relics associated with the Cross as documentation of the Lord's Passion. To grasp the absurdity of this poisonous reasoning one need only remember that the *Titulus* fragment explicitly identified the crucified Christ as a Jew, the 'Nazorean'.

From 1492 to the present day, the *Titulus* and the other relics have been technically accessible more or less without interruption. That said, they have never really been on full public display. Until 1520, St Helena's Chapel was part of a building complex, which could only be reached through the main monastery. Women were barred from these chambers, except on one day of the year, 20 March. After 1570 the relics were taken to another room in the monastery and shown to the congregation on certain other designated days. But Pope Innocent III's supposedly spontaneous visit to the church three months after the discovery ensured that the existence and whereabouts of the headboard were generally known. On 12 March 1492 he went to Santa Croce and prayed in front of the *Titulus*. Four years later, Pope Alexander VI declared it an authentic relic[65] and, in the manner of the time, promised a full indulgence to everyone who venerated the *Titulus* on the last Sunday in January. Since 1575 and to the present day, Santa Croce has been one of the seven churches in Rome where a pilgrim's visit and certain ritual actions gain an indulgence. In 1930 work on the new purpose-built side chapel was begun; when it was completed in 1952, the relics had at last found their permanent home.

With all these changes of location, and the intermittent public display of the *Titulus* after 1590, further damage to the wood was unavoidable. There are (and were) letters right up to the edges, but these have in places been worn down by centuries of handling – some of it no doubt rough in its emotion. Even so, it is possible to advance a surprisingly precise description of what is on the *Titulus* from the marking that remains; the following observations are based on our own investigation of the fragment on several occasions, most recently on 22 November 1998, on invaluable new photographs by Ferdinando Paladini[66] and on an analysis of what few existing studies there are:[67]

– It is made of wood, a kind of wood which was common in the Near East, so-called walnut wood or *iuglans regia*.[68]

– It weights 687 grams, measures 25.3 centimetres by 14 centimetres at its widest points and is 2.6 centimetres thick.

– The wood was originally painted white, which conforms to the Roman practice of whitening such publicly displayed placards, the *alba* or *tabulae dealbatae*.

– The letters, which are carved into the wood, show traces of what looks to us like a very dark red colouring, but which others have described as black. We assume that it once was indeed red and has taken on a blackish hue over the years. Red, but occasionally also black, would be in accordance with Roman practice.

– There are three lines of fragmentary writing, Hebrew or Aramaic (not enough has survived to offer certainty), Greek and Latin. We assume that Hebrew was the language of the first line, for the historical reasons explained above.

– Damaged as the fragment is, there can be no doubt about the sequence of the three languages: Hebrew (or Aramaic), Greek and Latin. To any reader of the Greek New Testament in our standard editions, this is in itself an extremely strong argument against a late forgery. As we have seen, the order in St John, according to the critical text, is Hebrew, Latin, Greek; the longer version of St Luke, meanwhile, has Greek, Latin, Hebrew. By the time of Helena's discovery, copies of the Gospels existed in abundance, all over the Roman Empire, and the first two great codices (ancient books), the Sinaiticus and the Vaticanus, were just being written. All of them have the order Hebrew, Latin, Greek for St John. And the earliest manuscript of St Luke that mentions the three languages, the Codex Sinaiticus, was indeed roughly con-temporary to Helena's visit, but has the order Greek, Latin, Hebrew. It goes without saying that a forger, working for Helena or for the Chris-tian community of Jerusalem, would have followed the order of lan-guages suggested in one of these two Gospels. To have invented a new order of languages patently at odds with the records in the Gospel would have been an act of absurdity for a craftsman striving for the appearance of authenticity. What this means, in effect, is that – what-ever else it is – the Santa Croce *Titulus* is very, very unlikely to be an artefact of the fourth century. Any contemporary looking at it – and comparing it with the Greek text of the Gospels – would have cried foul (one can imagine the jealous Eusebius, desperate to undermine Macarius, doing just that).

This, then, is our scenario: the *Titulus* was discovered at Golgotha, by Helena's team, in c.326. At that stage it was still complete. A comparative glance at a Gospel codex would have confirmed that this was more or less St John's text rather than St Luke's (but not quite, as we shall see further down), with a different sequence of the second and third languages. It would have been assumed that the *Titulus* reading was older and that the variant reading found in the St John codex was to be explained as a slip of memory committed by an eyewitness whose recollections were true in spirit rather than word perfect. Even so, the variance created a problem in a growing faith where precision of eyewitness detail was of the essence. The only solution was to introduce an official codex with this variant reading and to make sure that it would generate further copies, which would be spread through the Empire. It would have been considered a legitimate correction to make, on the assumption that the text on the *Titulus* was the authentic version of the Roman inscription. This is exactly what happened. In the early fifth century a carefully crafted, beautifully written codex of the Greek Bible was published, the Codex Alexandrinus. After the Sinaiticus and the Vaticanus, it is the third-oldest extant Bible codex. Other codices followed its example and finally it became the received reading of the Byzantine 'Majority Text', which was and remained the norm until, and including, Erasmus's first printed edition of the Greek New Testament. Hence, it is the sequence which appears in the first English translations and still is the accepted text in the Authorized Version and in the Book of Common Prayer.[69]

– The Hebrew line is so badly damaged, by constant handling in previous centuries, careless conservation, or a simple accident when the part destined for Rome was cut out (assuming that the fragment is authentic), that nothing but six, perhaps seven elongations of letters below the line have survived. Since such extensions can belong only to a limited number of Hebrew/Aramaic letters, and since possible reconstructions where the suggested Hebrew/Aramaic letters must of course match the places of those elongations can be attempted on the basis of the other two lines, an educated guess might be possible.

– Extraordinarily, the Greek and the Latin lines are written from right to left. What was and is correct in Hebrew is exceptionally odd in these two languages. There are old Etruscan texts and ancient Greek inscriptions with right-to-left words or letters, but there is no con-temporary or near-contemporary evidence for a whole text executed in this way. Again, this very odd reverse writing style is powerful evidence against the previous assumption that the Santa Croce *Titulus* is a forgery of some kind. A falsifier working, say, on behalf of Helena or Macarius, or for a medieval cardinal, would simply not have risked something so abnormal if his purpose was to establish the supposed authenticity of his work. If anyone had ordered the production of a *Titulus*, he would not have asked for a fragment to begin with. And he would have provided the writer with a model, a text to be copied. It is inconceivable that a later text or copy would have been written from right to left. Much more likely that the man who wrote the original *Titulus*, on Pilate's orders and perhaps to his own dictation, simply wrote it like that and that it was too late to correct the mistake when it was noticed. And here we get closer to the heart of the case: who would have spotted the error, at the time, in AD 30? Certainly not the Hebrew readers, for they had their first line, correctly written from right to left, and would not have bothered to read on and notice anything peculiar further down. The Greek- and Latin-reading onlookers would have been bemused, of course – but the text remained legible and understandable, if extremely eccentric. In other words, the message Pilate wanted to get across, the deterrent *causa poenae*, would not have been lost on his core audience. We can even suggest a possible profile of the writer: he was a Jew, brought up as a Hebrew/Aramaic speaker, employed or kept as a slave by Pilate, a court employee at hand when the *Titulus* had to be inscribed in the short period of time left between the final verdict and the crucifixion. Pilate dictated his text in Latin, which was the official language of the Roman administration. But since the principal group to which his inscription was addressed were the Jews of Jerusalem, he ordered the scribe to begin with the Hebrew line. This he did. He then continued writing hurriedly from left to right on the subsequent lines. Perhaps he was trying to direct a little scorn at the Jewish way of writing. Possibly he was simply confused. More probably his command of Latin and Greek was poorer than his command of Hebrew and while he was able to form the letters as indicated, he failed to write them in the correct order. And should he have hesitated when he wrote the last line, he may have felt, justifiably, that continuing like this to the very end at least made the *Titulus* look aesthetically harmonious. This is speculation, of course. Of all the mysteries of the Santa Croce *Titulus* this is the greatest. But what we can be sure of is that it is not a pattern a forger would have sought instinctively to employ.

– The Greek line reads: BCγNEPAZAN. All letters – with the exception of 'z' – are mirror imaged from right to left, and the γ stands for 'Y' or 'OY', that is, in Greek, *Ypsilon* or *Omikron* + *Ypsilon*. Therefore, since we are reading from right to left, what we have is: NAZAREN (O) YC B ... In English, this is 'Nazarene ("of Nazareth") K ...' (i.e. completed to read 'K[ing of the Jews]'. As 'Nazarene' never occurred without 'Jesus' preceding it, we can also tentatively add the Greek IHCOYC, *Iesous*: '[Jesus the] Nazarene, K[ing of the Jews]'.

Only St John's version has 'of Nazareth'. However, all manuscripts of his gospel have 'NAZWPAIOC', not 'NAZARENOYC'. The latter variant does occur in the Gospels, spelled with 'O' (Greek *Omikron*), but not in St John's.[70] And where it does occur it is not linked to the cross and the *Titulus*. Therefore, 'Nazarenos' was a linguistically legitimate form, but unrelated to any Gospel text with the inscription which a potential forger would of course have used. It follows that we have yet another piece of circumstantial evidence in favour of authenticity.[71]

It has been suggested that the Greek spelling is merely a Latinism, which is to say that the scribe, working from a Latin note or dictation, but not particularly at home in Greek, simply wrote in Greek letters what he knew in Latin – a so-called transliteration.[72] Such a supposition may make sense if one works on the basis that a correct Greek spelling would have had an 'O', and not a 'Y' or the diphthong 'OY', which could only have been written by someone thinking Latin ('Nazarenus'), but transferring his thoughts to Greek ('Nazarenos') and ending up with 'Y' in a rare but well-documented form, or even a mixture (technically, a 'ligature') of 'O' and 'Y'. However, there must have been something conscious about his decision, since he employed a letter, γ, which is not modelled on Latin (see below). The scribe may have been influenced by the Latin text elsewhere: whether for reasons of limited space, Latin influence or lack of Greek competence, he omits the definite article '*ho*' ('O' in Greek) before BACILEYC, 'King'. There are no definite articles in Latin, but they are normal in Greek and all manuscripts of St John's Gospel have it in this verse.

NAZAPENγC should of course be written with an 'H' (*Eta*), not with an 'E' (*Epsilon*). Our scribe's spelling is, however, hardly remarkable. At the time, *Eta* and the long *Epsilon* were pronounced almost the same way. There are literally hundreds of examples, particularly in Greek texts derived from Latin. Although the technically correct spelling would have been 'H', no one would have minded when 'E' was written – or indeed, in other cases, when it was done the other way round.

And then there is the striking γ. For the first century, it is documented in Greek texts for the single letter 'Y', but also for the diphthong 'OY'.[73]

A Jewish scribe of whatever ability would have been familiar with the sign, as it had been in use, since pre-Herodian times, as the abbreviation for *Shekel*.[74] Scholars who have researched the origins of this sign have suggested that 'it seems to signify the royal emblem, and thus royal approval'.[75] It was an apparently deft flourish by our Jewish scribe: by using the γ, he not only solved the problem of his (supposed) uncertainty about the correct Greek spelling by using a letter which could be read as 'Y' and 'OY'. He also symbolically reiterated the *causa poenae*, the 'royal' claim 'King of the Jews'. Perhaps this was the overriding reason behind his choice. Perhaps there was another, more subtle reason: there were, as we know beyond doubt, many Jews who believed in Jesus as the Messiah, those who did not cry 'crucify', men like Joseph of Arimathea and many others. One such messianic Jew could conceivably have been the very employee or scribe who incised the text into Pilate's piece of wood. Without causing offence to his employer, who would have been completely unaware of this symbolic nuance, he might have used the γ to make a subtle statement of faith.

Those onlookers who were neither bilingual nor familiar with monetary symbols and their meaning would still have understood the word and the line. γ was well known in Greek writing at the time, not least for the diphthong 'OY', and there is at least one surviving contemporary first-century Greek inscription, found on Rhodes, which includes it.[76] Again, there is not a single Gospel papyrus that uses this symbol, although other forms of abbreviations, so-called *Nomina Sacra* (or Holy Names) had been introduced towards the end of the first century.[77] No forger could have invented or copied this version from any known text of the Gospels. Again, and to an extent never before appreciated, the weight of evidence suggests that the *Titulus* at Santa Croce is not the work of a fraudster.

– The Latin line reads: ERSVNIRAZAN, in mirror-image writing from right to left. This is '... NAZARINUS RE[X] ... or, in English, '... Nazarene (of Nazareth), Kin[g] ...'. Plausibly reconstructed, it gives us the Latin equivalent to the Greek line 'IESUS NAZARENUS REX IUDAEORUM': 'Jesus of Nazareth, King of the Jews'. Here we may have a case of a so-called 'Itacism', familiar from countless other examples: the pronunciation of 'E' and 'I' was often identical. It is therefore hardly noteworthy that the scribe of the *Titulus* seems to have preferred 'I' to 'ε'. (The 'ε' on the engraving of a reconstruction above the *Titulus* in Rome is an invention.) However, there may be even more to it, if we look at the spelling from a Roman perspective. Today, mainly thanks to the Latin *Vulgate* version of the Bible, we are used to the *-enus* spelling. But in fact this is not correct in literary or epigraphical Latin. The usual suffix of a place-name is *-inus* or *-ensis*. In other words the familiar *Nazarenus* is probably derived from the Greek ending, with its *Eta* pronounced and understood as a long 'ε'. To put it differently again, there is nothing wrong with the scribe's Latin line (as far as it has been preserved) and this correct classical 'i' in the word *Nazarinus* supports our proposition that the original language of Pilate's order was Latin. We may even suggest, on the strength of this case, that the Latin line was given to the scribe in writing, rather than as a dictation. In any case, the 'i' is another important stone in the mosaic of authenticity. A forger would of course have copied the known biblical Latin version, with its 'e'.

As we saw when we investigated the remarkable γ in the Greek line, contemporary inscriptions can be extremely useful in such contexts. A survey of extant texts of the same period and from the same region, in Greek and Latin, suggests that the letters on the *Titulus* conform to established forms.[78] Since we know that the original headboard was a legal Roman text, formulated in Latin by the prefect, it is worth taking a closer look at the one other text indubitably associated with Pontius Pilate, the dedicatory inscription from the Tiberieum at Caesarea Maritima. Three fragmentary lines have survived:]TIBERIEUM /]NTIU-SPILATUS /]ECTUSIVD[AEA]E]: '... Tiberieum / ... (Po)ntius Pilatus / ... (Praef)ectus Iud(aea)e'. Of the letters which occur in both texts, the 'A', the 'R' (allowing for its reversed writing on the *Titulus*), the 'I', the 'V' and the 'E' are identical. The 'S' is very similar (again allowing for its eccentric reversed form on the *Titulus*). Only the second 'R' of the *Titulus* is slightly different; it is more elaborate than the first and the 'R' from Caesarea, with a rounded beginning of the diagonal stroke, betraying a scribe who was happier with parchment and papyrus than with wood or stone.

It is interesting to note that the scribe, working for a Roman prefect, was at least trying to adhere to Roman norms. He felt less inhibited when he wrote the Greek line. Even the same letters vary: in the Greek line, his 'ε', which is basically an identical-looking capital letter in

Greek and Latin, has an almost playful air about it. And two letters later, we encounter the intriguing γ.

What, then, is our verdict on the basis of this technical philological analysis? There is absolutely no reason to think that the *Titulus* at Santa Croce is a forgery, either from Helena's time, or from the Middle Ages. The style of writing on the piece of wood closely resembles the letter forms of the first century. Whoever wrote this text was not a copier or forger. This does not *prove* the authenticity of the fragment in Rome. But there is no reason a priori to exclude this piece of wood from future historical investigation of archaeological remnants, which may have survived two thousand years of European history. There is a great difference between forming an opinion about the historical origin of an artefact on the one hand and demanding its veneration on the other. To argue for the authenticity of an ancient object is not, in itself, a theological statement; it has nothing to do with credulity or fundamentalism.

Ideally, the church of Santa Croce in Gerusalemme and the Foreign Ministry of the Vatican (who have the last say in this matter) will one day commission a bio-technological analysis. Pollen, seed and other organic material must be hidden in the cracks and indentations of the wood. Their provenance can be determined. Some will ask for a dendrochronological study.[79] Others will demand a radiocarbon (^{14}C) analysis.[80] Whatever may eventually be permitted, there is, as it stands, a single fragment which claims to be what is left of the *Titulus* above the True Cross of Jesus. Our tools, the classical tools of historiography and philology, have presented future scholars with a strong preliminary verdict.

5

Jews and Romans in Jerusalem: The Titulus, *God, the Lord and the Saviour*

I published some tracts upon the subject myself, which, as
they never sold, I have the consolation of thinking were
read only by the happy few.

Oliver Goldsmith, The Vicar of Wakefield

Historiographical analysis is limited by the quantity of
surviving records, by their state of preservation, and by the
historical probability or accident of their survival.

Gabriele Boccaccini, Beyond the Essene Hypothesis

A Hebrew God

We do not know what the text of the first line on the Santa Croce
Titulus originally said. Nothing but a few lower strokes have
survived and the Gospels, even the two which explicitly refer to
the existence of a Hebrew line (whether first or last), quote or
paraphrase only the Greek text. But the challenge remains: can
scholarly detective work bring us close to what the scribe wrote?
It is, indeed, a question crucial to our understanding of the early
Christian communities in Judaea which, it is a central contention
of this book, venerated the Cross to an extent that has never been
fully grasped.

More than once, scholars have tried to reconstruct the Hebrew
text on the basis of the Greek one: 'Jesus the Nazarene/Nazorean,
the King of the Jews'. What would this look like in Hebrew?
The first who tried to do so were the medieval monks of Santa
Croce themselves. Their effort is still displayed on a wall of the

side chapel; at the very least, it is an imaginative completion of the whole *Titulus*. The most elaborate such study was published in Paris by Rohault de Fleury, under the title *Mémoire sur les instruments de la passion de notre Seigneur Jésus-Christ*. In practice, however, he merely repeats the Santa Croce formulation, making reference to Rufinus who, having seen the Jerusalem fragment, recorded that the languages were Hebrew, Greek and Latin.[1] He also quotes a strange rendering by a *'M. l'abbé Sionnet'* in the *'Auxiliaire catholique'* of 1845, who thought that the complete Hebrew text – written by him in Latin letters – was 'ISCHOU NTSRNOUS'.[2]

However, the only publication which has seriously tried to tackle the question was the *Annales de philosophie chrétienne* in 1839.[3] The provenance of the article is in itself a fascinating example of scholarly cross-fertilization: the editors of the *Annales* supply a foreword; they explain to their readers that the article is an extract from a book which *'le savant M. Drach'* had sent to them from Rome, in the form of a letter addressed to a *'M. l'abbé Liberman'*, an *'israélite converti'*. From the epistolary introduction, we gather that *'le savant M. Drach'* was himself of Jewish origin: he describes the Jews as *'notre nation'*; it appears that both the author and his addressee know some Hebrew. Drach explains that the remnants of the Hebrew letters – and in 1839, over one and a half centuries ago, he would have been able to discern more than has remained visible today – looked familiar to him from Hebrew coins minted in the Maccabean period. Obviously, neither the Papyrus Nash nor the all-important Dead Sea Scrolls had been discovered when he conducted his research;[4] coins were the most widespread comparative material. He does not think that the few surviving traces are lower elongations below the bottom line of what once was the Hebrew text. In his reconstruction they are middle and lower parts of letters *on*, rather than *below*, the imagined line. And he concludes that the spaces between the remnants, if combined with the traces themselves, yield a form of Hebrew, which was what he calls the 'corrupted' Syriac spoken during the time of Jesus – not, he hastens to add, *syriaque classique*. What he really means is a regional dialect of Aramaic. His consequent reconstruction is: '*Ye-ch-u-ang no-st-r-i me-lè-hh Y-e-hu-da-y-a'*.

This was clearly semi-educated guesswork and probably too clever by half. But Drach also refers to Leonardo di Sarzana who had seen the *Titulus* in 1492, then bearing a Hebrew line, which was apparently even less damaged than it was in 1839.[5] This Leonardus Sarzanensis described the line in a letter to Jacob of Volterra, on 4 February 1492.[6] But since Leonardo's deciphering does not match Drach's reconstruction in one case – the spelling of 'Jesus' – Drach judges that his medieval predecessor had 'certainly not read [the text] well'. He is convinced that Leonardo misread the spelling of the first word and that the fragment breaks off before the last word, 'of the Jews'. The case is complicated further by Leonardo's handwriting: Drach states that Leonardo copied the line in the cursive handwriting of Portuguese Jews and promised Jacob a later, more exact copy with the true letters in their original style. No trace of this second missive has survived.

As a matter of fact, 'Jesus', the first word in a text which, as we have seen, was written from right to left, is *not* preserved in the Greek and Latin lines.[7] There is, therefore, no reason to suppose that the corresponding Hebrew letters, which would have been exactly above the Greek part, were legible at any time. They presumably did exist on the larger fragment witnessed in Jerusalem, but none of those who saw it – all of them Latin- and/or Greek-speaking – felt obliged to quote the Hebrew line. Leonardo di Sarzana's reading and Drach's attempts must be, alas, pure fantasy.

Two much more recent reconstructions have more to offer. First, there is the German scholar Gerhard Kroll who, in a book updated no fewer than eleven times before his retirement,[8] opts for an Aramaic version: '*Yeshua Nazoraia Malka Diyehudaye*', or, in Hebrew/Aramaic letters, 'שועצזיאמסלבבאדיהודא'. If we suppose, for the sake of argument, that the last letter of *Yeshua* was preserved on the fragmentary Hebrew line, we would have an *Ayin* (ע) at the far right. A cut in the wood could theoretically be interpreted as such an elongation of the *Ayin*. But the gap between this hypothetical ע and the twin elongations further to the left is too narrow for what we would expect in Kroll's Aramaic reconstruction. Furthermore, the indentation, which would have to be a bottom part of a ע at the right-hand edge, is too high to correspond to the other remnants of letter elongations on or rather below that line.

Should we therefore assume a different, Hebrew, spelling? An inscription in marble, found at Caesarea Maritima in 1961, may give us a clue. Dated to the third century AD, it is a fragment of a list of priestly families, one of which was resident in Nazareth. Here we have an authentic writing of the place-name, with *Tsadeh* (ע) rather than *Zayin* (ז) as third letter.[9] And if therefore N-Z-R-T or נצרת was the Hebrew spelling of Nazareth, the form NZR or *'Nozri'* for 'Nazorean' suddenly seems plausible enough, not least in view of the fact that Rabbinical writings and Jewish parlance to this very day refer to Christians as Nazoreans, *'Nozrim'*, or, in Hebrew letters, נוצרים.[10] An alternative, shorter, spelling would have been נצרים. In each case the final *Mem* (ם) determines the ending of the plural; we would therefore not expect it in a text about the *Nozri* or Nazorean Jesus in the singular. It may be expected that the definite article was added (*the* Nazorean) in Hebrew by a *Heh* (ה). The two most likely readings of the Hebrew letters, corresponding to the place in the Greek and Latin lines underneath, would thus have been הנצרי, from right to left: *Heh-Nun-Tsadeh-Resh-Yod*, or, in the longer version, הנוצרי, *Heh-Nun-Vahv-Holem-Tsadeh-Resh-Yod*,[11] – *'H(a)N(o)zri'*, the *Nozri*, the Nazorean/Nazarene.

Strikingly, the first clearly visible traces on the Hebrew line, above the 'Z' of Greek *'Nazareno(u)s'*, look like the lower elongations of a *Heh*. (What may appear to be a horizontal bar linking the two vertical lines is nothing but a damaged part of the wood.) What follows, after a tiny gap which could signify that the scribe knew he was going from the definite article to the noun,[12] could be identified as the straight elongation of the right-hand part of a *Nun*, which was typical of the so-called 'simplified square' style of Hebrew at the time. Consequently, the next vertical line can be identified as the straight elongation of the *Vahv-Holem* in simplified square writing, with the scribe's idiosyncratic tendency to give all his letters a cursive drift to the left. There is an indentation to the bottom right of the stroke; this, however, is no linked-up part of the letter but one of many scratches in the wood, as the original fragment clearly confirms. What follows, after a small gap, looks like another cursive elongation, going to the left and up again. It is clearly the remnant of one of the two common forms of writing the Hebrew letter *Tsadeh* in simplified square. Even the small gap between the *Vahv-Holem* and the *Tsadeh* makes sense: the cursive square *Tsadeh* turns into a right diagonal stroke at the top, for which there had to be space. In other words, since we only have the lower part of the letter extant on the fragment, it merely *looks* as if there is a gap. In reality, with completed letters, there is not. Finally, after the *Tsadeh* we have a shorter, apparently higher elongation. This could easily belong to a *Resh* which, in simplified square, has exactly such a rounded right-hand stroke. To sum up: the fragmentary traces of the Hebrew line can indeed be read as '... *HaNozr* ...', הנוצר.

Letters as preserved

Letters reconstructed

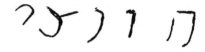

Again, this highly technical analysis confirms a much more general conclusion. No medieval forger would have invented these gaps, fragmentary elongations and remnants of rounded strokes, which modern scholarship allows us to identify clearly as a Hebrew script contemporary to the time of Jesus. These letters could not have been constructed by anyone without a textual model which included at least the words 'HaNozri' in simplified square, and with an eccentric scribal characteristic, the cursive drift to the left, which any forger, careful to get as close to utterly conventional forms as possible, would clearly have avoided.[13]

It is, at any rate, possible to advance a sensible theory about the nature of the Hebrew line. However, we still do not know the precise wording of the missing part. A fascinating solution was suggested by a Jewish scholar who had not seen the *Titulus* in Rome, but worked on the basis of the Greek text in John 19:19. Shalom Ben-Chorin surmised that the following was the Hebrew line (and the letters which we reconstructed on the actual *Titulus* are in bold type): *Yeshu* **HaNozri** *V_eMelek HaYehudim*.[14] Translated, this means: Jesus the Nazorean and King of the Jews. Ben-Chorin does not explain the philological aspects of his suggestion: obviously, it is not a word-for-word translation of the Latin, which must have been the source language of Pilate's order. But we can accept it as a Hebrew rendering which makes considerable sense: first, name and identification, Jesus the Nazorean, with a normal definite article, *Ha* = the. Then, the legal *causa poenae* 'King of the Jews', both parts linked with a grammatically correct 'and' (*V_e*). Another definite article *Ha* was not needed before *Melek* ('King') – even less so as 'King of the Jews' or '*Rex Iudaeorum*' was the *causa poenae* taken from Latin, a language without definite articles. Why does Ben-Chorin think that this was the Hebrew text? Consciously or not, he argues, the scribe was offering a rendering that began each new word with highly charged letters. If, as he presumes, *Yeshu, HaNozri, V_eMelek* and *HaYehudim* were understood as four groups of words, the initial letters were *Yod, Heh, Vahv, Heh*. And this was the Tetragram, the four letters of the holy, unpronounceable name of God: יהוה.

We could assume that the scribe did not know what he was doing. But we could just as easily assume that he did, if, as we speculated in the last chapter, he was one of those Jews who believed in Jesus. Any Jew who had heard Jesus say those decisive words, which contributed to his sentencing by the Sanhedrin and consequently to his death, 'I and the Father are One'[15] and who believed these words, might easily be inspired to incorporate the Tetragram into the Hebrew line on the *Titulus*. Small wonder, in any case, that the chief priests protested vehemently. 'Do not write "The King of the Jews", but, "This man said, I am King of the Jews"' (John 19:21).[16] Ben-Chorin suggests two possibilities: either they protested against the royal dignity bestowed, even if only ironically, upon Jesus by Pilate; or they protested because they recognized the profanation, as they would have seen it, of the Tetragram. Perhaps they did so for both reasons.

Interestingly, this controversy did not generate a tradition in early Christianity: 'King of the Jews', the *causa poenae* in all three languages, remained a criminal allegation. No church, no community turned it into a Christological title[17] – another argument against the supposition that the Santa Croce *Titulus* is a late forgery.

At Cross Purposes in Jerusalem

How much do we know about the earliest Christian community in Jerusalem, the languages they spoke, their culture and their ability to hand down reliable information about the sites and artefacts dearest to their nascent faith? How did the message about the Cross and the empty tomb spread to the first pilgrims, the same sort of believers who left their graffito in what today is called St Vartan's Chapel underneath the Church of the Holy Sepulchre? Should we look many years before, to those Jews who had come to Jerusalem, to celebrate *Shavuot*, the Feast of Weeks, in AD 30 and heard St Peter talk about the Cross, the empty tomb of Jesus, and who then returned home to Rome and other cities of the Roman Empire, some of them energized and converted, ready to spread the good news? These questions are at the heart of our exploration and they involve real, troubled, deeply political figures of the first century, sanitized in our culture's collective memory by sainthood but, in fact, actors on the stage of a true human drama.

Shavuot, the Feast of Weeks, was and is a major Jewish festival. Fifty days after Passover, it celebrates the Giving of the Law. The scroll of the biblical Book of Ruth was – and is – read, along with the Ten Commandments. Hundreds of thousands of pilgrims flocked to Jerusalem, from all over the Roman Empire, to join in the festivities in and near the Temple.[18] St Luke, a circumspect historian and narrator if ever there was one, has a scene where such pilgrims suddenly understand the supposedly uneducated followers of Jesus, 'filled with the Holy Spirit', in their own languages:

Now there were devout men present in Jerusalem from every nation under heaven ... and each one was bewildered to hear these men speaking his own language. They were amazed and astonished. 'Surely,' they said, 'all these men speaking are Galileans? How does it happen that each of us hears them in his own native language? Parthians, Medes and Elamites, people from Mesopotamia, Judaea and Cappadocia, Pontus and Asia, Phrygia and Pamphylia, Egypt and the parts around Cyrene, residents of Rome – Jews and proselytes alike – Cretans and Arabs: we hear them preaching in our own language about the marvels of God' (Acts 2:5–11).

This list of regions from which the pilgrims originated is likely to be accurate; if anything, it probably suffers from omissions, since Jews from Athens, Thessalonica, Corinth, and from other cities and regions of the Roman Empire would have been there as well. One of the resident Jews, a certain Simon Peter (or Shimon Kephas) of Bethsaida, addressed the crowd, presumably in the vicinity of the Temple:

Brothers, no one can deny that the patriarch David himself is dead and buried: his tomb is still with us. But since he was a prophet, and knew that God had sworn him an oath to make one of his descendants succeed him on the throne, he spoke with foreknowledge about the resurrection of the Christ [in Hebrew: of the 'Messiah']. He is the one who was not abandoned to Hades, and whose body did not see corruption. God raised this man Jesus to life, and of that we are all witnesses. Now raised to the heights by God's right hand, he has received from the Father the Holy Spirit, who was promised, and what you see and hear is the outpouring of that Spirit. For David himself never went up to heaven, but he said: 'The Lord declared to my Lord: take your seat at my right hand, till I have made your enemies your footstool.' For this reason the whole House of Israel can be certain that the Lord and Christ whom God has made is this Jesus whom you crucified (Acts 2:29–36).

There could scarcely be a stronger statement of the core facts of the new faith: the physical reality of Jesus's crucifixion and resurrection. Peter's injunction to the pilgrims is to go and see for themselves. Jesus has fulfilled Davidic prophecy: while the forefather's tomb is there, intact, the tomb of his descendant is open and empty.

Clearly, whatever its theological content, such a forthright declaration would have made sense only if the sites in question were known and those whom Peter was addressing would have been able to inspect them for themselves. St Peter could not have risked pronouncing utter lies to so committed a group of worshippers.[19] One is reminded of a passage in St Paul's first Epistle to the Corinthians, where the apostle mentions that the majority of those who had seen the risen Christ were still alive.[20] Paul's message is clear: if you do not trust me, journey to Jerusalem, go to Golgotha, see that the tomb is empty and speak to the witnesses themselves. His letter is also full of juridical terminology, as if to underline the forensic character of his claims.

It is possible that some members of the audience to which St Luke refers had settled in Jerusalem, but were still known by their native districts. Simon of Cyrene, for example, the man who carried the crossbeam for Jesus (Mark 15:21), had originally come from the Cyrenaika, between Egypt and Tunisia. Jews from that region had their own synagogue in Jerusalem. One of the two sons of Simon, Alexander, was buried in the Holy City; his ossuary with an inscription which identifies him was rediscovered by archaeologists of the Hebrew University, Jerusalem.[21] St Stephen, too, the leader of the Greek-speaking Jews who had become followers of Christ (Acts 6:1–7), was an immigré; and the Jewish 'Hellenists' had at least one synagogue of their own in Jerusalem. But while St Luke's wording could hint at a mixture of resident Jews and *Shavuot* pilgrims, he singles out those from the capital of the Empire and explicitly calls them 'residents of Rome'. They, at any rate, would return home after the Feast of Weeks.

St Luke suggests that 'about three thousand' were converted by Peter's speech (Acts 2:31) – not many, from hundreds of thousands. But some time later we read that 'the total number of men had now risen to something like five thousand' (4:4). Those who returned to Rome would have seen Golgotha, with the vertical beam of the Cross probably still standing, and the empty tomb, and perhaps, during clandestine meetings in the famous 'Upper Room', even the *Titulus* itself, which documented the name 'Jesus the Nazarene'. They would have known, too, that the Romans had been

responsible for his death. This, after all, was how St Peter began
his speech:

> Men of Israel, listen to what I am going to say: *Jesus the Nazarene* was
> a man commended to you by God by the miracles and portents and
> signs that God worked through him when he was among you, as you
> know. This man, who was put into your power by the deliberate
> intention and foreknowledge of God, you took *and had crucified and
> killed by men outside the Law* (Acts 2:22–3).[22]

What this suggests is of great importance: the holy sites of the
new faith appear to have been established at a very early stage.
More importantly, the knowledge of their whereabouts was being
exported to towns and cities throughout the Roman Empire, not
least to its very capital, as early as AD 30. From then on, three
cultural strands were interacting: there was a continuous local
tradition among Jewish Christians in Jerusalem, which even a
short exile[23] could not disrupt; there were theological opponents
who had every chance to prove the Christians wrong about the
sacred sites but did not do so, or at least did not do so successfully;
and there were all those in other parts of the germinating Christian
world who were to hear the stories from Jerusalem, told by returning pilgrims. Of the last group, at least a certain number we can
assume would have been curious enough to find out more about
this crucified and risen Messiah to see for themselves at a pilgrimage festival.[24] The Feast of Tabernacles (*Sukkoth*), in September–October, was the next-best chance. Then there was the
following year's Passover (*Pesach*, the Feast of the Unleavened
Bread), and again *Shavuot*, the Feast of Weeks, the modern Christian Pentecost.

Local Jews and seasonal pilgrims interested in *Yeshu HaNozri*
and his sites had several groups of people to whom they could
address their questions. There was the immediate family of the
fallen leader – Mary, James and others; there were the women who
had been the first to see the empty tomb; there were the eleven
disciples; and there was Matthias, the successor to Judas who
had been elected not least because he fulfilled the one decisive
criterion, that of having been an eyewitness from the first hour of

Jesus's public ministry.[25] Their witness was not, of course, above suspicion. But there was one participant in the Passover events of AD 30 who stood out from the others: Joseph of Arimathea, the man whom we identified, in the previous chapter, as the most plausible first custodian of the *Titulus*. Since he was not a Jerusalemite by birth, he has always been associated with his native town, Arimathea, which most historians today locate fifteen kilometres north-east of Lydda. The Greek spelling '*Arimathaia*' is probably a translation of *HaRamatha*, plural '*Ramathaim*', the 'twin peaks', a city mentioned in 1 Samuel 1:1 and in the apocryphal book of 1 Maccabees 11:34.[26] *Ramathaim*, or Arimathea, had a long past: it was the birthplace of Elkanah, the father of the prophet Samuel, and probably of Samuel himself,[27] suffered occupation under the Syrians, and was liberated and returned to Judaism by the Maccabean Jonathan in the mid-first century BC. In Luke's Gospel we are reminded that Joseph's place of origin was indeed, and in the most hard-won sense of the word, 'a Jewish town' (Luke 23:51).

To be 'of Arimathea', therefore, was a distinction. And Joseph was also materially successful. He had acquired personal wealth – Matthew describes him as 'rich' (Matthew 27:57), he was respected (Mark 15:43) and just (Luke 23:50), and above all, he had reached the pinnacle of a Jewish career: he was a member of the Sanhedrin, the higher court of law.[28] Our sources seem to imply that he belonged to the Great Court in Jerusalem; this traditionally numbered seventy sages, although there were also smaller law courts of twenty-three members each, which met in the cities, including Jerusalem. The high priest presided as head of the Great Sanhedrin.[29] By the time of Jesus, most members were Sadducees, although the influence of the Pharisees was increasing. Decisions of the Sanhedrins did not have to be unanimous. Since Joseph of Arimathea objected to their actions against Jesus (Luke 23:51), we can either count him as a minority voter in the Great Court, or as a member of one of the Small Sanhedrins not directly involved with the case. The situation was sensitive enough: voting against the high priest's unambiguous wishes may have been technically within the rules, as Gamaliel was to demonstrate a few weeks later (Acts 5:33-40). But the consequences could be dangerous. If

Joseph was a follower of Jesus, he had to maintain secrecy (John 19:38) and assist, using all the resources of his power base without endangering it.

As a member of the Sanhedrin, Joseph was fully entitled to go to Pilate and ask the prefect to give him the corpse of the crucified man for a traditional Jewish burial. Even an executed criminal had to be buried properly, on the day of his death. Paradoxically, this requirement of Jewish law may have disguised the intensity of Joseph's commitment; according to Deuteronomy, a person who carried out such a burial was not necessarily a friend or relative of the dead person, but simply a Jew obeying the law:

> When someone is convicted of a crime punishable by death and is executed, and you hang him on a tree, his corpse must not remain all night upon the tree; you shall bury him that same day, for anyone hung on a tree is under God's curse. You must not defile the land that the Lord your God is giving you for possession (Deuteronomy 21:22–3).[30]

Even enemies of the people – which was how the majority of the Sanhedrin saw Jesus – were not excluded from this scriptural guideline.[31] There is no reason why Pilate should not have consented to Joseph's request; he would have recited the ancestral law to the prefect, which Pilate probably knew already from previous crucifixions of Jews, conscious that there was no point in aggravating sensitivities on the eve of the Sabbath, after a crucifixion which the prefect must have felt had strengthened his position in Jerusalem.

According to a later Talmudic text, bodies of criminals could be buried in a mass grave provided by the Sanhedrin.[32] Interestingly, the only two first-century cases of which we know eschewed this option. The corpse of the crucified Yehohanan from Givat ha-Mivtar must have been buried on its own or in a double chamber tomb, otherwise his dry bones could not have been collected, some time later, for the customary second burial in a small ossuary where they were found many centuries later by archaeologists. And in Jesus's case, Joseph of Arimathea offered his own tomb, a newly hewn one, as John makes clear.[33] We should not suppose, however, that Joseph was prepared to cede his tomb for ever. First, even in a private family tomb there was usually more than one bench; and second, corpses decayed quickly. A few weeks or months later, in normal conditions, the dry bones would have been ready to be transferred to a small ossuary, which would then be placed on the floor. While Joseph's actions were doubtless morally courageous, his bequest of space in the tomb would not have attracted particular attention. The precedent of Yehohanan shows that even a crucified man could be buried with dignity, according to the ancient traditions.

Joseph did not act alone. Nicodemus joined him at the tomb, with the ritual myrrh, aloes and linen sheets (John 19:40).[34] Unlike the other three Gospel authors, John had a special interest in mentioning the presence of Nicodemus: this man had played an important role twice before in his account, as a Pharisee and member of the Sanhedrin who came to Jesus by night (John 3:1–21) and as an enlightened advocate of Jewish law (John 7:50–1). Joseph of Arimathea and Nicodemus were colleagues, brought together by their interest in the person and the teaching of Jesus – probably at the trial or during the clandestine events preceding it.

The presence of Nicodemus is parenthetically interesting in our exploration of the reliability of local tradition. Unlike Joseph, he is not identified by a place name, partly, no doubt, because his name was so unusual.[35] His name, which means 'conqueror of the people' is Greek, furthermore, not Hebrew or Aramaic – in which case the nearest phonetical equivalent would have been Naqdimon. Greek names were not, of course, unusual in first-century Judaism. Andrew and Philip, two of the disciples, had such names, as did Stephen, the leader of the hellenists, Aeneas, a Jew healed by St Peter, and many more memorialized on tombstones and inscriptions. But the rarity of this particular name, which has no precedent in the Greek Old Testament or in Jewish folklore, suggests that Nicodemus had a genuinely international provenance; his parents could have come from the Diaspora and their native language may have been Greek. It is quite conceivable that he was one of the representatives on the Sanhedrin of the two Greek-speaking synagogues in Jerusalem. If so, he would have been a natural person for pilgrims from Greek-speaking Diaspora regions to approach, for it seems that such visitors sought out

fellow Jews who spoke their tongue. A good example is given
in St John's Gospel, when 'some Greek-speaking' Jews came to
Jerusalem for the Passover Festival, planning to meet Jesus. They
instinctively approached Philip, the one disciple whose name and
native tongue were Greek. In his turn, Philip immediately went to
another disciple from Greek-language Bethsaida, Andrew, Simon
Peter's brother, and together they told Jesus (John 12:20–3).

Joseph and Nicodemus personify a tendency within the Jewish
law courts which, in its response to Jesus, dissented from the strict
majority opinion of the Sanhedrin. It was later said apocryphally,
that Joseph had been a friend of Pilate's and became a missionary,
custodian of the Holy Grail and founder of the first church in
Glastonbury; Nicodemus was also said, in much later accounts,
to have been a disciple of St Peter and St John and, later still, the
author of a Gospel.[36] Such whimsy has little relevance to our
quest. What matters, though, is the presence of these men in
Jerusalem and of others like them. At least two men of very high
standing were close to Jesus and to his followers. They would have
been regarded as extremely trustworthy sources. Jewish pilgrims
coming from abroad would naturally have sought out these two
Jewish sages, who would have been able to recount their experiences and show them the sacred sites. Just as Paul invited the
Corinthians to go to Jerusalem and consult eyewitnesses, so the
Jerusalemite Christians could have sent sceptical Jewish visitors
to see Joseph and Nicodemus.

Blue Plaques and Graffiti

The Christian faith has always been linked with holy sites. The
Gospels insist time and again on their importance, from Bethlehem via Nazareth and Caesarea Philippi to the Temple, Golgotha
and the Tomb. It was evidently considered of the highest importance by the Evangelists to record that a certain event happened at
a certain place. For centuries, some of these place-names have
retained their evocative character without any archaeological evidence to show where they might have been. Recent excavations
have solved many puzzles, settling, for instance, where Cana really

Struck at Siscia in AD 326–7, when Constantine began the construction of the first Church of the Holy Sepulchre in Jerusalem, this gold medallion portrays the emperor with his eyes turned heavenwards. According to his biographer Eusebius, this symbolized prayerful piety. As Constantine did not want to offend his non-Christian subjects, most of his coins did not overtly signal his conversion. There is only one known example of an indisputably Christian coin: minted at Ticinium in 315, it shows the emperor with the Chi-Rho symbol on his head.

A modern statue of Helena, who was declared empress (Augusta) in 325, portrayed in regal posture, at Santa Croce in Gerusalemme, Rome. Many coins of Helena survive, but no contemporary statues.

Deep below today's Church of
the Holy Sepulchre, the Crypt
of St Helena is believed by
thousands of pilgrims to be the
place where the True Cross
and the Titulus were found by
the empress and her excavators. The rockface to the right
belongs to the lower slopes
of the rock of Golgotha.

Pilgrims leave pieces of paper
with prayers behind the glass
which protects a badly damaged fresco depicting Helena
in the crypt.

The *Titulus* at Santa Croce in Gerusalemme, Rome. Only under exceptional circumstances has the protective glazing been removed to allow closer inspection. This photo was taken on one such occasion in 1998. In spite of the damage the fragment has suffered over the years, the remnants of the Hebrew line and the surviving Greek and Latin letters can be seen clearly in their present state of preservation.

Behind the present church of Santa Croce in Gerusalemme, excavations have brought to light the remains of the imperial 'Sessorian Palace', Helena's lodgings in Rome.

The north-west façade of Santa Croce preserves the original wall of the palace's atrium and of the first church built in the fourth century AD.

The entrance to Santa Croce in Gerusalemme is partly 12th century (the Campanile), partly baroque, created by Domenico Gregorini between 1743 and 1750. Since 1561, the church has also been a Cistercian monastery.

The Church of the Holy Sepulchre in Jerusalem and its surroundings. Photo taken from the tower of the Church of the Redeemer in the Muristan Quarter.

A board on display at the Church of Santa Croce in Gerusalemme, with the traditional but erroneous reconstruction of the Titulus.

The stone lid which covered the lead box of the Titulus in a wall at Santa Croce between 1140 and 1492. The Latin inscription reads TITVLVS CRVCIS, 'T

The oldest undisputed pictorial example of the Cross in a Christian context. Found on the Palatine in Rome, it is a mocking graffito incised into the wall of the third century Roman Army cadets' garrison. Dated to c. AD 220, it shows a crucified person with the head of an ass, and standing next to it, a young man, with the Greek text 'Alexamenos sebethe theon' (Alexamenos worships [his] God). Christians had often been accused of venerating an assheaded God. The Roman graffito is clear archaeological proof that believers in Christ proclaimed the Cross as the central symbol of their faith – even in public – long before the time of Helena and Constantine.

Constantine's pride in his vision of the Chi-Rho was emulated by his successors. His son Constans, who ruled from 337 to 350, is shown on this silver medallion struck at Siscia in c. 340, holding a standard with the Chi-Rho on the 'Labarum'. The coin was found at Kaiseraugst (Augusta Raurica) in Switzerland. The inscription calls Constans the 'triumpher over the barbarian peoples'.

Outside the church at Piesport (Moselle), a former Roman garrison town where excavations have revealed traces of wine growing and production at the time of Constantine, this memorial standard shows the Greek text of Constantine's vision, according to Eusebius, and the form of the Chi-Rho as he describes it. According to a late tradition, Constantine had his vision not far from Piesport, on a hill above his residence at Neumagen (Roman Noviomagus), when he assembled his troops before marching on Rome. To this day, the hill is called Constantine's Hill (*Konstantinhöhe*).

was, but have left others unanswered, such as the riddle of the location of Emmaus. Sometimes the results of such digs can be breathtaking: the rediscovery of the fishermen's town of Bethsaida and of a fishing boat near the town of Migdal/Magdala (Kibbuz Nof Ginnosar) are only two examples. Another is the ongoing work at Caesarea Philippi in the north, not far from Dan below Mount Hermon, where a whole first-century vista, including a pagan shrine dedicated to the godhead Pan, a temple of Emperor Augustus and one of the sources of the River Jordan, has become visible again.

This last site – now called Banjas, an Arabic form of the old Greek name 'Paneas', after Pan – encapsulates the importance of place to nascent Christianity. The site had been one of the most popular pilgrimage destinations in the eastern Roman Empire since the third century BC.[37] The sheer size of the area, and the re-excavated shops and amenities in front of the shrine, indicate a flourishing business. And it was here, in c.AD 29, that Jesus asked his disciples who the people thought he was and who they themselves thought he was.[38] Evidently it was no accident that this religious revolutionary chose this particular site to pose these particular questions. According to the Gospels a man called Simon, son of Jona, proclaimed Jesus the Messiah at a place where the universal Greek God of 'All'[39] was venerated next to a temple of Emperor Augustus: the pagan cult and the imperial cult as next-door neighbours were thus confronted by Jesus, the Anointed One of God, standing near a source of the river of his baptism. Indeed, Pan, like Augustus, had places of worship elsewhere in the Roman Empire, some only a couple of days' journey away – one dedicated to Pan is known to have existed in Ashkelon, while another Augustus temple was at Caesarea Maritima. Pilgrims knew where to go, where the sacred places of their faith were alleged to be.

Among the many locations associated with Jesus, two were of the greatest importance: the place of his crucifixion and the place of his resurrection, Golgotha and the empty tomb. His disciples and first followers, all Jews, though some with a Greek background, knew of course that the precise location had to be remembered and that this knowledge had to be passed on from generation to generation; it had to be secured and its transmission guaranteed.

What was required was the historical equivalent of the blue plaque. In ancient times the normal method was to incise names and exclamations into the stone. The ossuaries we encountered above carry the name of the dead person and often his or her father's name as well. The family tomb of Caiaphas, discovered in the southern suburb of Talpiot, or the ossuaries found near the church of 'Dominus flevit' on the Mount of Olives, provide us with numerous examples. Those unearthed near Dominus flevit are Jewish and for some of them a Jewish-Christian context has been claimed (see chapter 6). Two further ossuaries, excavated in Talpiot, have been dated by their discoverer, Eliezer L. Sukenik (the father of the famous soldier and archaeologist Yigael Yadin) to the early Forties of the first century, AD 50 at the latest, and were identified by him as Jewish-Christian.[40]

But these are movable objects. What about the scenes of the events themselves? Martin Biddle, the Oxford archaeologist, has reconstructed the architectural history of the tomb in the Church of the Holy Sepulchre with the latest techniques of archaeology and computerized photogrammetry, and is a scholar respected by all Christian denominations in Jerusalem, by the Muslim guardians of the key to the church and by the Israelis. He is also certain that further restoration work will be carried out, particularly on the floor of the Rotunda.[41] He has been heard to say more than once that this will be the moment when an important missing link might be found: inscriptions from local Christians or pilgrims. Any inscription that is older than the time of Hadrian would be the decisive 'blue plaque', which all scholars of the Cross and Holy Sepulchre seek. It would provide us with something visible, to help us accept that this particular area of the church rather than, say, the so-called 'tomb of Joseph of Arimathea', a few yards behind the Coptic chapel in what once was the 'garden' of tombs in the first century, is the exact tomb of Jesus, the one which local Christians could show to visitors until Hadrian built his temple above it. Biddle's guarded confidence is not without basis – for there is a first-century precedent not far away: the so-called Tomb of David at the Cenacle on Mount Zion.

Archaeologists agree that this building is not the true tomb of King David, which was in his own city on the eastern hill called

Ophel.[42] A group of orthodox Jews has turned the false tomb into a synagogue and at the northern wall there is a giant sarcophagus, covered by a valuable carpet with symbols and stars of David. However, there is just as little ground for claiming this to be David's sarcophagus as there is for venerating the room as his: it is nothing but a twelfth-century Crusader's cenotaph. What is really remarkable is the niche, alcove or apse for the 'Aaron Ha Kodesh', the ark which contained the sacred scrolls. In synagogues outside Jerusalem this was, as a rule, directed towards the Holy City. In Jerusalem the natural direction would have been towards the Temple, or, after the conflagration of AD 70, its former site.[43] However, the compass needle confirms a striking deviation: this niche is facing in the direction of the area of Golgotha and the tomb. We have checked this ourselves and the exactness of the line plotted is remarkable. And a view over Jerusalem from the Haas Promenade, where the sites of the 'Tomb of David' syna- gogue, the inner Temple precinct (now occupied by the Dome of the rock) and the Church of the Holy Sepulchre are easily distinguished, supports the co-ordinates of any good map of ancient Jerusalem: no one standing at the 'Tomb of David' could or can mix up the location of the Temple with that of Golgotha. In other words, the direction of the niche was not accidental.

This observation is one of several arguments for a theory first suggested by Bargil Pixner, a Jerusalem archaeologist. Pixner iden- tified the building as a Jewish-Christian synagogue, constructed by believers in Christ after their return from voluntary exile in Pella, during the mid- and late Seventies of the first century. We portrayed one of them, Symeon Bar Cleopas, in the previous chapter. Pixner went on to claim that the Judaeo-Christian syna- gogue was built in this particular area of Mount Zion because it had been the site of the Last Supper, destroyed during the revolt against the Romans. His suggestions met with doubt and oppos- ition, but he has been able to establish his case over years of study, not least with colleagues.[44] It is, however, a second argument for Jewish-Christian habitation which interests us most.

In 1948 a Jordanian mortar grenade hit the building. An Israeli archaeologist, J. Pinkerfeld, was appointed to analyse and repair the damage. In 1951 he found the niche of the Torah scrolls and two different layers of flooring underneath the present surface: Byzantine-late Roman and, deeper still, 70 centimetres below the present floor level, the original surface with remnants of stone slabs.[45] Pinkerfeld's most important discovery were pieces of plasterwork from the first building, on the oldest level, with Greek graffiti. Pinkerfeld was killed before he could publish them. An Italian archaeologist, Emanuele Testa, was the first to reproduce and interpret these drawings.[46] None of them is formal, in a style known from official inscriptions. Abbreviated and hastily written, their handwriting reminds one of those last-minute inscriptions on ossuaries, added in the moments before the container was placed in the tomb chamber.[47] One of them is clearly an appeal to Jesus. It reads, in Testa's deciphering, which has been corroborated by Pixner, Riesner and others: *ΙΟΥ ΙΗΣΟΥΣ ΖΗΖΟ ΚΙΡΙΕ ΑΥΤΟΚΡΑΤΟΡΟΣ*: O Jesus, Lord of the Ruler, may I live'. Others have translated it as 'O Jesus, that I may live, Lord of the Autocrat'.[48] This invocation of Jesus seems to allude to the beginning of Psalm 109/110, which was interpreted by Christians as a messianic prophecy as early as St Peter's speech at Pentecost in Jerusalem: 'The Lord said to my Lord, sit at my right hand ...' The strange 'autokrator', (self)ruler, or 'autocrat' of our graffito was a term known to Greek-speaking Jews at least from an apocryphal book of the Bible, 4 Maccabees, where it occurs five times. In each case it means master or ruler.[49] But 'Autokrator' was also one of the many titles of the Roman Emperor at the time of Jesus and his first followers. To call Jesus 'Autokrator' was at least as poignant, in political terms, as calling him 'Son of God', which was also, as we have seen, one of the official titles of the Emperor.[50]

The exact identification of the graffiti from the first level of the synagogue on Mount Zion is a matter of scholarly dispute, but seen in the context of the archaeology of the site and of the niche for the Torah, the very strong likelihood is that they are Judaeo-Christian. At the very least they can be said to be of first-century origin and to appeal to something or someone, and at a place of worship – which this building soon became if it had not been one from the beginning. Whether we opt for the most or least bold interpretation, the graffiti are obviously an important hint of what further excavations may reveal – similar inscriptions, drawings or graffiti, which may indeed be found during the eagerly anticipated restoration work on the floor of the tomb of Christ in the Church of the Holy Sepulchre.

Tantalizingly, we shall have to wait until the work of Martin Biddle, his wife Birthe and their multidenominational team begins. In the meantime, there is one remarkable Christian inscription in Jerusalem which predates the time of Helena's discoveries and Constantine's building work; we referred to it briefly in the previous chapter: underneath the Church of the Holy Sepulchre, following the steps to St Helena's chapel, the visitor reaches a plateau, which belongs to the chapel of the Armenians. To the left there is a closed door, which the Armenians open on rare occasion. Behind that door, steps lead to a deeper, cave-like room: we have reached the area of the rock of Golgotha, which once would have been in the open, not yet obscured from sight by Hadrian's temple. The Armenians found it almost by accident, during restorations, when they happened upon a hollow space behind a wall. They call it the Chapel of St Vartan and the Armenian Martyrs, and here they made a surprising discovery. On a stone they saw a boat and a Latin inscription underneath. Before the whole area was properly restored, a member of the British School of Archaeology came and suggested that the line, in capital letters, read ISISMYRIONIMOS, 'Isis of the thousandfold names', one of the titles given to the Egyptian goddess. It was a wild guess, as the letters of the second word do not remotely resemble MYRIONIMOS (apart from the fact that there is an 'M' and an 'S'), and given that comparable inscriptions do not speak of the goddess as ISIS, but address her as ISIDI. Furthermore, the boat above the line would be a meaningless element in connection with Isis. Emanuele Testa suggested a reading, which conforms to the letters as they actually are and does justice to the drawing of a boat above them. He read DOMINEIVIMUS, i.e. *Domine ivimus*: Lord, we have arrived. Those who had been convinced by the 'Isis' interpretation asserted that Testa had changed or falsified the letters during restoration and charged him with fraud. The specialists of the Criminal Investigation Bureau, a branch of the National Police, were called in, and on 12 January 1977 they finally established the integrity of Testa's work, and the authenticity of the drawing and of the Latin line (whatever its deeper meaning – that was not the business of the Israeli police to decide).[51]

The translation of *Domine ivimus* presented no problems. Nor was it difficult to see that it alluded to the pilgrimage psalm 121/122, verse 1: '*Laetatus sum eo quod dixerint mihi in domum Domini ibimus, stantes erant pedes nostri in portis tuis Hierusalem*', which means 'I rejoice that they said to me, *Let us go to the House of the Lord. Our feet are standing at your gates, Jerusalem!*'. These pilgrims have followed the injunction of the psalm: they have gone and they have arrived. A single letter, 'b/v', often pronounced identically at the time, turned the future tense of *ibimus* into the fulfilment. Interestingly, even the Jewish scholars who investigated the text and its context never suggested that it could be a Jewish rather than a Christian inscription. The site of the discovery, at the feet of Golgotha, would rule this out. It is also, in fact, unlikely that Jewish pilgrims would have chosen Latin, rather than Greek, which remained the Jewish language of communication even in Rome and elsewhere in the Diaspora. However, Christians in the West soon began to use Latin, first as an alternative to Greek, finally as the majority language. By the mid-second century AD, Latin was an acceptable language for Christian literature. In c.AD 180 a contemporary account of a martyrdom in Scilli (modern Tunisia) presupposes the existence of Latin scrolls with St Paul's letters; towards the end of that century, the great apologist and theologian Tertullian was writing exclusively in Latin.[52] In other words, we would expect a pilgrimage inscription from this era to be written in Latin.

What sort of date can we ascribe to the image? It is a small Roman trading vessel; its bow has the shape of a goose's head; the sail is rolled up behind the mast and bound together with red ropes. The mast itself has been brought down – the boat, we are meant to understand, has arrived in its safe haven, at the site of the Lord's death and resurrection. A powerful pictorial language, achieved by simple means.

As Magen Broshi has shown (see note 51), this type of trading ship was in use from the second to the fourth centuries. Thus, drawing and text could be as early as the mid-second century or as late as the fourth. The style of the inscription favours an earlier date, but given its rough and unprofessional form, precise dating is impossible. Other historical factors are of some assistance. However, a date after 326, the period of Helena's visit, must be ruled out. Any pilgrim would have been able to reach the hillock of Golgotha and the stones of the empty tomb as soon as Hadrian's temple had been torn down. Conversely, any date prior to the building of Hadrian's temple, c.AD 135, must be ruled out for the same reason. Whoever came to see these two sites, from near or far, would have had access to them. And, as we saw above, it is unlikely that Jewish – or 'pagan' – Christian pilgrims would have written a Latin invocation before Hadrian's time.

We can say with certainty that the boat and inscription were incised between AD 135 and AD 324. Can we be more precise? They are likely, by definition, to date from a period when Christians were at liberty to travel and to be seen to be Christians, a period free from local or empire-wide persecutions. From this perspective the most likely moment is some time in the late second and early third century. Although there were always shorter periods of relative calm, what the Italian historian Marta Sordi calls the 'de facto toleration from Septimius Severus to Elagabalus',[53] one era looks particularly likely: the reign of Philip the Arab, Marcus Iulius Philippus, Roman Emperor from AD 244 to 249. As an Arab from Shabba, south-east of Damascus, he came from a religiously tolerant region. His acts of administration encouraged Christians and it has been suggested that he was a Christian himself, if only in secret.[54] With Decius after him, some sixty years of insecurity and concentrated persecutions set in, until Constantine and Licinius declared Christianity a tolerated religion in 313, at the imperial court of Milan. Tentatively, therefore, we suggest the time of Philip the Arab at the latest, or any time under the Severan dynasty before him.

In any case the pilgrims subtly protected their graffito against destruction by hostile Jews or persecuting Romans. By writing 'DOMINE', they used a term which a Jew could see in the context of Psalm 122 and a simple Roman as an invocation of the Emperor: *Dominus* (and in Greek, *Kyrios*) was one of those titles and forms of address the emperors demanded for themselves.[55] Why should the Christians not follow a word of their Lord Jesus: 'Look, I am sending you out like sheep among the wolves; so be cunning as snakes and yet as innocent as doves' (Matthew 10:16)?

But whatever the year, month, week and day of arrival of those Christians may have been, they must have met other Christians in Jerusalem who were able to show them the place. To repeat a point central to our thesis, there is no reason to doubt a continuous local tradition, from the moment of crucifixion and burial, to the day when Empress Helena arrived on the scene. Beginning with those at the Cross, via Joseph of Arimathea and Nicodemus to Symeon Bar Cleopas, from the Judaeo-Christians in the synagogue on Mount Zion to the seafaring pilgrims with their graffito at Golgotha, we encounter people who could read and write in more than one language and who were guarantors of a reliable local tradition. When the tomb was found in c.AD 326 the onlookers were of course surprised. But their astonishment had nothing to do with the location; it was the surprise of those who had not dared to hope that they would find it in pristine condition, in spite of Hadrian's activities, exactly where the 200-year-old tradition said it would be.[56]

Much of what once existed was lost or destroyed in later centuries. The conquests of the seventh century and the wanton acts of destruction at the tomb of Christ and the whole church 'of the Resurrection', with its Christian symbols, which had been ordered by Caliph al-Hakim bi-Amr Allah in 1009 and dutifully carried out by Yaruk, the governor of Ramla,[57] had left the sites in a state of disrepair, which the Crusaders merely covered with their new Church of the Holy Sepulchre. There must have been more inscriptions and signs which were visible prior to Hadrian's building work, and then again after the excavations ordered by Helena. What we can see today, even perhaps what we can uncover with the most scientifically sophisticated excavation, is a tiny proportion of what once was. Even so, the quality of what remains is astonishing, more so than many historians of the Holy Sepulchre and other Holy Land sites are minded to admit. This is the echo that rings down the centuries of men and women who believed they knew what had happened and, more important, where. The *Titulus* is only one part of this rich and strange tradition.

6

The Earliest Christian Symbol:
Believers under the Cross

When I survey the wondrous Cross
 On which the Prince of Glory died,
My richest gain I count but loss,
 And pour contempt on all my pride.

> Isaac Watts (*Hymns Ancient & Modern*)

The centrality of the cross...

> Hugh Montefiore, *On Being a Jewish Christian*

A Shorthand Symbol from Heaven?

It has long been orthodox, as we have already noted, to suppose that the Cross became a central feature of Western symbolism during and after the reign of Constantine. It is true that the sudden increase of crosses and Chi-Rho monograms on inscriptions, lamps, amulets and ampullas in the fourth century is remarkable. Something must have happened to encourage this proliferation, some act of political will. It is quite wrong, however, to conclude from this new liquidity that the market did not exist at all before – a point we made in chapter 1.[1] This is a misapprehension which has proved enormously influential. Whenever a cross or Chi-Rho monogram is discovered on an ossuary, an inscription, or on a papyrus, and dated to the third or second centuries, it is stated almost as a matter of course that it is not a Christian symbol. Alternatively, the symbol is taken to be of a date later than the beginning of Constantine's reign in the fourth century.

This circular form of argument has also been influential in other areas of Christian archaeology. In precisely the same way, it is still considered a scholarly heresy to suggest that separate Christian church buildings could have existed prior to Constantine: this in spite of the fact that there is at least one quite clear archaeological case – the mid-third-century church at Dura Europos (modern Qalat es Salihiya) in the East. There is also literary evidence for the existence of such buildings from the late third century in a neglected statement by Lactantius, the tutor of Constantine's son Crispus.[2] But as a rule, ancient Roman buildings which look like churches are necessarily assumed to be later than c.314, or, if they are obviously older, assumed not to be churches at all. Since there are certain architectural similarities between these early Christian structures and temples of Mithras or Roman basilicas (a term which originally meant nothing but 'royal hall'), this has been an easy, if misleading, position to adopt. Only small buildings – too small to be royal halls, or not ostentatious enough to be associated with the established cult of Mithras – have been categorised as possible churches: a profoundly misleading criterion. One such example of a very early church is almost certainly the building at Silchester, near Reading, which is late third century and closely matches the description of a church as suggested by Lactantius.[3] It even has a mosaic in the form of a black-and-white cross in the apse. And it is here at Silchester that we begin our quest for traces of the earliest Christian symbol.

Would we expect early Christians, in uncertain times prior to the toleration edict of AD 313, to use the cross as their motif? And if so, how? The Silchester cross is a brilliant example of disguised candour. The uninitiated would see black and white stones in an interchanging pattern. No 'triumphal cross' – that would have been quite unthinkable at this point. But it is a cross nonetheless, with all sides of equal length – a so-called 'Greek Cross', the form still used by the International Red Cross, and in the national flag of Switzerland. In the four quadrangles, above and below each 'arm', the pattern was repeated. Much later, after the Crusades, this form of five crosses in one (four above and below the equidistant central arms) became known as the 'Jerusalem Cross'. At Silchester, it is a deft picture puzzle – as cunning as other elements of this church, such as the separate area for a movable, and therefore easily concealed, baptismal font,[4] east of the church's entrance. While the apse faced west (only later was it made more or less obligatory that it should point towards Jerusalem), the baptismal area was facing east, towards the geographical location of Jesus's own baptism.

Not far from the Basilica (not the church) of Silchester or, to give it its Roman name, Calleva Atrebatum, a lead seal was discovered. On it, the monogram of Christ or Chi-Rho is clearly visible: an X and in it a P, with the rounded part of the P above the upper ends of the X. As we have already seen, this sign owes its name to the Greek letters *Chi* and *Rho*, written X and P, which are the first letters of Christ (XPICTOC) in Greek. To the left and right of the X, there are the Greek letters *Alpha* and *Omega* (A and ω). The *Alpha* is damaged and almost illegible, but other archaeological discoveries which have been made all over the Roman Empire enable us to reconstruct it. Such a seal implies the stamp of officialdom. The obvious conclusion to draw would be that it cannot be older than the age of Constantine, when Christians could become civil servants and were in a position to use such seals. Again, however, it would be wrong to assume that the shift in practice happened only in his reign. Under Constantius Chlorus, Constantine's father, who ruled as Caesar of the West (which included Britannia) from AD 293 to his death on 25 July 306 in York, Christianity was already tolerated in practice. Constantius may have had personal reasons for adopting this stance: the wife he married after his separation from Helena, Theodora, bore him a daughter they called Anastasia, 'the resurrection'. So a Christian in imperial employment could easily and quite legitimately have used such a seal at the time and, when Diocletian's persecution began, he might be expected to have thrown it away, near the basilica where it was discovered by archaeologists so many centuries later.

Let us consider the background: The two letters A and ω, *Alpha* and *Omega*, had a symbolic meaning, which was well known to all Christians, long before Constantine the Great had his visions and despatched his mother on her holy mission. They occur in the book of Revelation, at the end of the New Testament: 'I am the Alpha and the Omega, says the Lord God, who is, who was, and who is to come, the Almighty' (Revelation, 1:8). And: 'Look, I am coming soon, and my reward is with me, to repay everyone as their deeds deserve. I am the Alpha and the Omega, the First and the Last, the Beginning and the End' (Revelation, 22:12–13). The first and the last letter of the Greek alphabet symbolized beginning and end in Christ, the incarnate Son of God, and therefore the omnipresence of God himself. It was, in the truest sense of the word, an awful symbol, but also, for those who used it on seals or inscriptions, a sign of hope. Sometimes, as on the Icklingham baptismal tank and on some funerary inscriptions elsewhere in the Roman Empire, the order of the letters was reversed: ω and A. The point of this occasional inversion was quite clear. As in baptism, so in death, the end is the beginning. In baptism, a life outside the community of believers has ended, and the new life in Christ has begun. With death, life on earth has come to an end, but life eternal, the new beginning, has set in.

'The Revelation of St John the Divine', as the Authorized Version of the Bible calls it, is commonly dated to the end of the first century, but may be some thirty years older.[5] In any case, it existed at least two hundred and thirteen years before the toleration edict of Constantine and Licinius. Is it really credible that no Christian had the idea of using *Alpha* and *Omega* before AD 313? The symbolism was there to be used, readily available in the poetic rage of Revelation, from the end of the first century, probably as early as AD 68.

And the Chi-Rho? Our earliest papyri of the New Testament, it is true, abbreviate the Greek form of Christ, like all other 'Holy Names' or *Nomina Sacra*, with the first and last letter, but not with the first two.[6] Thus, we find XC for XPICTOC, but not XP, the letters of the Chi-Rho. However, there are two notable exceptions: the papyrus classified as P45 of the late second, early third century, which abbreviates XP (in Acts 16:18), and – particularly fascinating in the context of our observations on the *Alpha* and *Omega* in the book of Revelation – the papyrus P18, of the third century, a small fragment with Revelation 1:4–7, which abbreviates *Christos*/XPICTOC as XP in chapter 1:5.[7] This latter example is all the more important as the name of Christ occurs only once in this tiny fragment, at the very beginning of the book, in chapter 1, verse 5, where it is abbreviated XP. Thus, it is fair to assume that this was the spelling throughout the codex, the rest of which is lost. In other words, we have pre-Constantinian manuscript evidence for the Chi-Rho abbreviation and, in one case, this evidence occurs in the very book of the New Testament which introduces the *Alpha/Omega* symbolism.

It was not a great step to proceed from the XP abbreviation, with the usual horizontal bar above the letters, to a form where these two letters were intertwined. Not that we would expect to find this in papyri, where letters were kept separate, linked in ligatures, or re-created as abbreviations, as in the γ of the Titulus, but – as a rule – not symbolically intertwined. However, the use of these powerful symbols in early papyri is quite clear: *Alpha* and *Omega*, XP for *Christos*. On tombstones or other inscriptions, and even on seals, the creative freedom to link and combine these elements was inspired by the text of a biblical book and by the example of early manuscripts.

One thing is certain: the use of the Christogram with XP cannot have been the consequence of Constantine's vision in early 312. Lactantius, who gives us a detailed description of this vision, is adamant that the sign was an upright cross, not an X, with the top of the vertical bar turned round to form a P.[8] The way he describes it does full justice to a many-layered symbolism: 'Constantine was advised in a dream to mark the heavenly sign of God on the shields of his soldiers and then to engage in battle. He did as he was commanded and by means of a slanted X [*transversa X littera*] with the top of its head bent round, he marked Christ on their shields. Armed with this sign, the army took up its weapons'.[9]

The historian Andrew Alföldi interprets the description thus: 'According to Lactantius, the sign was represented by a vertical stroke, rounded at the top, drawn through the middle of the *Chi*. We must interpret this to mean that the *Rho*, hastily painted on the shields, took the form of a round-headed pin.'[10] Lactantius says it all: 'the heavenly sign of God' – that is the Cross of Jesus, the 'slanted X'. The X with the top of its head bent round is the beginning of Christ's name. On 28 October 312, Constantine defeated the troops of his opponent Maxentius at the Milvian Bridge north of Rome, Maxentius died, and the way for the acknowledgement of Christianity was paved, to Rome and beyond. We have every reason to trust Lactantius. His account is sparse, without the heated language of some of his mystic contemporaries, and he describes a form of the monogram which is not the one that was soon to become familiar on the earliest coins and inscriptions. In other words, he did not copy common Christian coinage, but gave an independent account which must have had the support of Constantine himself. His book *On the Deaths of the Persecutors* was published in AD 314–15, some two years before he became the tutor of Constantine's son Crispus. It is inconceivable that the Emperor would have entrusted Lactantius with such a delicate task if he had failed to get the basic facts about the heavenly sign right.

It may even be possible to demonstrate how Constantine might have used the sign for the shields of his soldiers without offending their traditional sensitivities: for there is a type of Roman standard finial which resembles circles drawn around a vertical beam or stem. A well-preserved example numbered PRB 1927.12–12.6 is on display in the Weston Wing of the British Museum which houses the finds from Roman Britain. It probably once belonged to the top of a wooden shafted military standard. Formed like a cross it has a wider and a smaller circle just under the top of the finial, looking almost like a reticle (Fig.1). If one covers or deletes part of the circles and most of the left-hand side, what remains looks precisely like the vision described by Lactantius. In other words, it is not a completely new sign, but the altered form of a well-known type (Fig.2). As a hardened soldier, Constantine would have recognized it well enough, and his soldiers would have grasped that the new symbol was close enough to something they had seen before: comfortably traditional, and yet from one perspective completely new.

The introduction of new practices by the mutation of existing traditions has been a feature of military organization through the ages – not least in the amalgamated regiments of the British Army. And it may not be accidental that the device on the cruciform crest of the Chaplains' Department of Her Majesty's Armed Forces is the English text of Constantine's Latin vision: *In hoc signo vinces*, in this sign conquer.

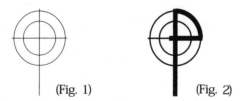

(Fig. 1)   (Fig. 2)

It seems, at any rate, that the sign put on his soldiers' shields was, in a way, a typical Constantinian compromise: there was an obvious Christian message to those who saw it, but to those who did not (or did not want to) see it, the sign was a mere variation on a theme.

In contrast, Eusebius wrote his extended version in his biography of Constantine, the *Vita Constantini*, after the Emperor's death in AD 337, in an undisguised attempt to glorify his master's memory. Hence his description conforms to the stylized type of the Chi-Rho established in the late Twenties of the fourth century. Eusebius describes how the Emperor tells his artists about the details of his vision, and how they make the shaft with the sign:

> The sign was formed like this: A long, gilded shaft of a lance had a crossbeam and was thus shaped in the form of a cross. At the top, there was a garland attached, made from jewels and gold, and in it was the sign of the name of the Saviour – two letters, the initial letters which signify the name of Christ, with the *Rho* crossed in the middle by the *Chi*. From that day on, the Emperor wore those letters also on his helmet. On the crossbeam there was a linen cloth of valuable fabric, which was interwoven with gold and studded with colourfully mixed jewels which glittered in the sun – a glorious view for every beholder. This linen cloth which hung from the crossbeam of the shaft was square.[11]

Eusebius goes on to say that there was, between the cloth and the cross, the golden portrait of the Emperor and his sons. This is a tell-tale error: in 312, Constantine had only *one* son and he was not yet a co-regent who could be portrayed in such a way. However, the many examples of the shaft, technically called a *Labarum*,

which came into being after 327–8 show precisely the form which
Eusebius described, many of them with the imperial portraits. In
327 and after, this was politically correct: after the execution of
his son Crispus and his second wife Fausta in 326, there remained
three sons, Constantinus (born in 316), Constantius (born in 317)
and Constans (born in 320). Constantinus was installed as Caesar
one year after his birth in 317, Constantius followed in 324, while
Constans had to wait until 333. Crispus, the first son, had been
elevated in the same year as Constantinus, AD 317. Only then, at
the earliest, was there a justification for Eusebius's plural, the
'sons', which he saw above the cloth. It is clear that – char-
acteristically – Eusebius embellished his sources. He followed the
accepted type of coinage and inscriptions, which was in use from
AD 327 and may be conceivable from AD 317 at the earliest, five
years after the vision and the battle at the Milvian Bridge. But if
there was a change in the form of the Chi-Rho, from the simple
'round-headed pin' to the Greek X and the Greek P as the intertwined first letters of *Christos*, in a circle or wreath or garland,
what caused it?

The Chi-Rho of Lactantius was a cross, visibly and unmistakably. There is no reason to doubt that this is what Constantine
saw, or thought he saw, in his dream and vision: not for the first
time, of course, since he had been aware of the Christian faith
and Christian practice for decades, and had a half-sister called
'Resurrection'. And, as we have already seen, there was every
reason for the Emperor to cast his spiritual net as widely as seemed
expedient. Looking for divine guidance and support, an army com-
mander who lived in a world of plural, competing religions, a
worshipper of the Invincible Sun, the 'Sol Invictus', did not doubt
the significance of signs from above, and could not afford to dispute
the possibility that another god, the Christian one, might try to
communicate with him.

This did not mean, however, that Constantine had complete
freedom of manoeuvre. The majority of the Senate remained
staunchly attached to the old religions. There was not a single
Christian symbol or reference on the triumphal arch dedicated to
the victorious Constantine. Indeed, as we have seen, the Emperor
seems to have pursued a careful middle course, whatever the

strength of his private belief: encouraging the Christians, helping them into positions of influence and power, but without alienating the old families and undermining the old structures too soon and too vigorously. His initial approach was conspicuously gradualist. The Emperor's mints continued to produce coins with the symbols of the Sun god, next to those with the Chi-Rho and the 'Labarum'. As such the new form of the monogram of Christ appeared to be a politically astute compromise: it was no longer a simple cross, but an X and a P, and outside Christian circles this had no obvious or offensive religious connotation.

Or did it communicate a message after all? Constantine was not a particularly literate man, but he surrounded himself with highly educated advisers. Anyone acquainted with Greek literature knew the Chi-Rho in the intertwined XP form: it was a very common symbol called *Chrêsis*, *Chrêsimon* or *Chrêston*, which was written in the margin of lines of special value, suitable for quotation. There are examples of this as early as the first century BC.[12] The three Greek terms for this sign, all spelled with a long 'E' (*Eta*) mean 'useful', 'helpful', 'good' or (*Chrêsis*) 'borrowing' (as in: for a quote). Employed on coins or standards, it became a kind of recommendation, or annotation, recognizable to the literate and utterly uncontroversial. However, to all Christians the subliminal message was clear: not only were these indeed the first two letters of Christ's name, the technical term *Chrêston* was of course also the neuter of *Chrêstos*. And in Greek pronunciation, the long 'E', the *Eta* of *Chrêstos*, was virtually interchangeable with the 'I' or *Iota*. Write *Iota* for *Eta*, and what you get is *Christos* – Christ.[13] To put it another way, the Chi-Rho, known from Greek papyri, could be understood either as a Christ monogram because of the two initial letters, or as an innocuous literary device.

But Constantine's advisers, as we saw in chapter 1, did not invent the Christian meaning of the Chi-Rho. There are other, apparently older examples, and one such which can be dated with archaeological certainty to the period well before Constantine, and which uses the Chi-Rho in a Christian context.[14] It was found in the Hypogaeum of the Acilians, the late second–third-century part of the Priscilla Catacombs in Rome. The text, in clumsy Greek, reads: 'O Father of all, who you have created and taken [up

to heaven] Eirene, Zoe and Markellos, to you the Glory in Christ.'
The last words, 'in Christ', are written *'en'* (in), followed by the
Chi-Rho monogram of 'X' with 'P'.

What about the sign described by Lactantius? The Cross monogram – or 'Staurogram' as it is often called, from the Greek word
for cross, *stauros* – was known among Christians at least forty
years before Constantine's vision. An indisputably Christian
inscription at a burial place in Rome, between the Via Appia and
Via Latina, and safely dated to the period before AD 270,[15] has this
monogram twice underneath the name of the buried person. It
must be Christian, since it is accompanied by the typical symbols
used on the burial inscription of that faith: Jona (whose reappear-
ance from the whale was compared by Jesus himself to his own
resurrection, Matthew 12:40), the Good Shepherd and the anchor
as a sign of hope (Hebrews 6:19). Elsewhere, the dates are less
certain: for example, numerous inscriptions with the intertwined
Chi-Rho and one with the Christ monogram were found on the
so-called Red Wall in the Vatican necropolis, not far from the
'Tropaion', the tomb memorial for St Peter which definitely
existed in this place before AD 200. As we saw in chapter 1, the
graffiti have been dated to 290–315,[16] certainly prior to 322 when
Constantine began the construction of the first church of St Peter,
and we may assume that at least some of them precede the date
of the battle at the Milvian Bridge, 312. However, the 'Staurogram'
is undoubtedly an even earlier Christian symbol, about one and a
half centuries older than Lactantius's account of Constantine's
dream: it occurs in New Testament papyri, the oldest being a
papyrus codex of St John's Gospel, the P66 at the Bibliotheca
Bodmeriana in Cologny near Geneva. Its traditional date, *'c.200'*,
is much too late, and it may in fact be as old as *c.*AD 125–50.[17] In
almost all cases when the Greek words *stauros* (cross) or *staurôo*
(to crucify) occur, they are abbreviated. An initial letter or two
and one or two end letters remain in full writing, but in the middle,
for the rest of the word, there is the symbolic Staurogram.[18] A few
decades later, another codex of St John's Gospel and St Luke's, the
P75, also housed at the Bibliotheca Bodmeriana, has the same
Staurogram abbreviation. The extant pages of St John's Gospel
contain no *staur*-words, but the St Luke section is full of them.

Thus we have two gospels, two different scribes, over a span of perhaps half a century, using this abbreviation as a matter of course. Without going into the details of other papyri and their transmission, it can be asserted with confidence that Christianity did not have to wait for Constantine (or Lactantius, for that matter) to invent this monogram or proselytize it. Lactantius in particular, the learned man, would have understood its significance completely and it is extremely unlikely that he did not know what he was doing when he described Constantine's dream the way he did. These architects of modern Christianity knew the existing power of the stones with which they were building.

We have assumed that there was a reason for the change from Staurogram to Chi-Rho monogram some time after 317, and that it was political. We also found that the use of the Chi-Rho in existing Greek papyri proved to be a useful secular smokescreen for a symbol which was, of course, avowedly religious. Was there anything comparable for the Staurogram? Some scholars have thought so. First, there is the evidence of the papyri again. The cross, resembling a T, and the *Rho* developing out of the vertical beam turned right into a loop, could be used as an abbreviation for the word τροπος (character, custom): the first two letters are T and P. Scrolls of Philodemus (*c*.110 BC–*c*.35 BC), a popular philosopher from Gadara, ten kilometres south-east of the Lake of Galilee,[19] were discovered at Herculaneum – and therefore written before the destruction of the town in AD 79. They have the sign, together with the Chi-Rho as an abbreviation of χρονος (time).[20] The other related symbol was also religious, and it came from Egypt: the so-called ankh cross, a symbol which means life, popular even in Roman times.

However, both cases differ from Constantine's Staurogram: here the upper part of the vertical beam is bent round in such a way that the lower part of the loop forms the crossbeam. In other words, there are not two separate letters or signs but a single hybrid symbol. The two papyri at Cologny also hint at this visual concept, although they extend the crossbeam slightly to the right to make the horizontal bar more straight. The TP abbreviation, on the other hand, distinguishes between two letters. The round top of the P is clearly separate from the T, and the T has its own crossbeam. Such a form was used for the cross monogram on a pre-Constantinian inscription from Gabbari, a suburb of Alexandria – unrelated to Lactantius and Constantine since it is some seventy years older. It commemorates two Christians called Theodora and Nilammon, has been dated to the period of Emperor Gordian (AD 238–244) and ends in the Staurogram, with *Alpha* and *Omega* to its left and right.[21]

The interesting point is that Lactantius insists on a Christian vision which differed, to a certain degree from existing practice, while building upon it. How much easier it would have been for him to 'adjust' his master's vision just a little bit to make it fit existing models. But he did not. The similarities with symbols in existing papyri and on inscriptions, between pagan and Christian signs, were self-evident. But the nuances beyond the similarities were the key: the Emperor's vision had to be rendered truthfully, in all its God-given singularity. Obviously Constantine accepted this account as an authentic rendering of his experience, otherwise – as we noted above – he would hardly have employed Lactantius as tutor of his son only a few years later. Conversely, we can understand all the better why it may have seemed expedient to prefer a less ostentatious version of the monogram not much later, for political reasons.

A Secret Delta

The most intriguing example of a Chi-Rho monogram has puzzled scholars ever since its discovery. It was found on a leather fragment in Greek shorthand (so-called 'tachygraphy'). And the discovery was made at the most improbable place, in the Wadi Murabba'at near the Dead Sea, between Qumran and En Gedi. Its probable date is c.AD 135 at the latest, before the end of the second Jewish revolt, under Bar Kokhba against the Romans (AD 132–5). This is the date of all non-tachygraphic manuscripts found nearby. It was published in 1961, and classified as P. Mur. 164.[22] There are two fragments, in darkened brownish colour, crumpled and extremely difficult to read. But fragment *a*, measuring 30 centimetres by 23.5 centimetres, offers a surprise in line eleven: there is a clear, unmistakable Chi-Rho. We studied the original at the John Rocke-feller Museum in Jerusalem, not only with the naked eye but also under a microscope. The material used is indeed leather, not parchment or papyrus. It has been assumed that the Qumran Essenes – the scribes of the Dead Sea Scrolls – further north preferred leather because it was purer, 'holier' and more durable than the alternatives, but the more prosaic truth is that parchment production was complicated and comparatively time-consuming, and papyrus had to be imported from northern Egypt. Why pay for costly imports or spend time on parchment production when goats and antelopes, kosher animals, were living nearby anyway and could be kept in herds, ready to yield the skin needed for leather scrolls?

The first editors of the document, in 1961, noticed that it was a shorthand text, and that the shorthand was Greek: there are, they observed, some complete Greek letters, like the *Delta*, *Theta* and *Phi* – and we could add *Alpha* and *Epsilon* – and certain shorthand signs known from other Greek manuscripts. They also noticed the Chi-Rho in line eleven of fragment *a*, called it, in French, a '*sigle*', but did not hazard any comments. In fact, and somewhat absurdly, they abandoned any attempt at analysing the text, on the grounds that they simply did not have enough time ('*nous n'avons pas eu le loisir de tenter*').[23] Admittedly, it is very difficult to make sense of the letters because of the damaged state of the leather. And it must be said that the scribe used a somewhat eccentric, irregular shorthand.[24] We are currently developing a computerized programme which will help us to read such texts – a problem comparable to the deciphering of cuneiform tablets or Egyptian hieroglyphs. But the highly personalized style of this particular manuscript clearly does not adhere to a recognizable system of any kind. Thus, progress is slow.[25]

Tachygraphy was an ancient art: there is a reference to it in the Greek translation of Psalm 44/45:2 (third century BC) and Cicero's secretary Tiro was a virtuoso whose name was given to a particular system, the 'Tironian notes'. Titus – the man who destroyed Jerusalem in AD 70 and went on to become Roman Emperor – was another acknowledged master of the art.[26] It has been suggested that some New Testament authors and writers knew shorthand,

P. Mur. 164 (Drawing, after DJD II, 275–7)

and in at least two cases this would not be surprising at all.[27] But whatever the skills of Christian scribes might have been, it would appear to be unlikely that a Christian leather fragment with the Chi-Rho suddenly turned up among the Jewish texts of the Wadi Murabba'at. Unless, of course, fragments *a* and *b* were not associated with the other finds at all: as the first editors suggested, their peculiar state of preservation may suggest that they were glued or sewn together to form a receptacle for other objects, probably letters. If this was the case, these fragments are at least moderately older than the other finds in the same wadi and they could have come from anywhere, reused as such manuscripts often were, without any regard to their contents. But even so, someone must have written them in the first place. Tachygraphy was not normally used for correspondence. Could it be that these leather scrolls, recycled as letter pouches, were the spoils of an attack by the Bar Kokhba revolutionaries on a Jewish-Christian community? Such attacks were, in fact, a common enough occurrence, since the Christians refused to participate in this revolt against the Romans.

But this is conjecture. As things stand, we cannot decipher the whole text, nor can we determine its origins. However, there is another striking letter which occurs a number of times, and in one case it is only three letters to the left of the Chi-Rho. It is a Greek *Delta*, and Benoit et al., in their first edition, identified it as such. Having consulted Milne – the standard textbook in this field – and studied the type of handwriting, they did not think it was a shorthand symbol. And yet, in this arcane code, even a simple *Delta* may be more than it seems: if we look at the tiny papyrus fragment P29, with verses from the New Testament book of Acts (26:7–8/26:20), written towards the end of the third century – c.AD 275 –[28] we find it twice, once on each side. The scribe of this manuscript, which is the oldest surviving papyrus of the book of the Acts of the Apostles, achieved a double feat of symbolism. First, he abbreviated the Greek word *Theos* (God) as a Christian *nomen sacrum* or 'Holy Name', by its first and last letters: *Theta* and *Sigma* in line five of the 'front page' or recto, and *Theta* and *Nu* in line four of the back, or verso (since here the word is in the fourth case, *Theon*). To mark it as a *nomen sacrum*, he drew the usual horizontal line above both letters. But then he shaped his *Theta*, which is usually written as an 'O' with a horizontal bar in its centre – Θ – like a *Delta*, which looks like a triangle: △. There is still the horizontal bar in the middle, so that readers cannot mistake it for a simple *Delta*. The scribe did it twice, on both sides of the fragment (and therefore would probably have done it throughout the codex). Thus, it cannot be a mistake or the accidentally misshapen figure of an 'O'. The first editors, Bernard Grenfell and Arthur Hunt, noticed that the text on the fragment 'is tantalizing, for it belongs to an abnormal recension of Acts';[29] they also noticed that *Theos* (Θεός) 'is contracted, as usual'. But although they published a plate of the recto of the papyrus, where the *Delta* at the beginning of the contracted *Theos* can be seen in pristine clarity, they did not notice this deviation from normal practice. To make sure, we studied the original papyrus at the Bodleian Library, Oxford and compared it with a new photograph of both sides, made on our behalf. Neither the old plate in Grenfell and Hunt's edition, nor the new photograph, nor, above all, the original itself, leaves any room for doubt. It is a deliberate *Delta*, distinguished from the usual Greek letter by the horizontal stroke in the middle. In other words: the scribe did intend to write a typical *nomen sacrum*, but also wanted to convey a message.

In early Christianity the triangle symbolized the Trinity. It was 'the most widely disseminated' symbol of the Trinity, but 'was exposed to the verdict of Augustine, because it had been used by the heretical Manichaeans'.[30] In fact, the Manichaeans were a popular gnostic movement founded by the Persian teacher Mani (AD 216–c.AD 276) who saw himself as a combination of the Paraclete prophesied in St John's Gospel (14:16; 14:26), the Maitrya of the Buddhists (the Buddha who will come next) and the Usetar Bamik of the Zoroastrians (the saviour who will bring the Last Judgment and the coming of a new world). Writings addressed to Christians call Mani an 'apostle of Jesus Christ'. But they were at best syncretistic, and St Augustine saw the danger posed by them more clearly than many modern theologians. He was particularly annoyed by the Manichaeans' trinitarian teaching.[31] They taught that the sunlight came to mankind through a triangular window in heaven; God the Father was in the light, the might of God the Son was in the Sun (an idea which was appreciated by Emperor Constantine who wanted to link his old faith in the invincible Sun God with his new faith in Christ) and the Holy Spirit was in the Air. St Augustine condemned this imagery as mystical speculation, and his influence stopped the spreading of the trinitarian triangle in the form of the $\triangle$ until the Middle Ages. Only isolated examples have survived. But we should not assume that St Augustine's strictures were universally respected. First of all, there were those who were attracted by Manichaean symbolism, even though they would have resisted the syncretism of that sect as it manifested itself in its general theology. The papyrus P29 belongs to the period of Mani's death and growing posthumous fame; it may be the oldest surviving Christian manuscript including this trinitarian idea, some one hundred years before St Augustine wrote his treatise *Contra Faustum Manichaeum*.

A couple of decades later, probably before the end of the third century, another surviving papyrus, also found in Egypt, displays the same triangular Delta: the papyrus Chester Beatty I or P45, with partly damaged parts of the four Gospels and Acts. It is interesting to follow the present debate about the redating of the earliest New Testament papyri. If the latest tendency to date P29 and P45 to the late second or early third century (see note 28 above) should prevail, the introduction of the trinitarian Delta would belong to the period of orthodox theologians like Clement of Alexandria, preceding the Manichaeans by far. St Augustine's resistance would have been directed against its misuse, rather than its use as such. And this would indeed make sense: after all, the man from Hippo appreciated the trinitarian triangle in other contexts. In his 'Treatise on St John', 122:8, he explained that 153, the number of fish caught by the disciples in St John 21:10–11, is the sum of all numbers from 1 to 17, and if one sets a dot for each number, beginning with 1 in the first line and ending with 17 dots in the last line, one gets a perfect triangle.

There was also Mar ('St') Saba (AD 437–532), an influential monk who founded the monastery near Bethlehem which is named after him – still one of the most surprising and uplifting sights in the desert, with a magnificent library. Mar Saba wrote a whole treatise about the trinitarian triangle, and he did so because it had retained

a theological and visual presence in spite of St Augustine.[32] This
highly educated desert monk explained and defended the trinitarian △ triangle in the old Christian tradition which, in turn,
derived its impetus from the Greek mathematician Pythagoras and
his school. Plato's philosophy was much appreciated by Christian
thinkers like Clement of Alexandria (c.AD 160–c.AD 215), who
taught in Egypt and discussed the idea in his *Timaeus* (53,5);
Plutarch (c.AD 50–c.AD 125), a non-Christian philosopher, thought
he had identified an Egyptian concept of Osiris, Isis and Horus
symbolized by a triangle.[33] But although not a shred of visual
evidence, archaeological or literary, has been found for such an
Osiris–Isis–Horus symbol, we can understand how the cunning
Christian mind responded to 'pagan' triangles, as it did in so many
other cases to popular, non-Christian imagery. It was part of the
early Christians' jackdawish genius to turn what already existed
to their own ends – a technique cultural historians describe as
'transvaluation'. The triangle was neither an abstract or math-
ematical cosmic idea, nor was it tarred by direct association with
particular goddesses and godheads. Christianity proclaimed a God
who acted in history, a Son who was an historical person and a
Spirit which continued to be at work in men and women, as Jesus
had promised it. What stronger, more poignant way of underlining
this teaching could there be than the trinitarian triangle as it is
found in unmistakably Christian contexts, such as fragment P29?
What better place for it could there be, moreover, than the home
country of Egyptian myths, where P29 was read and rediscovered?

   To return, then, to the shorthand fragment from the Wadi Murabba'at, it is not hard to envisage a scribe using the *Delta* triangle
precisely to denote God as the head of the Trinity, as did the
scribes of P29 and P45. By AD 135, the approximate date of the
shorthand leather fragment, more than one hundred years after
death and resurrection of Jesus, the teachings of the Pythagorean
school, Plato or Plutarch were known at least in some Christian
circles. Indeed, as early as c.AD 50, St Paul had quoted the Greek
natural philosopher Aratus in his address in Athens, on the invi-
tation of the Areopagus, the Athenian philosophers' assembly.[34]
Without a complete decoding of the shorthand text, it cannot be
proved beyond doubt that this is the Christian symbol. But our

hypothesis is, at the very least, plausible – all the more so as the Chi-Rho monogram which inspired our investigation in the first place is plainly not a scribal note in the margin, a *Chrêsimon*, *Chrêston* or *Chrêsis*, alerting readers to an important, quotable text in the ensuing line. It occurs roughly in the middle of line eleven, surrounded by tachygraphic letter symbols. Nor is it in any way embellished, larger, higher or wider than other signs used in the manuscript. There is a sign which looks like a full stop, after the Chi-Rho. Thus, the Chi-Rho, for XPICTOC, Christ, could have been the last word of a sentence which also included God or a reference to the Trinity. There are many examples of this, not least in the pages of the New Testament. Romans 15:6 is one such instance.[35] Another instance is 2 Corinthians 4:5 – in the very Letter from St Paul which preserves one of the oldest explicit trinitarian formulae in the New Testament.[36]

As we noted earlier, most scholars argue strongly that the cross was a post-Constantinian symbol rather than an awesomely significant image from the earliest years of Christianity. Yet here we have evidence of a Christian Chi-Rho as early as *c.*AD 135 or even earlier, a stark contradiction of the scholarly orthodoxy. What is truly odd, as we argued in chapter 1, is that this orthodoxy should ever have arisen. It goes without saying that Constantine gave enormous impetus to the use of the cross as a Christian image, hitching it to the star of his own imperial and dynastic glory. But, as we have shown, he was building on sturdy foundations. That this is so is clear from the famous mocking crucifix which was found near a Roman garrison on the Palatine in Rome.[37] Dated to the late second or early third century, it was a graffito discovered in 1857 on the wall of the imperial 'Paedagogium', the school for Roman pages. It would seem that one of them was a Christian who had talked about his faith in the crucified Jesus. The figure of a young man is on the left and his name, Alexamenos, appears in the text. One of the other pages mocked him by drawing his fellow student pointing to a cross on which a crucified person with the head of an ass can be seen. The text in Greek, reads: '*Alexamenos sebete theon* (Alexamenos worships [his] God)'. It is clear that there were times in Rome, well before Constantine's reign, when a Christian could attend the imperial Paedagogium where it was possible to be open about one's faith – and to have it mocked. Some sixty years before this particular image was drawn, the Roman lawyer, Minucius Felix, a Christian, refers to the accusation that Christians worshipped an assheaded god in his dialogue 'Octavius' and at about the time of the graffito, Tertullian, the first Latin-writing Christian apologist, mentions and attacks the slander too.[38] It was not even particularly original: the Jews had been accused of similar things before.[39] The novelty here was the cross.

One of the reasons why many scholars have assumed that Christian worshippers and artists initially shrunk away from the shame of the cross is the fact that there are no murals with the cross or the crucified Christ in the catacombs, prior to the Constantinian era. But this a fallacious argument. Death on the cross, after all, was unlikely to be depicted in circumstances where hope in the resurrection and its pictorial expression was obviously of the essence. The visual programme of the catacombs is marked by biblical and non-biblical scenes which underline the reality of life after death – Jonah and the fish, the men in the fiery furnace, Jesus as Orpheus, the raising of Lazarus and so forth. And there are scenes which celebrate communion in Christ: eucharistic meals and *agape* (love) meals, fish, bread, wine. Other scenes depict Adam and Eve, Abraham and the three men at Mamre (a trinitarian symbol), the near-sacrifice of Isaac by Abraham, Moses and the rock, the adoration of the Magi, Mary and the child with the prophet Balaam, the baptism of Jesus (complete with dove), Jesus and the Samaritan woman, the healing of the lame man, Jesus and the haemorrhagic woman, the miraculous multiplication of bread and fish, Jesus with the twelve apostles, Christ as *Helios* (the Sun God), the Good Shepherd and the shepherd as teacher, praying men and women (so-called *Orantes*). Towards the end of the third century Christ as Ruler, with the apostles St Peter and St Paul, started to be depicted. But the image of crucifixion or the cross would not have been appropriate in the catacombs which was a burial place and never – contrary to widely held opinion – a hiding place for persecuted Christians.[40] The same visual code applied to the decoration of sarcophagi, needless to say – although when Christian symbolism later became the official symbolism of the state, some sarcophagi were adorned with the Triumphal Cross.

However shameful or indeed insane their adversaries found the centrality of the cross to the new religion, the early Christians never distanced themselves from it. How, indeed, could anyone become a follower of Jesus in the first place, without believing that the Redeemer was someone whom the Romans had crucified like a common criminal? In the dialogue 'Octavius' by Minucius Felix, the Christian speaker, Octavius Ianuarius, accepts the importance of the cross but states that Christians do not adore or venerate it.[41] The cross must be honoured, but physical objects themselves are not to be worshipped. It is Jesus, not his cross, to whom veneration is due. Octavius turns the tables: you 'pagan' Romans, he says, pray to wooden 'crosses' which are part of your statues and you adore triumphal standards looking like gilded crosses. And, he adds poignantly, 'the sign of the cross is made when a man venerates God with a pure mind and raised arms'[42] – an image familiar from the catacombs, and present in a mural discovered at Lullingstone in Kent which can be seen in the Weston Wing of the British Museum. At Herculaneum, destroyed in AD 79, the cross on the wall of an upper room – the traditional meeting place of Christians as described in Luke 22:12 and Acts 1:13 – of which only the mark on the wall has survived, would have been simple and modest.[43] This inconspicuous and yet fearless way of dealing with the cross can also be detected in the so-called SATOR palindrome. One was found in Pompeii, in the vicinity of Christian graffiti, and must predate AD 79 – the year of the destruction of the town during the fatal eruption of the Vesuvius volcano. Others have been found in many parts of the Roman empire, two of them, both dated to the second century, in Britain – on a rubbish heap in Roman Manchester (Mamucium) and on the wall plaster of a house in Cirencester (Corinium Dobunnorum).[44] They read:

ROTAS
OPERA
TENET
AREPO
SATOR

– literally: the wheels/carefully/holds/Arepo/the sower. Which-ever way the letters are read, they always yield the same meaning. The reason it has been interpreted as a Christian message employ-ing the motif of the cross is simple: the two central words, to be read from top to bottom, bottom to top, left to right and right to left, form a so-called Greek cross (with equidistant arms). The first and last letters are a 'T' – the closest equivalent to a cross in Latin. The lines, whichever way they are read, yield a Latin word, 'tenet' (he holds). Who is 'he'? The word in the left and right vertical lines is SATOR which may simply mean, 'sower', but also CREATOR: the creator who 'holds' his creation. The innocent-looking personal name AREPO, which means, if read backwards, OPERA ('with care'), and also the works (of creation), begins and ends with A and O: this is the *Alpha* and *Omega*, beginning and end, of God's Creation. A and C surround each of the four Ts of the 'Tenet' cross. Was it such a palindrome cross which Caecilius Natalis, the non-Christian speaker in Minucius's dialogue 'Octa-vius', had in mind when he accused the Christians of recognizing each other by 'secret symbols and signs'?[45]

The simple cross, unadorned, was a sign which occurred in the most varied of contexts, before, as well as after, Christianity was born. Even the Hebrew *Taw* could be interpreted as a symbol of deliverance and indeed for the name of God. If it is written side-ways, it looks like a Greek *Chi*. In the great Isaiah scroll from Qumran Cave 1, classified as 1QIs[a], it occurs eleven times and has been interpreted as a sign in the margin to mark references, direct or indirect, to the Anointed One of God, the Messiah. Again, Jewish Christians could use this *Taw* sign for their own purposes. If it was seen and written like a *Chi* (as it was in the Isaiah scroll and on numerous ossuaries), it was of course the first letter of XPICTOC, Christ, which was the word used in the pre-Christian Greek translation of the Hebrew Old Testament, the 'Septuagint', for Messiah.[46] Whether the *Taw* was written **+** or X, Jewish Chris-tians could transfer its symbolic meaning from God to Christ and, more than that, they could use it to imply that Jesus, the Christ, *was* God. The practical problem for archaeologists and epi-graphers, however, is obvious: it is almost impossible to be certain whether an ossuary or inscription from the early Christian period, found in Jerusalem or anywhere in the Holy Land, is Jewish or Jewish-Christian.[47] All one can say with any degree of certainty is that the sign was indeed used by Jewish Christians.

Elsewhere, a very recent archaeological discovery may shed further light on the Christian use of the unadorned cross by the early Christians. During the ongoing excavations in Bethsaida, the home town of St Peter and St Andrew, a house with a cellar was found, and in the cellar some wine jugs, together with the small sickles used in harvesting. Next door, there was a courtyard of 12 by 12.9 metres. And north of it, in another room, the most surprising of all Bethsaida finds was made: in 1994 Gloria Strickert, the wife of Fred Strickert, one of the archaeologists in charge of the Bethsaida excavations, discovered a piece of pottery. On it is a cross. Fred Strickert describes it as follows:

> The somewhat rough and imperfect cross inscription measures $4\frac{1}{4}$ inches by $5\frac{1}{2}$ inches although the top portion has broken off. It is composed of a circle in the center with four extended arms each made up of two connected parallel lines. The 'circle' in the center is imperfect with a 1.65-inch horizontal diameter contrasting a 1.42-inch vertical diameter. Yet all three complete arms extend 2.12 inches from the center. Fainter lines continue another 1.30 inches from the lower arm which alter the appearance from a 'Greek cross' – all arms equidistant – to a 'Roman' cross – horizontal arms intersecting the vertical at a distance of one third from the top. Therefore the cross presents some sort of sophistication and planning in spite of its crude appearance.[48]

The shard would have come from a storage jar, of a type common between 100 BC and AD 70. Since it was found *in situ*, in the vicinity of the wine cellar pottery, some of it complete, Strickert sees a 'sealed locus for the destruction of the house' in the context of Bethsaida and argues for a first-century date. In fact, the dating of the comparable pottery, 100 BC to AD 70, suggests that, in this case, 'first century' means 'not later than AD 70'.

Such an early date would make it the most ancient Christian cross found anywhere in the world, predating the one in Herculaneum, if only by some nine years.[49] Understandably therefore, Strickert hesitates to commit himself. He notes that there is no inscription to identify it beyond doubt and he refers to the paucity of crosses in visual art prior to the time of Constantine. And yet he concludes with a cautiously positive verdict:

> The possibility of early crosses need not be totally unexpected. The design of the Bethsaida fragment is unparalleled in pre-Constantinian figures ... The key to interpreting this cross is the presence of arms extending out in four directions from a central circle. The circle thus denotes wholeness and unity and the arms denote diversity. The diversity is fitting for a multicultural center where the imperial cult and Judaism were practised as well as Christianity; where the disciples had Greek names; and where Greeks sought to see Jesus. The wholeness and oneness could even point to the common loaf in a commemorative meal. The same focus of unity and diversity is linked with crucifixion in the John 12:24 saying of Jesus so that the death of a single grain produces diverse fruit.[50]

We have quoted Strickert extensively, not least to show how a renowned archaeologist, working with Jewish and Christian colleagues at the same site, weighs the evidence with all due care. One of his fellow archaeologists at Bethsaida, Bargil Pixner, had discovered a basalt stone with a small cross at the southern slope of Bethsaida-et-Tell as early as 1982. He resisted the temptation to date it, assuming that it might theoretically belong to later Byzantine Christian activity.[51] The archaeological dating of the pot shard discovered in the very centre of the old fishing settlement to before AD 70 made him reconsider his position. He suggested that the cross on the shard was originally meant to symbolize the sun as a crosslike symbol of Christ, the invincible sun taking over from the pagan 'Sol Invictus'. The artist, not quite satisfied with the result, extended the horizontal beam – it is obvious that an extension was carried out at some stage – to turn it into a proper 'Latin' cross. Why all the effort? Perhaps because this was a very special jug, used for the wine of the commemorative Lord's Supper, the Eucharist or Holy Communion.[52]

It would not have been difficult to interpret the sun as a symbol of God and Christ at a very early stage: Psalm 84:11 specifically said it ('For the Lord God is a sun and shield'), and this was

certainly good enough for Jewish Christians. There is also
Matthew 17:2: 'And he [Jesus] was transfigured before them, and
his face shone like the sun, and his clothes became as white as
the light'. St Luke described Jesus, put on a par with God, as 'the
rising sun which will come to us from heaven' ('Zechariah's Song',
Luke 1:78, referring to a prophecy in Malachi 3:20). In Revelation
1:16 we read (in the powerful Authorized Version): 'And he had in
his right hand seven stars: and out of his mouth went a sharp two-
edged sword: and his countenance was as the sun shineth in his
strength'.

All this perhaps before AD 70. And yet such a conclusion should
not come as a surprise. For, after all, even without the archaeological and papyrological evidence for crosses and crosslike
signs, even if there were not a single surviving piece of evidence,
it would seem only logical that they existed. How could Christians
not have used the cross, knowing as they did, for instance, this
passage from St Paul's First Letter to the Corinthians: 'For the
message of the cross is foolishness to those who are perishing, but
to us who are being saved it is the power of God ... We preach
Christ crucified: a stumbling block to Jews and foolishness to
Gentiles, but to those whom God has called, both Jews and Greeks,
Christ the power of God and the wisdom of God' (1 Corinthians
1:18, 23–4)? The Gospels themselves, meanwhile, ascribed the
injunction to Jesus himself: 'If anyone would come after me, he
must deny himself and take up his cross and follow me' (Mark
8:34).

The conclusion is inescapable, though controversial: the Cross
of Christ was honoured, visualized and depicted from the very
earliest years of the new faith. The first Christians did not have
to wait for Helena to rediscover the True Cross, or for her son to
have his vision. The Empress's rediscovery and her son's experience, with its theological and political consequences, were not
the beginning of a tradition, but the culmination of one. They
were, indeed, a turning point for Western civilization, the birth,
one might argue, of Christendom itself. But it was the True Cross
of the Gospels, of the Epistles, of daily worship in Jerusalem,
Bethsaida, Herculaneum, Rome and so many other places, which
underpinned and legitimized their achievement. Without this

legacy, without the ingenuity and resolve of the earliest believers in Jesus, Helena and Constantine would never have achieved what they did.

7

The Lasting Quest

A clue is something which opens the way to understanding a mystery. But what do they look like? How do you recognize a clue when you see one?

Alister McGrath, *Bridge-building*

True reverence involves personal honesty, not pious pretence.

Joy Tetley, *Encounter with God in Hebrews*

VANBRUGGHE. Have I told you this story? When a Widow, hearing in a Sermon of the Crucifixion, came to the Priest after, dropped him a Courtsie and asked him how long ago this sad Accident happened? When he answered, about 15 or 16 hundred Years ago, she began to be comforted and said, Then by the grace of God it may not be true.

Peter Ackroyd, *Hawksmoor*

Not all quests end in arrival at a clear destination or in a moment of unambiguous resolution. Mysteries and riddles survive many an intellectual journey. Our purpose in this book has not been to offer absolute answers to the questions which hover over the True Cross – for how could such answers be forthcoming? – but to challenge the settled orthodoxy on the subject. By retracing Helena's steps and by exploring the history of the cross as symbol and artefact, we have tried to offer a corrective to the scholarly assumptions we encountered and to stimulate fresh debate. No study of a voyage which took place seventeen centuries ago, or of the fate of a piece of wood 2000 years old, can claim a monopoly of truth, any more than a modern biography of Alexander the Great or a critical analysis of Virgil can do so. Nonetheless, each generation is entitled to test and to challenge the intellectual consensus it inherits. This has been our objective.

Necessarily, some of the methods deployed in this book are highly technical. The deciphering of ancient texts and symbols has never been straightforward, and is becoming more complex – as well as more exciting – as the potential of modern forensic science to transform the field becomes clear. Those who go in search of the origins of Christianity are now as likely to be found in the laboratory as the library. Technology is no less important than philology to the historian of the early Church. But these methods are a means to an end, rather than an end in themselves. They are merely tools in the quest to find the deepest roots of Christian civilization. The intricacy of some of these arguments should not obscure the simplicity of our conclusions.

The Empress Helena, as we noted in chapter 2, is best known today as the subject of Evelyn Waugh's classic devotional novel, first published in 1950. Waugh predicted to the Catholic luminary Ronald Knox that his book would be one 'which absolutely no one will be able to bear', and it was, indeed, savagely received by many critics, adversely compared to the more complex Catholic novels of Graham Greene. Even so, Waugh regarded Helena as 'the best book I have written or ever will write'.[1] It is not strictly biographical, and imports much anachronism and pure fiction to the legend of the Empress's discovery. Nonetheless, Waugh was right to be proud of his novel, in the sense that it took seriously a story which has been almost universally scorned by the modern mind since Edward Gibbon's famous strictures.

What we have tried to demonstrate is that the surviving historical sources provide a seam of entirely plausible evidence for Helena's discovery. It is true that Ambrose of Milan's funeral oration for Theodosius the Great of the 390s is the earliest surviving record of the Empress's part in the *Inventio Crucis*. But that text does not read like a work of adventurous fabrication;

indeed, it would have been bizarre, not to say foolhardy, of Ambrose to unveil a complete contrivance at such a politically sensitive event as Theodosius's funeral. How much more plausible it is that the astute Bishop of Milan was trying to please his aristocratic and learned audience by drawing on the reassuring familiarities of established tradition. He spoke of Helena's discovery because his listeners would have expected him to do so.

In this context, it is hard to exaggerate the importance of the testimony of Cyril of Jerusalem. As we remarked in chapter 3, the great churchman, who was bishop of Jerusalem for more than two-thirds of a century, provides ample evidence that something resembling the True Cross had been discovered at the Holy Sepulchre as part of the Constantinian excavations. It seems perverse to read Cyril's witness in isolation from the Helena legend. Eusebius, of course, chose to disengage himself entirely from the discovery of the *lignum crucis*, at least in his biography of Constantine. But, as we have seen, this notoriously selective author had extremely good reasons to make his famous omission. In other contexts, furthermore, Eusebius seems to confirm that the Cross was, indeed, unearthed at the Holy Sepulchre in the 320s.

The exultation which Cyril encouraged and the pilgrim Egeria so vividly felt was the culmination of a centuries-old tradition. The first Christians venerated the site of Jesus's crucifixion, as one would expect them to. They passed on this most sacred knowledge from generation to generation so that, even when Golgotha was covered by the Emperor Hadrian's buildings, pilgrims gathered as close as they could to the original site: DOMINE IVIMUS, 'Lord we have arrived', they wrote in the rock of what is now the Chapel of St Vartan and the Armenian Martyrs.

Elsewhere, the sign of the Cross in its many forms had taken root long before Constantine made it the symbol of his divine imperialism. The Cross mosaic at Silchester and the lead seal found near its basilica show that the sign was in use by the late third century. Papyrus evidence – specifically the manuscripts called P29 and P45 – shows that the Chi-Rho was in use as a Christian symbol a century earlier. From a similar period, there is the mocking crucifix found on the Palatine in Rome. The mysterious leather manuscript unearthed in the Wadi Murabba'at, which bears a Chi-Rho, is almost certainly older than AD 135. We can be sure that the cross-palindrome at Pompeii predates AD 79. The Bethsaida shard, incised with a Roman cross, is even older: the Christian who made this sacred mark did so only a few decades after Jesus's ministry.

Amassed in this way for the first time, the archaeological and papyrological evidence undermines quite clearly the orthodoxy that the Cross only became an important symbol during Constantine's reign. One of the most eminent scholars of early Christianity has claimed that 'no "Chi-Rho" sign has been found in a Christian context which is datable with certainty to the years before Constantine's vision'.[2] This, we have shown, is simply not the case. The sign of the Cross was at the heart of Christian culture and belief from its earliest times.

And so too was the physical Cross itself, or rather faith in its survival. The Crusaders who perished on the field of Hattin in 1187 – the moment when the Cross itself was lost for ever – were responding to an impulse as ancient as Christianity itself. They believed that the wood they defended to the death was the very wood on which Jesus had died; the same belief had animated the first Christians in Jerusalem and further afield – as John Chrysostom would later assert. His account of the early followers of Christ first distracted by the turmoil within their communities and then retrieving the physical remains of the Cross matches what else we know of their early history.

This is why the Santa Croce *Titulus* is such an important and tantalizing artefact. It is assumed, as a matter of course, to be a risible forgery, redeemed only by the sincerity of its curators. But in chapters 4 and 5, we tried to show how misguided this assumption is, closing off as it does an avenue rich in intellectual possibility. The order of languages on the Santa Croce fragment – Hebrew, Greek, Latin – is, as we have seen, crucial evidence that the *Titulus* is not a Constantinian forgery. Indeed, the extraordinary reverse writing style in the Greek and Latin lines suggests instead that the scribe was familiar only with Hebrew script and perhaps writing in great haste. Certainly, these two lines do nothing to support the view that he was a fourth-century or medieval fraudster. The striking spelling of the word 'Nazarenos', meanwhile, points to a first-century origin. The style of writing on the wood, particularly the Hebrew script, closely matches the letter forms of this time. Whatever else it may be, the *Titulus* bears none of the hallmarks of a forgery.

Does any of this matter, in a secular age? In our time, as Ruth Harris remarks in her brilliant book on Lourdes, the culture of pilgrimage, holy places and relics is seen as nothing more than 'a lingering cultural manifestation of a remote, impoverished and illiterate world ... a form of right-wing leisure activity'.[3] We have tried to show, however, that the traditions which modern pilgrims uphold in their journeys to Jerusalem have a sound historical basis. These traditions are neither 'impoverished' or 'illiterate': quite the opposite, in fact.

Perhaps, indeed, they matter even more in the secular age than they did in the pre-Enlightenment era. 'Pilgrimage', the columnist and author Simon Jenkins has written, 'is never more alive than now. As the sense of locality and community gradually ebbs from everyday life; as it becomes more difficult to extend your web of acquaintance; and as the sense of authenticity in objects and experiences diminishes in an endlessly reproduced world, so people hunger for the real thing at which thousands of others are there to share it with them'.[4] Jenkins was writing of the millennial project which eventually became the Greenwich Dome. But the distinctively modern impulse to which he referred is felt no less keenly by the pilgrims who descend upon the Holy Sepulchre today.

This is not, however, a religious book, but a book about religion. The distinction is important, for our purpose has not been to advance a theological position or a spiritual claim, but to make an historical case.

In our first book, *The Jesus Papyrus*,[5] we tried to sketch out the beginnings of a 'new paradigm' in New Testament scholarship and early Church history. 'Its essence', we contended, 'is a renewed attention to the date of the Gospels, rooted in the forensic evidence of papyrology, and an open-mindedness to the potential implications of redating for our understanding of the Gospels' origins.' In this book we have tried to extend this approach to the first symbols and sacred artefacts of the early Christian communities; to show the antiquity and deep significance of those symbols, and the care with which holy objects would have been safeguarded; and to demonstrate the absolute importance in early Christianity of such objects, of sacred locations and of their preservation. Naturally, legends, rumours and pure falsehoods accrued to their memory. But not everything that was said and written about holy relics and places was false.

It is in the nature of intellectual culture to swing from one extreme to another. There was a time when the literal truth of the Bible was taken for granted; in the pre-modern West the so-called 'verbal inerrancy' of the Bible was an article of faith. The achievement of Enlightenment scholarship was to release the Word of God from the iron grip of the Church and to apply the critical methods of scholarly investigation to the earliest Christian texts.[6] This was a leap forward of the greatest importance. But in the twentieth century the spirit of the Enlightenment mutated into a sometimes pathological scepticism. The New Testament became an object of cultural suspicion and was automatically distrusted as an historical source. It has been taken for granted that the Gospels are deeply unreliable texts and that a thick veil stood between the historic Jesus and the communities that later worshipped him. Scholars who question this consensus have routinely been accused of 'fundamentalism' or bovine conservatism.

Needless to say, those who examine alleged relics in anything other than a spirit of utter scorn are courting even harsher judgement. It has become axiomatic that such artefacts are fake, that the survival of genuine relics is, almost literally, a philosophical impossibility. The great scholar of the saints, Hippolyte Delehaye, mocked this intellectual fallacy when he said that 'not every relic that is above all doubt is false'. But his irony has fallen, for the most part, on deaf ears.

The radiocarbon dating of the Shroud of Turin in 1988 was apparently a complete vindication of the sceptical instinct. It seemed to show that the Shroud's raw material had been made into linen in or around the year AD 1325 and that the famous image of a crucified man was therefore a medieval fake. This may be so and there are many in the Catholic Church, alarmed by the hysterical pitch of the centuries-old controversy over the Shroud, who hope that the matter has, indeed, been settled once and for all.

And yet it does not appear that the 1988 dating was the end of the matter. In 1998, the distinguished Shroud scholar Ian Wilson published new evidence in a book entitled *The Blood and the Shroud*, suggesting that the question is very far from resolved.[7] Among Wilson's revelations was the finding of human blood and DNA on the Shroud and a 'bioplastic coating' of living micro-organisms, which might suggest a much older origin than that advanced by the carbon dating in 1988. Wilson is scholar enough to acknowledge that his new evidence poses as many questions as it answers. 'If you are a thinking person,' he writes,

> ultimately you do have to decide in your own mind whether you believe the Shroud to be just a mediaeval fake – in the words of the American writer John Walsh 'One of the most ingenious, most unbelievable products of the human mind and hand on record' or 'the most awesome and instructive relic of Jesus Christ in existence', imprinted with a 2000-year-old photograph of him as he lay in death. Those are the two stark alternatives that the Shroud presents, and although it was some thirty-five years ago that Walsh penned those words they remain every bit as valid today.[8]

It is precisely this sort of open-mindedness that we had in mind when we first called for a 'new paradigm' in a field tyrannized by faddish theory and post-modern scepticism. And there are, indeed, encouraging signs of a gradual shift in early Church and New Testament studies. When *The Jesus Papyrus* first appeared, the international controversy which it generated encouraged strong reaction, ranging from rapturous support to hate mail. Some scholars refrained entirely from joining the fray – in one case, commenting that it would take at least ten years for a new consensus to emerge about the dates of the Gospels and the communities which produced them. Many still cling to the old orthodoxy: that the Gospels are late creations, that two or even three generations stood between them and the events they described, that the texts were not written by individual authors and that they have no claim to authenticity whatsoever. But this orthodoxy is under increasing pressure from classical philologists, historians, papyrologists and even a growing number of theologians.

It should, indeed, be possible to assess Luke as a writer in the same way as one would assess, say, Tacitus, without being accused of 'fundamentalism'. The Gospel according to St John deserves to be read as the masterpiece of an individual author, rather than the composite creation of a Palestinian focus group. Increasingly, philologists are drawing the conclusion that we have inherited the Gospels more or less as they were first written, rather than in hopelessly bowdlerized form. A recent study by Ulrich Victor, an acknowledged expert in the field of Greek philology and textual criticism, effectively sounded the knell for the schools of so-called 'form criticism' and 'redaction criticism' (both of which staunchly attacked the view of the Gospels as historical narratives).[9] The implication of this highly technical analysis could not be more straightforward or more profound: we are once again entitled to treat the Gospels as serious historical sources rather than literary contrivances born of unreliable oral tradition.

Part of the problem is the refusal of the modern mind to understand that the partition between the natural and the supernatural in ancient times was not as clear as it seems today. It goes without saying that the stories told about Christ – and indeed about Helena three centuries later – were not historical biographies in the contemporary sense. The belief that all legends are literally true has been described as the 'euhemeristic' fallacy, after the Sicilian Euhemerus who claimed in the fourth century BC to have discovered that Zeus had been a real man, Cretan by birth. Clearly, it is wrong to read ancient texts in this over-literalistic, credulous way.[10] The legends of Helena's life and the Gospels themselves make use of mythic and figurative language, steeped in allegory and allusion. But that does not mean that they are pure fabrication. The challenge in reading the legends of any culture is to judge what core of historical reality lies within them.

In the case of the Gospels, historians have added their weight to a process of reassessment launched by papyrologists and philologists. In Italy, Marta Sordi and Ilaria Ramelli have shown that St Mark's Gospel had been assimilated to the Graeco-Roman canon before the mid-Sixties of the first century, read (and occasionally parodied) by authors like Petronius.[11] Jewish scholars like Shemaryahu Talmon have argued with ever greater conviction that an early Gospel like St Mark's could easily have been studied and catalogued in the archives of the Essenes at Qumran – the home of the Dead Sea Scrolls – before its destruction in AD 68.[12] The great Finnish pioneer of papyrus reconstruction, Heikki Koskenniemi, has even compared the identification of the Dead Sea Scroll fragment 7Q5 as St Mark 6:52–3 – meaning that this Gospel *must* have been composed before the Romans overran Qumran in 68 – with the identification of the famous 'Linear B' script.[13] A Spanish scholar who teaches in Israel, Joan M. Vernet, recently analysed and compared all the studies on Qumran and the origins of St Mark's Gospel, including our own and those of our more outspoken opponents like Emile Puech and Vittoria Spottorno. Vernet concluded unequivocally that the Gospels must have been written in the eyewitness period and that the papyrus evidence demonstrates this beyond reasonable doubt.[14]

At the centre of this unfolding debate has been St Matthew's Gospel, the oldest surviving fragments of which – the so-called 'Jesus Papyrus' – are kept at Magdalen College, Oxford and the Fundación S. Luca Evangelista in Barcelona. The vast majority of recent scholars have dated St Matthew to the Eighties of the first century. In our first book we redated it to a period some twenty years earlier, well before the destruction of Jerusalem and the Temple in AD 70, and thus before the flight of the first Christian community from the Holy City in AD 66. And in recent years numerous studies, by Heikki Koskenniemi and others, have corroborated this claim.[15]

A year after our book's publication, a new papyrus of St Matthew was found among the Oxyrhynchus discoveries at the Ashmolean Museum, Oxford: the fragment classified as P.Oxy.4404 or P104. It is a small scrap bearing verses 21:34–7 and 21:43–5. Comparative analysis of its handwriting – the standard method of dating employed by papyrologists – shows that it belongs to the early second century. Indeed, its striking similarity with the non-biblical first-century papyrus P.Oxy.225 may suggest an even earlier date. Thus, after the Magdalen and Barcelona manuscripts, the

Ashmolean fragment is the second-oldest surviving text of this Gospel and quite possibly the second papyrus of St Matthew from the first century to be unearthed. Like the Jesus Papyrus, the surviving script shows that the earliest copies of the Gospel were free of stylistic additions: they were sparse, sober and unembellished in tone.

In our analysis of the Magdalen College fragments we demonstrated that this papyrus, together with two other old and commonly overlooked manuscripts (P37, P45), provides us with a better, more original text of Matthew 26:22. The twelve disciples do not speak 'one after the other', when Jesus predicts his betrayal by Judas, but agitatedly all at once.[16] Similarly, the new discovery, P104, omits verse 44 of Matthew 21:43–5 on the back, the verso, of the fragment. Many scholars have argued that verse 44 was a late and spurious addition. P104 proves them right.

There will certainly be further discoveries of papyri – unearthed, not from archaeological sites, but in archives, libraries and the unedited heaps of fragments in the great collections of Vienna, Munich, Berlin and Oxford. As this work progresses, the frame of reference to which papyrologists have to refer will almost certainly shift back in time. The astonishing advances made in forensic technology will transform the field. This trend – already visible, as we have noted – has profound implications. The immensely technical field of papyrology will continue to yield findings which alter perceptions of the Gospels, their origins and their value as historical sources.

But why revisit the question of papyrus evidence at all, in the context of a study of the Cross? The answer is that the history of the early Church, its achievements and its culture, cannot be understood without reference to its most ancient manuscripts. From our comprehension of the Gospels all else flows. Unless one takes these books seriously as sources, all subsequent questions about Jesus's life, deeds and the artefacts he may have left behind are irrelevant to the historian. If the Cross never existed, then the quests we have described in this book – Helena's, the Crusaders' and our own – were quite pointless.

But that is a counsel of despair. In the field of ancient history there are few proofs and many probabilities. And what we have tried to show is this: that it is not wholly improbable that the Cross, or rather fragments of it, survived the stormy night on Golgotha, perhaps for many centuries. We can be sure, at the very least, that the first Christians would have tried to preserve the Cross. We know that they and their successors held dear the knowledge of the site of the crucifixion: so much so that the Emperor Hadrian built over it, obscuring Christianity's holiest site until the excavations of Constantine. We have shown that, to a much greater extent than has been grasped by previous scholars, the Cross was a central Christian symbol from the earliest times.

At the centre of this historical and cultural web is the Santa Croce *Titulus* itself, guarded by its Cistercian custodians, guarding its own ancient secrets. Have we proved that this wooden fragment was the headboard of Christ? Of course not. But we have, we hope, restored it to its rightful place in the spectrum of historical probability. Bertrand Russell said that 'it is undesirable to believe a proposition when there is no ground whatever for supposing it is true'.[17] But from this it follows that propositions should be taken seriously when there are at least some grounds for believing them to be true. When there is good reason to reassess a theory – in this case, that the *Titulus* may be very old indeed and bears none of the hallmarks of a medieval forgery – one should do so without fear or favour. Subsequent scholars will doubtless learn more about the precise nature of this extraordinary object, as and when the Church grants them access to the reliquary of Santa Croce. Our primary objective has been to rescue the *Titulus* from the condescensions of centuries-long academic neglect.

To take an artefact such as this seriously is not idolatry; still less is it pointless antiquarianism. Just as the Gospels are the building blocks of Christianity, so the holy places and relics of that faith are at the heart of its historical distinctiveness. From the earliest times, the new faith depended upon the empirical: memory, eyewitness accounts, sites that could be visited, objects that could be touched. Time and again, the New Testament writers make clear the importance of first-hand witness, of physical presence at an event – when the successor to Judas is chosen as the new twelfth disciple (Acts 1:21–2), when Luke describes the scholarly method of his Gospel writing (St Luke 1:1–4), when

John and those who published his Gospel affirm the truth of his
testimony (St John 19:35; 21:24), when the apostle Peter dif-
ferentiates between the myths followed by others and the veracity
of his own account (2 Peter 1:16). Go and ask the witnesses, Paul
tells the readers of his first Letters to the Corinthians: most of the
five hundred who saw the risen Christ are still alive. Take the
boat to Yafo or Caesarea and speak to them, he says, if you do not
believe me, a humble apostle.

This was Christianity's most powerful claim and also its most
contestable. Faith cannot be verified, but facts can. The Emperor
Constantine knew the risks implicit in his conversion. He was,
after all, building churches on venerated graveyards and tearing
down ancient temples to make way for his new Christian
edifices. Had the Christian claims for these sites been spurious,
the Emperor would never have endangered his credibility in this
way. Indeed, it is certain that his researches were painstaking:
he could not afford needlessly to alienate those in the Roman
élite who still followed the old religions. The founder of established European Christendom had to be sure that its historical
basis was sound. Although a warrior rather than a theologian
by inclination, he was present when the Credo was formulated
at Nicaea and it is no accident that this founding text of the
Christian faith makes so much of the historical context from
which it sprang – mentioning, for instance, the name of the
Roman prefect Pontius Pilate.

But, as we have tried to show, Constantine and Helena knew
that the risk was worth taking. Christianity's historical basis was
its great strength, the defining feature which made it unique. By
declaring himself a Christian emperor, Constantine had become
the chief benefactor of a religion rooted in the historical writings
of identifiable authors, in places, events and artefacts. Christianity
was not only a belief-system: it was a map, a reliquary and a
library. It offered its adherents a vision of time and space in which
they could, quite literally, locate themselves in relation to the
coming of their Saviour. As anyone who has seen Christian pilgrims in the Holy Land can attest, this remains the central drama,
the emotional force of the faith even today, seventeen centuries
after Constantine. For, no less than Helena, Egeria or the thou-

sands who thronged in their wake, today's pilgrims believe that God Incarnate sat on those stones, walked that road, was crucified on that hill, with a *titulus* above his head.

And in Rome, in the cold side-chapel of a Baroque church, once the palace of an ageing Empress, they can see an incised wooden fragment described as the physical remains of that same headboard. Its history is as mysterious as the words carved in three ancient languages into its worn fibre. Its twelfth-century custodian, Gerardo Caccianemici, the cardinal of Santa Croce, safeguarded the precious relic in a lead casket. It was recovered by accident during restoration work in 1492. Since then it has been a silent witness to centuries of change in Christianity's capital city, treated in modern times as little more than a quaint trophy.

Yet, as we have shown, it is evidently something much more than that, a quite remarkable artefact which can no longer be dismissed as a Constantinian or medieval forgery. In the reliquary of Santa Croce, this unadorned treasure, bearing three simple lines of mockery, still draws the eye and probes the mind. In the impenetrable quiet of the chapel, one is compelled to ask what the *Titulus* really is, and what ancient passions brought it to this sequestered setting. Behind plate glass, and very rarely removed, it is both tangible and beyond reach. To each it represents something different. For the believer, it is physical evidence of Christianity's darkest moment. For the historian, it is best seen, perhaps, as a symbol of the Empress's genius and the ancestral link she renewed between the two most sacred cities of her faith, between Rome and the Holy Land.

General Charles Gordon, who wrote a famous account of Jerusalem's holy places in 1885, is best remembered for the mistakes he made about the city's past. But he was not wrong in every respect. 'These sites are in each of us,' he wrote.[18] In each of us: Christian and non-Christian alike, we bear the imprint of the faith these places spawned, the civilization which Helena and her son built on the rough-hewn rock of Golgotha and the mystery of the wood they unearthed there. The True Cross was the most bleak and yet also the most uplifting emblem of Christianity's historical past. It was dread proof of a hideous means of execution, but also an inspiring symbol of the Christian belief that death had been conquered. It was both real and symbolic, an object to be touched with awe and depicted in reverence. It represented the link between past and present, between the physical and emotional, between a faith born among a colonized people and the faith it became under a mighty empire.

It spoke, above all, to the human desire to know. 'I want knowledge,' says the knight Antonius Block in Ingmar Bergman's masterpiece, *The Seventh Seal*. 'Not faith, not presumption. Knowledge.' It is an ancient human weakness and a forgivable one. For what else drove the Crusaders so many centuries ago and still drives the pilgrims who creep down the stairs at the Holy Sepulchre to Helena's chapel today? It is the wish to match belief with experience, conscious that the leap is always hard and sometimes never achieved. But it is the hope that the leap is possible, now as before, which makes the quest worthwhile.

NOTES

INTRODUCTION

1 Carsten Peter Thiede and Matthew d'Ancona, *The Jesus Papyrus*, London, 1995; revised edition with Afterword, 1996; the American edition of the book was entitled *Eyewitness to Jesus*. For the controversy over the Qumran fragment, 7Q5, and the Magdalen College St Matthew papyrus, P64, discovered by the Victorian missionary Charles Huleatt in Luxor, see Graham Stanton, *Gospel Truth? New Light on Jesus and the Gospels*, London, 1995. However, Stanton's objections are dealt with comprehensively in chapters 3, 4 and 5 of our book.

2 Edward Gibbon, *The Decline and Fall of the Roman Empire*, II, p. 382, Everyman Edition, London, 1979.

3 For two such observations, separated by more than a century, see W. C. Prime, *Holy Cross: A History of the Invention, Preservation, and Disappearance of the Wood Known as the True Cross*, London, 1877, p. 68: 'I am not aware that any careful examination has been made of this old piece of wood in modern times, and no publication which I have been able to find has given any account of it since the seventeenth century'; Paul L. Maier, 'The Inscription on the Cross of Jesus of Nazareth', *Hermes* 124, 1996, p. 73 n. 60: 'apparently, the TITVLVS CRVCIS has never been accorded a serious investigation, which would be a desideratum.'

I   THE TREE OF LIFE: A BRIEF HISTORY OF THE CROSS

1 For a useful analysis of its theology, see Alister McGrath, *The Enigma of the Cross*, London, 1987. For an exploration of the symbolic associations of the Cross, see John Baldock, *The Elements of Christian Symbolism*, Shaftesbury, 1990.

2 Quoted McGrath, op. cit., p. 9.

3 Translated in Lavinia Byrne, *The Life and Wisdom of Helena Mother of Constantine*, pp. 63–70; see also *Anglo-Saxon Poetry*, London, 1997, ed. S. A. J. Bradley, pp. 159–63.

4 See below, chapter 3.

5 Zoe Oldenbourg, *The Crusades*, London, 1998, p. 418.

6 Quoted Oldenbourg, op. cit., p. 420.

7 For an account of the battle, see Steven Runciman, *A History of the Crusades*, vol. 2: *The Kingdom of Jerusalem*, pp. 436–73.

8 The best account of this is Martin Hengel, *Crucifixion in the Ancient World and the Folly of the Message of the Cross*, London, 1977. See also Joseph A. Fitzmyer, 'Crucifixion in Ancient Palestine, Qumran Literature and the New Testament', *Catholic Biblical Quarterly* 40, 1978, pp. 493–513; J. F. Strange, 'Crucifixion, Method of', supplementary volume to *Interpreter's Dictionary to the Bible*, pp. 199–200.

9 Hengel, op. cit., pp. 10, 18.

10 For the historical value of New Testament texts see *The Jesus Papyrus*, passim.

11 Josephus, *Bellum Judaicum* (many editions), 5:449–51.

12 Fitzmyer, art. cit., p. 503.

13 Cited in Hengel, op. cit., p. 25.

14 See N. Haas, 'Anthropological Observations on the Skeletal Remains from Giv'at ha-Mivtar', *Israel Exploration Journal* 20, 1970, pp. 38–59.

15 On this subject, Paul L. Maier's article 'The Inscription on the Cross of Jesus of Nazareth', *Hermes* 124, 1996, pp. 58–75 is indispensable.

16 R. Bultmann, *The History of the Synoptic Tradition*, New York, 1963, p. 272.

17 Cited by Maier, art. cit., p. 59.

18 See Maier, art. cit., p. 63.

19 Cited by Maier, art. cit., p. 60.

20 1 Corinthians 22:24.

21 Galatians 6:14.

22 See Cyril E. Pocknee, *Cross and Crucifix: In Christian Worship and Devotion*, London, 1962, p. 33.

23 See Pocknee, op. cit., p. 36.

24 Jan Willem Drijvers, *Helena Augusta: The Mother of Constantine the Great and the Legend of her Finding of the True Cross*, Leiden, 1992, p. 81. In other respects Drijvers's book is masterly in its command of detail.

25 Michael Grant, *The Emperor Constantine*, London, 1993, p. 142.

26 Pocknee, op. cit., p. 33; see also Robin Lane Fox, *Pagans and Christians*, London, 1986, p. 616: 'no "Chi-Ro" sign has been found in a Christian context which is datable with certainty to the years before Constantine's vision'.

27 See Pocknee, op. cit., plate 2.

28 See George Pitt-Rivers, *The Riddle of 'Labarum'*, London 1966, for the eccentric claim that the Chi-Rho was simply a pre-Christian symbol indicating a good passage in a text. Cf. however, for a correct understanding of the context, Jack Finegan, *The Archaeology of the New Testament*, rev. ed. Princeton 1992, 354-355.

29 See Matthew Black, 'The Chi-Ro sign – Christogram and/or Staurogram', in *Apostolic History and the Gospel: Biblical and Historical Essays presented to F. F. Bruce on his 60th Birthday*, eds. W. Ward Gasque and Ralph P. Martin, London, 1970. Black argues that this dual meaning would have been an attraction to the Emperor: 'the "sign" by which he conquered was the sign of the cross, a *staurogram*, but at the same time this was ingeniously combined with the *christogram* symbol in the artistic reproduction of the "divine sign" ' (p. 323).

30 See Thiede, *Heritage of the First Christians: Tracing Early Christianity in Europe*, Oxford, 1992, p. 94.

31 See Jean de Savignac, 'Le Papyrus Bodmer XIV et XV' in *Scriptorium* 17, 1963, pp. 50-6: 'Il faut en conclure que le monogramme ... date, en Egypte tout au moins, du IIe siecle' (p. 51).

32 Margherita Guarducci, *The Tomb of St Peter*, London, 1960, p. 99.

33 Guarducci, op. cit., p. 117.

34 See Thiede, op. cit., p. 83 for examples of the Chi-Rho monogram found near Shepton Mallet in Somerset in 1990 (but recently disputed) and Walter Newton in 1975.

2   QUEEN HELENA AND THE BIRTH OF CHRISTIAN EUROPE

1 The main excavations of the mausoleum were conducted by Friedrich Deichmann (1940 and 1954-8) and the Ecole Française (since 1975). These digs revealed a circular building 25.5m high, with an outer diameter of 27.74m. See C. P. Thiede, op. cit., pp. 134-5.

2 Robin Lane Fox describes her aptly as 'the most tireless worker for Christianity since St Paul': *Pagans and Christians*, London, 1986, p. 658.

3 Three relatively recent scholarly monographs are available. Jan Willem Drivers, op. cit., Stephan Borgehammar, *How the Holy Cross Was Found: From Event to Medieval Legend*, Stockholm 1991, and Hans A. Pohlsander, *Helena: Empress and Saint*, Chicago 1995; they are indispensable guides to primary sources for Helena's life, while shying away from the radical conclusions which can be drawn from them. R. Couzard, *Sainte Hélène d'après l'Histoire et la Tradition*, Paris 1911, remains a useful primer.

4 E. Waugh, *Helena*, Penguin edition, 1963, p. 9.

5 For a helpful *tour d'horizon* of recent scholarship see Hans A. Pohlsander, *The Emperor Constantine*, London, 1996. A. H. M. Jones, *Constantine and the Conversion of Europe*, London, 1948 is a useful introduction to the subject, as is Michael Grant, *The Emperor Constantine*, London, 1993. For intellectual exploration of Constantine's world, T. D. Barnes, *Constantine and Eusebius*, Harvard, 1981 and *The New Empire of Diocletian and Constantine*, Harvard, 1982 are masterly. In contrast, those books which do appear on the Empress tend to be of an almost exclusively devotional character – a recent example being Lavinia Byrne, op. cit.

6 See Borgehammar, op. cit., p. 10 ff.

7 Quoted in Drijvers, op. cit., pp. 79–80.

8 For the resilience of this tradition see Winifred Joy Mulligan, 'The British Constantine – an English Historical Myth', *The Journal of Medieval and Renaissance Studies*, 1978, and V. Burch, *Myth and Constantine the Great*, London, 1927.

9 Quoted in Mulligan, art. cit., p. 264.

10 Mulligan, art. cit., p. 266.

11 Mulligan, art. cit., p. 270.

12 When this Elen's husband, Magnus Maximus, went to Gaul to claim the *imperium* in 383, she stayed with him at Treves. Here, she developed a reputation for holiness, which encouraged Sulpicius Severus to write a hagiographical account of her life.

13 See Drijvers, op. cit., chapter 1, and J. Vogt, 'Helena Augusta, the Cross and the Jews: Some Enquiries about the Mother of Constantine the Great', *Classical Folia* 31, 1977.

14 See Drijvers, op. cit., p. 24, and Thiede, op. cit., pp. 108–10.

15 See Hans A. Pohlsander, 'Crispus: Brilliant Career and Tragic End', *Historian* 33, 1984, pp. 79–106.

16 Both passages quoted in Pohlsander, op. cit., p. 53.

17 For its transformation see Richard Krautheimer, 'The Constantinian Basilica', *Dumbarton Oaks Papers* 21, 1967, p. 115 ff.

18 See Drijvers, op. cit., p. 42: 'It was obvious to those into whose hands [the coins] came that Helena and Fausta were being presented as protected and pillars of the new Constantinian society.'

19 Drijvers cites as an example of this the advancement of Flavius Optatus, consul in 334, a relative by marriage of the Empress, op. cit., p. 43, n. 21.

20 See chapter 6, p. 192 and note 9.

21 See A. H. M. Jones, *Constantine and the Conversion of Europe*, London, 1949, p. 96.

22 Trajan's column, for instance, depicts the shields of troops marked with a thunderbolt, symbol of Zeus.

23 See R. H. Storch, 'The Trophy and the Cross: Pagan and Christian Symbolism in the Fourth and Fifth Centuries', *Byzantion* xl, 1970, pp. 105–17. 'By elevating the *labarum*-trophy-cross to so prevalent a place in the *Vita*, Eusebius makes it the physical representation of the heavenly military alliance between Constantine and the Christian God.' (p. 114).

24 One author has aptly referred to the sign's 'victory-mystique': see Diana Bowder, *The Age of Constantine and Julian*, London, 1978, p. 24.

25 See Lane Fox, op. cit., p. 618: 'The proof of a god is best found in his protection.'

26 Ramsay MacMullen, 'Constantine and the Miraculous', *Greek, Roman and Byzantine Studies* 9, 1968, p. 81.

27 MacMullen, art. cit., p. 96: 'We must suppose that Constantine's contemporaries (why not himself then?) did in truth fear antagonistic wizardry, did put their faith in supernatural aid to be exerted visibly on the very field of battle, accepted without skepticism the powers claimed both for Maxentius' sacrifices and for the symbol of the cross, and looked on the whole struggle of old against new religion as being greater than, but no different in kind from, the operation of magicians' spells and counter-spells.'

28 For these divisions, see Lane Fox, op. cit., p. 609 ff.

29 For this argument, see Barnes, *Constantine and Eusebius*, p. 26.

30 Quoted in Grant, op. cit., p. 154. But see Barnes, *Constantine and Eusebius*, p. 43: 'In the ultimate reckoning, however, the precise details of Constantine's conversion matter little. After 28 October 312 the emperor consistently thought of himself as God's servant, entrusted with a divine mission to convert the Roman Empire to Christianity.'

31 See R. Couzard, op. cit., pp. 10–12.

32 Vogt, art. cit.

33 See Henry Chadwick, 'The Fall of Eustathius of Antioch', *The Journal of Theological Studies* 49, 1948, pp. 27–35: 'The emperor's mother had a past which could provide an easy opportunity for some sarcastic reference on the part of the Bishop of Antioch, who appears from his attack on Origen's interpretation of the witch of Endor to have combined a mordant tongue with a rationalistic attitude rare in the fourth century' (p. 34).

3   THE DISCOVERY OF THE TRUE CROSS

 1 See E. D. Hunt, *Holy Land Pilgrimage in the Later Roman Empire AD 312–460*, Oxford, 1982, p. 246: 'The pilgrim needed to live at the end of a reliable continuum.'

2 See E. D. Hunt, op. cit., p. 15: 'Palestine of its own accord began to act as a natural, but unwitting focus for those changes that Constantine's accession brought to the world-wide Church.'

3 See H. A. Drake, 'Eusebius on the True Cross', *Journal of Ecclesiastical History* (36), 1985, p. 4: 'The agony of the Christian community at the proximity of such a goddess to Christ's tomb would alone have been sufficient to keep the memory alive: in a cruel sense, no better landmark could have been wanted.'

4 Eusebius, *The Life of Constantine*, translated by C. McGiffert and E. C. Richardson, in *Select Library of Nicene and Post-Nicene Fathers*, 2nd series, vol. I, New York, 1890, p. 530.

5 Eusebius, op. cit., p. 531.

6 See Hunt, op. cit., p. 37: the journey was 'a predominantly public activity, carried through according to conventional patterns but at the same time springing from an essence of individual conviction'.

7 Hunt, op. cit., p. 49.

8 See Henry Chadwick, *The Circle and the Ellipse: Rival Concepts of Authority in the Early Church*, Oxford, 1959, pp. 6–7; André Parrot, *Golgotha and the Church of the Holy Sepulchre*, London, 1957, p. 53; Hunt, op. cit., p. 4.

9 See chapter 5 below for discussion of the remarkable graffito of a pilgrim's ship in the Chapel of St Vartan beneath the Church of the Holy Sepulchre – further evidence of the veneration of the site from the earliest days of the Church.

10 See Chadwick, op. cit., p. 7: 'Constantine does not create the Jerusalem idea; he is dependent upon an existing way of thinking, a way of thinking illustrated by the widely held belief that Golgotha (rather than the Temple, as the Jews thought) was the site of Adam's grave and the very centre of the earth ... the original predominance of Jerusalem in the thought of the Church did not die with the surrender to Titus' legions or the Hadrianic war. The city remained at the very heart of things.'

11 As Stephan Borgehammar has shown: see *How the Holy Cross was Found: from Event to Medieval Legend*, Stockholm, 1991, p. 140.

12 See Lionel Casson, *Travel in the Ancient World*, Baltimore, 1974.

13 The so-called Bordeaux Pilgrim, who made a pilgrimage to the Holy Land in c.333, covered 3400 Roman miles between Bordeaux and Jerusalem in 170 days – that is, 20 miles a day.

14 Quoted Hunt, op. cit., p. 37.

15 Charles Couasnon, *The Church of the Holy Sepulchre in Jerusalem: the Schweich Lectures of the British Academy 1972*, London, 1974, p. 1; L. H. Vincent, quoted Parrot, op. cit., p. 66, n. 1.

16 *Egeria's Travels to the Holy Land*, tr. John Wilkinson, London, 1971, p. 127.

17 For the ideology of Constantine's architecture, see Richard Kraut-heimer, 'The Constantinian Basilica', *Dumbarton Oaks Papers* 21, 1967, pp. 115 ff.

18 Drijvers, op. cit., p. 5, n. 10.

19 See Hunt, op. cit., p. 28: 'It must be acknowledged from the outset that there is nothing in history to link Helena with the discovery of the true cross.'

20 There is no shortage of commentary on Eusebius. See, for example, R. M. Grant, *Eusebius as Church Historian*, Oxford, 1980; D. S. Wallace-Hadrill, *Eusebius of Caesarea*, Oxford, 1960. The analysis offered by Timothy D. Barnes in *Constantine and Eusebius*, Cambridge, Mass., 1981 is indispensable.

21 Michael Grant, op. cit., pp. 4–5.

22 Hunt, op. cit., p. 37.

23 There are honourable exceptions. See H. A. Drake, art. cit., and Borgehammar, op. cit.

24 On this subject see R. M. Grant, op. cit., p. 24 ff.

25 For this debate, see P. W. L. Walker, *Holy City, Holy Places? Christian Attitudes to Jerusalem and the Holy Land in the Fourth Century*, Oxford, 1990; H. A. Drake, 'Eusebius on the True Cross', *Journal of Ecclesiastical History* 36, 1985, pp. 1–22; Z. Rubin, 'The Church of the Holy Sepulchre and the Conflict between the sees of Caesarea and Jerusalem', *The Jerusalem Cathedra* 2, ed. Lee I. Levine, Jerusalem/Detroit, 1982, pp. 79–105.

26 See Borgehammar, op. cit., p. 118: 'We immediately sense what an acute embarrassment Christian symbols and monuments evoking the Passion of Christ could be to a bishop in the early fourth century who wanted to convince men of the educated class that Christianity was a doctrine as lofty as the purest philosophy.'

27 For this unconvincing explanation see Drake, art. cit., p. 20: 'Eusebius's silence . . . should be construed as mute testimony not merely to the novelty of the device, but also to the threat posed by Constantine's devotion to it.'

28 See Walker, op. cit., p. 258: 'As metropolitan bishop, he might . . . have been suspicious of the intentions of the Jerusalem Church: were they strictly honourable? If this wood could be a potent force within the life of faith, it could also no doubt be a powerful force within the world of ecclesiastical politics.'

29 J. H. Newman, *Two Essays on Biblical and Ecclesiastical Miracles*, London, 1875, repr. 1907, pp. 291 and 296. See Borgehammar, op. cit., p. 106.

30 See Thiede & d'Ancona, op. cit., pp. 190–1 for the importance of accurate transmission and learning by heart of holy tradition in the Jewish milieu of the first century AD. See also B. Gerhardsson, *The Origins of the Gospel Tradition*, London, 1979.

31 For examples, see André Parrot, op. cit., p. 50.

32 *Onomasticon* 74, pp. 19–21, quoted in Parrot, op. cit., p. 56.

33 Matthew 27:32; Mark 15:20; John 19:17.

34 Hebrews 13:12.

35 See Borgehammar, op. cit., pp. 96–8.

36 For discussion of Cyril, see Walker, op. cit., passim.

37 The limited bibliography on Cyril includes J. Mader, *Der heilige Cyrillus, Bischof von Jerusalem, in seinem Leben und seinen Schriften*, Einsiedeln, 1891; A. Paulin, *Saint Cyrille de Jerusalem Catechete*, Paris, 1959; E. Bihain, 'L'épitre de Cyrille de Jerusalem à Constance sur la vision de la croix', *Byzantion* 43, 1973, pp. 264–96; E. H. Gifford, *Cyril of Jerusalem*, Oxford, 1894; W. Telfer, *Cyril of Jerusalem and Nemesius of Emesa*, London, 1955.

38 Quoted in Drijvers, op. cit., p. 82.

39 Quoted in Drijvers, op. cit., p. 82.

40 Quoted in Wilkinson, op. cit., London, 1971, p. 20.

41 See Hunt, op. cit., p. 85: 'There was no limit to the possibilities of bringing the Bible to life before his eyes; the biblical associations (no matter how fragile) constituted the credentials of a pilgrim site, distinguishing it as a holy place.'

42 See J. F. Matthews's review of 'The Prosopography of the Later Roman Empire', in *Classical Review* (88), 1974, p. 104.

43 See Wilkinson, op. cit., p. 240.

44 *Patrologia Graeca* 48, p. 826.

45 See Hunt, op. cit., p. 129.

46 Quoted in Hunt, op. cit., p. 132.

47 Quoted in Hunt, op. cit., p. 92.

48 Quoted in Hunt, op. cit., p. 41.

49 Wilkinson, op. cit., pp. 136–8.

50 Wilkinson, op. cit., pp. 146–7.

51 Wilkinson, op. cit., p. 5.

52 See Hunt, op. cit., p. 124: 'The treachery of Judas or the sufferings on the cross were for the faithful no remote events of the past, but, through the medium of the location and the readings, vividly recalled in the present.'

53 Hunt's argument is that 'some formulation of how it had come to light was required' (op. cit., p. 40). But this assumes a gap where one did not necessarily exist.

54 See Kenneth G. Holum, *Theodosian Empresses – Women and Imperial Dominions in Late Antiquity*, Berkeley, 1982.

55 W. C. Prime, *Holy Cross: A History of the Invention, Preservation, and Disappearance of the Wood Known as the True Cross*, London, 1877, p. 87.

4 A KISS OF LIFE – JERUSALEM AND ROME, OR: HOW A PIECE OF WALNUT WOOD MADE HISTORY

1 There are many different editions of the Latin text, with or without translation. A reliable English edition is provided in J. Wilkinson, *Egeria's Travels*, Jerusalem, 1981, pp. 89–147. For the Latin text, see eds. A. Franceschini, R. Weber, *Corpus Christianorum Series Latina*, vol. 175, Turnhout, 1965, pp. 29–103.

2 M. C. Díaz y Díaz, ed., *Valerius, Epistula de beatissimae Aetheriae (s. Egeriae) laude*, Paris, Sources Chrétiennes 296, pp. 321–48.

3 1 Corinthians 15:6.

4 John 19:17, 41–2; Hebrews 13:12.

5 C. P. Thiede, *Heritage of the First Christians* ... pp. 141–7.

6 It is interesting to note that local tradition and physical evidence were – occasionally at least – regarded as less important than divine intervention. In some accounts of Helena's discoveries it is a sign from heaven which points to the place, and a healing miracle which helps to identify the True Cross.

7 2 Corinthians 13:13.

8 Matthew 28:19.

9 Cf. the research in E. Hello, *Physiognomie des Saints*, Paris, 1858; A. Legner, *Reliquien in Kunst und Kult*, Darmstadt, 1995, p. 63.

10 They were not the first to preach the Gospel in Rome, and Paul came after Peter, but Roman tradition, following a passage in Irenaeus, sees both apostles as the guarantors of an established community. Cf. C. P. Thiede, *Simon Peter – From Galilee to Rome*, Exeter, 1986, 2nd rev. ed. Grand Rapids, 1988, pp. 153–8, 171–93.

11 As to the chronology, we are following the reconstruction suggested by S. Borgehammar, *How the Holy Cross Was Found: From Event to Medieval Legend*, Stockholm, 1991.

12 *De Obitu Theodosii*, p. 47.

13 Details vary in different accounts, and those who wrote in the east of the Roman Empire loved theological embellishments. As we have seen, when Theodoret of Cyrrhus (c.393–466) tried to defend the somewhat extravagant equestrian fashion device of the Emperor's mother, he claimed in his *History of the Church*, pp. 1,17 that her use of (parts of) a nail of the Cross for the bridle of Constantine's

horse fulfilled a prophecy from Zechariah: 'When that day [of the eschatological battle] comes, the very bells on the horses will be inscribed with the words ... Sacred to Yahweh ...' (Zechariah 14:20).

14 See above pp. 52–4.

15 See J. Zias & E. Sekeles, 'The Crucified Man from Giv'at ha-Mivtar: A Reappraisal', *Israel Exploration Journal* 35, [1985], pp. 21–7; J. Zias, *'La prima cristianità in Terrasanta'*, in: A. Donati ed., *Dalla Terra alle Genti. La diffusione del cristianesimo nei primi secoli*, Milan, 1996, pp. 44–8.

16 Modern translations tell us that the risen Christ asked the disciples to see (and touch, in the case of Thomas) the wounds *in his hands*. The Greek word *cheir* can mean arm or hand; it is normally the context or additional words which help to define the precise meaning. Medical evidence and experiment leave no option – it had to be the arms, not the palms which were nailed to the cross and our translations of these Gospel passages should be corrected accordingly.

17 Perhaps a *clavus trabalis*, a strong nail used for beams (see, e.g., Horace, *Carmina*, 1,35,18 and the idiomatic reference in Cicero, *Against Verres*, 5,53: '*trabali clavo figere*' – 'to nail it down').

18 There were, at the time, the Chera, Chola and Pandya kingdoms in southern India. Thomas is linked with the north and north-west; so-called 'Thomas Christians' still flourish in the region of Malabar and Goa. Trade with Rome was intense and Roman artefacts have been found in the west and south.

19 The pilgrim Egeria was informed about these 'Acts' and the presence of the relics in Edessa when she visited the city in *c*.384: *Peregrinatio* 17,1; 19,3.

20 People were healed by touching the edge of the cloak of Jesus (Mark 6:56); a woman who touched the fringe of his cloak from behind was healed when he turned round and praised her faith (Matthew 9:20–3).

21 Cf. C. P. Thiede, 'The Search for the True Cross', in: *The Church of England Newspaper*, 19 March 1999, p. 18.

22 See above p. 14.

23 There is not the slightest reason to doubt the accuracy of this incident. Occasionally, New Testament scholars, following the fashion of doubting the accounts in St John's Gospel almost as a matter of principle, have argued that we do not know what happened in those hours after the death of Jesus. Was he really buried by Joseph of Arimathea in a new tomb not far from Golgotha (John 19:41), or was he, the executed criminal, thrown into an anonymous mass grave? The discovery of the ossuary of Yehohanan from Givat ha-Mivtar has provided us with the contemporary evidence: here was a crucified man who had not

only been taken from the cross and buried according to Jewish custom: his relatives or friends even took the bare bones – once the flesh had decayed – and buried them once more, following another typically Jewish custom of the time, in a small container (ossuary) with an inscription identifying the person inside. When it came to burial rites, a Jew was treated like any other Jew, regardless of the cause of death. A Roman crucifixion (and it had to have been a Roman crucifixion in the case of Yehohanan as well, since only the Roman occupying power had the privilege, in Israel, to execute people by crucifixion) made no difference.

24 It remains one of the strongest arguments in favour of the authenticity of Golgotha under the roof of today's Church of the Holy Sepulchre that the local Christian community insisted on it throughout the centuries, until Helena's arrival, even though the site was – to all appearances – 'wrong', since it was clearly inside the city, not outside (cf. also John 19:17; Hebrews 12:12). They had preserved an accurate memory of a topographical fact which only modern archaeology rediscovered and confirmed.

25 Ambrose, as above, in his funerary speech on Theodosius, and John Chrysostom, in his homilies on St John's Gospel in c.398 (*In Ioannem hom* 85).

26 Socrates Scholasticus, *Historia Ecclesiae* 1,17; c.439.

27 See above pp. 21–3.

28 *In Ioannem hom* 85; see note 25.

29 Acts 12:1–3.

30 Acts 12:6–17. See C. P. Thiede, *Simon Peter – From Galilee to Rome*, pp. 153–7; id., 'Babylon, der andere Ort: Anmerkungen zu 1 Petr 5,13 und Apg 12,17', in *Biblica* 67/4, 1986, pp. 532–8.

31 Euthychius of Alexandria, *Annales* 985, dates the return to Jerusalem to the fourth year of Emperor Vespasian, i.e. AD 73–4. Cf. B. Pixner, *Wege des Messias und Stätten der Urkirche*, Giessen, 3rd ed., 1996, pp. 300–4, with further literature.

32 Eventually, he did prove that he was the right man in the right place. Cf. M. Hengel, 'Jakobus der Herrenbruder – der erste "Papst"?', in E. Grösser & O. Merk eds., *Glaube und Eschatologie*, FS W. G. Kümmel, Tübingen, 1985, pp. 71–104; R. Bauckham, *Jude and the Relatives of Jesus in the Early Church*, Edinburgh, 1990, pp. 45–133; C. P. Thiede, *Ein Fisch für den römischen Kaiser, Juden, Griechen, Römer: Die Welt des Jesus Christus*, Munich, 1998, pp. 150–202.

33 As a brother of Joseph of Nazareth. Eusebius, *Church History* 3,11; 3,32,6, 4,22,4. Cf. John 19:25; Luke 24:18. See R. Bauckham, as in note 32, pp. 15–32; R. Riesner, 'Kleopas', in: *Das Grosse Bibellexikon*, Wuppertal/Giessen, 2nd ed., 1990, p. 794. Hegesippus, writing in c.AD

180, has been shown to be a reliable, extremely well-informed source. See, among others, B. Gustafsson, 'Hegesippus's, sources and his reliability', in: *Texte und Untersuchungen* 78, 1961, pp. 227–32; L. Herrmann, 'La famille du Christ d'après Hégésippe', *Revue de l'U-niversité de Bruxelles* 42, 1936–7, pp. 387–94.

34 Eusebius, *Church History* 3,11.

35 Or perhaps Tyche: some scholars have suggested that Eusebius (*Life of Constantine*, 3,26) merely confused the various deities represented in Jerusalem temples or consciously heightened the abomination, which was later redressed by Constantine when he chose Venus rather than the less despicable Tyche ('Fortuna', i.e. 'Luck' – a Greek word/term which does not occur in the New Testament, but several times in the 'Septuagint', the Greek Old Testament: Genesis 30:11; Isaiah 65:11; 2 Maccabees 7:37). Jerusalem coinage preserved from the time of Hadrian shows two temples dedicated to Tyche, but none to Venus/Aphrodite. For a discussion of the evidence, now see M. Biddle, *The Tomb of Christ*, Stroud, 1999, pp. 56–8.

36 A. K. Bowman & J. D. Thomas, *The Vindolanda Writing Tablets. Tabulae Vindolandenses* II, London, 1994, p. 18.

37 Cf. W. Eck, 'Inschriften auf Holz. Ein unterschätztes Phänomen der epigraphischen Kultur Roms', in: P. Kneissl & Volker Losemann eds., *Imperum Romanum*, FS Karl Christ, Stuttgart, 1998, pp. 203–17, here pp. 211–17.

38 See W. Eck, as in note 37 above, p. 206.

39 J. H. Oliver, *Greek Constitutions of Early Roman Emperors from Inscriptions and Papyri*, Philadelphia, 1989, No. 38.

40 W. Eck, as in note 37 above, p. 214. Sozomenus, an historian at Constantinople, wrote a 'History of the Church', probably between AD 443 and 450, which refers to the discovery of the Cross, the nails and the *Titulus*, and to the miraculous identification of the True Cross. Indebted to the earlier sources, he follows them with the exception of one addition: he writes that there was this piece of wood, on which were inscribed in white letters in Hebrew, in Greek, and in Latin, the following words: 'Jesus of Nazareth the King of the Jews' (*Church History* 2). The 'white letters' would appear to be an oblique reference to the type of inscription: the *Titulus* was a typical Roman whitened tablet, an album or *tabula dealbata*. He must have had accurate information about the inscription, since he gets the three languages right and does not copy the order as it is given in St John's Gospel (see below).

41 The Greek word is αιτια (*aitia*). Cassius Dio, *Roman History* 5,3,7; Mark 15:26; Matthew 27:37.

42 John 19:19: τιτλον.

43 Quintilian, *Declamationes minores* 274 (he suggests major cross-roads); John 19:19–20.

44 Casius Dio, *Roman History* 5,3,7; Suetonius, *Life of the Caesars, Gaius* 32; Eusebius, *Church History* 5,1,43–4.

45 Suetonius, *Life of the Caesars, Domitianus* 10.

46 The fragment in Rome does not preserve nail marks. Regardless of the question of authenticity, this should not be used to argue in favour of hanging: the place(s) where a nail or nails would have penetrated the wood are simply no longer extant.

47 The Latin ending – *ieum* – corresponds to the Greek ending – *eion* – and, in such contexts and combined with a personal name, designates temples. The historian Géza Alföldi has recently suggested that the inscription refers to one of two mighty lighthouse towers at the harbour of Caesarea, named after Drusus ('Druseium'), a brother of Tiberius who had died in 9 BC, and after Tiberius, the reigning emperor ('Tiberieum'). However, the only historical source, Josephus, does not mention the name of the second tower, which he would have done if it was a known – and indeed famous – imperial name. See W. Eck, 'Neue Deutung der Pilatusinschrift von Cäsarea', in *Welt und Umwelt der Bibel*, 15 (2000), p. 63.

48 Emperor Claudius elevated the office of the regional governor at Caesarea from Prefect to Procurator; thus Pilate was a prefect, but Felix and Festus, the two with whom St Paul had to deal, were already procurators. The New Testament does not confuse the terminology: the status of Pilate, Felix and Festus is described, in Greek, as 'hegemon', which covers both Latin terms.

49 Some scholars have argued that 'Hebrew' actually means 'Aramaic', which indeed it sometimes does, occasionally even in St John's Gospel. But here, on the *Titulus*, there is only one conceivable reason why Aramaic should have been preferred: comprehensibility. This, however, was guaranteed by the Greek line, since Jews in Jerusalem and elsewhere were bilingual or even trilingual, as has been shown more than once. Cf. C. P. Thiede and M. d'Ancona, *The Jesus Papyrus*, London, 1996, 115–23; see also S. E. Porter, 'Jesus and the Use of Greek in Galilee', in B. Chilton & C. E. Evans eds., *Studying the Historical Jesus: Evaluations of the State of Current Research*, Leiden, 1994, pp. 123–54. The few who did not know Greek were conservative enough to understand Hebrew. At the time of Pilate this still was the language which characterized traditional Jewishness. The prefect would have used it for the *Titulus* without hesitating.

50 This inscription can be detected behind the scene in Acts 21:28–31. Paul – who was clearly multilingual, as he proves a few minutes later (Acts 21:37–40!) – was accused of having brought an (uncircumcised)

Greek, the Ephesian Trophimus, into the Temple and a crowd of orthodox Jews was beginning to beat him to death, when the Roman temple cohort intervened. The two copies of the stone are at the John Rockefeller Museum, Jerusalem (a fragment), and at the Turkish National Museum in Istanbul (complete).

51 The oldest representative of the Majority Text is Codex Q, at the Herzog-August-Bibliothek in Wolfenbüttel, which, like the Alexandrinus, is fifth century. Although fragmentary, with damaged passages from St Luke and St John, its surviving pages include Luke 23:38.

52 Some of the manuscripts of Luke's Gospel with the longer text differ among themselves in certain respects of style and word order. None of them is identical with St John. The least one can say, therefore, is that there was an independent tradition associated with St Luke, insisting on a reference to the three languages and to Greek as the first one.

53 A revealing comparative example from the period of New Testament scholarship prior to the First World War, when most of the important codices and minuscules were known, but only a few papyri – those numbering P1 to P15 (none of them containing our passages) – Alexander Souter, a Fellow of Magdalen College, Oxford (where the oldest papyrus of St Matthew's Gospel, the P64 or Papyrus Magdalen Greek 17, is kept; cf. C. P. Thiede & M. d'Ancona, op. cit.) and Professor of New Testament Greek at Oxford University, edited the Greek New Testament on behalf of the Oxford University Press in 1910. He opted for the shorter version of Luke 23:38, but offers the available evidence for the longer reading in a footnote. As for John 19:20, he has the sequence Hebrew, Latin, Greek and is apparently so certain of its authenticity, and of the weakness of the alternative, that he does not even bother to refer to the variant reading in a footnote. And this in spite of the fact that all manuscripts which could be used to argue in favour of Hebrew, Greek, Latin were already known to him and appear in his list of consulted manuscripts. Some scholars have explained the later variation, Hebrew, Greek, Latin, in geopolitical terms: if Hebrew, Latin, Greek was 'the national language, the official language, the common language', then Hebrew, Greek, Latin 'were arranged in accord with a geographical order going from East to West': see B. M. Metzger, *A Textual Commentary on the Greek New Testament*, Stuttgart, 4th rev. ed., 1994, p. 217.

54 Ambrose, *De Obitu Theodosii*, pp. 45–6.

55 Suetonius, *Life of the Caesars, Augustus* 66; cf. Cassius Dio, *Roman History* 53,23,5; 53,24,1.

56 See Mark 15:32, where this is expressed quite unequivocally: 'Let the

Messiah, the king of Israel, come down from the cross. If we see that, we shall believe.'

57 See the evaluation by a contemporary author, Philo of Alexandria (d. c.AD 50), in his 'Legatio ad Gaium', pp. 299–305. Philo emphasizes that Pilate not only felt entitled to despise and maltreat the Jews, but also feared a wrong step which could alienate him from Tiberius's favour. Cf. also H. K. Bond, *Pontius Pilate in History and Interpretation*, Cambridge, 1998, pp. 36–48 and, for Josephus on Pilate, pp. 49–93.

58 Eusebius, *Church History* 5,1,44.

59 Several first-century ossuaries with 'Jesus' incised in Hebrew or Aramaic have been found in and near Jerusalem and Josephus, the Jewish historian who died in c.98, mentions no less than twenty-one different Jesuses in his two books, the *Jewish War* and the *Jewish Antiquities*, either prior to or contemporary with New Testament times.

60 See S. Goranson, 'Nazarenes', *The Anchor Bible Dictionary*, vol. 4, New York, 1992, pp. 1049–50; W. L. Petersen, 'Nazoreans, Gospel of the', *The Anchor Bible Dictionary*, vol. 4, New York, 1992, pp. 1051–2.

61 Cf., among others, the study of two leading archaeologists, E. M. Meyers & J. F. Strange, *Archaeology, the Rabbis, and Early Christianity*, Nashville, 1981 and the article by one of them, J. F. Strange, 'Nazareth', *The Anchor Bible Dictionary*, vol. 4, New York, 1992, pp. 1050–1.

62 The official nature of this report is emphasized in P. L. Maier's interesting paper, 'The Inscription on the Cross of Jesus of Nazareth', *Hermes* 124, 1996, pp. 58–75, here 67.

63 'Apology' 35,48. For the historicity of a reference to Jesus by Pilate in such *Acta*, it is of course irrelevant – fascinating as it would otherwise have been – that Pilate's *Acta* have not survived. In fact, not a single imperial Roman archive has survived. It is, however, important enough to realize that it must have existed, and that the old myth according to which 'the real world' did not take notice of Jesus and his little Jewish corner of the Empire is plainly wrong.

64 It may look as though Ambrose of Milan described the contents of the *Titulus*, in Latin, following the Johannine version. But he does not say that this is what he himself saw on the actual piece of wood; he merely tells his listeners, in that funeral oration for Emperor Theodosius, what the text of the *Titulus* on the Cross of Jesus said. Hence, he had to quote a complete text. How easy it is to jump to the wrong conclusions about what someone really said or wrote can be seen in Jan Willem Drijver's magisterial book about Helena. Having

quoted from Egeria's account, he comments: 'Egeria is the first to mention the presence in Jerusalem of the *Titulus* bearing the text: "Jesus of Nazareth, King of the Jews", written in Greek, Latin and Hebrew. According to the Gospel of John, this inscription had been attached to Jesus's Cross by Pontius Pilate' (J. W. Drijvers, op. cit., p. 92). But clearly – as he himself had just quoted correctly – Egeria does *not* refer to the text on the *Titulus* she saw in Jerusalem, nor does she mention the languages, nor is the order Greek, Latin, Hebrew the one recorded by John; it is, as we know, the order of the longer version in Luke's Gospel. Drijvers mistakenly incorporates into his statement information from different sources, which are unrelated to what Egeria herself wrote and yet, everything he says is correct in its own, different context.

65 Bulla 'Admirabile Sacramentum', 29 July 1496.

66 We are grateful to Michael Hesemann, Düsseldorf, who gave us the first of Paladini's photos and told us that the Abbot of Santa Croce, Don Luigi Rottini, had weighed and measured the fragment. Hesemann has recently published an account of his own investigation: *Die Jesus-Tafel. Mit einem Vorwort von C. P. Thiede*, Freiburg/Basel/Wien, 1999.

67 Special thanks are due to Stephan Borgehammar, Uppsala, author of the standard work on Helena and the True Cross (S. Borgehammar, op. cit.). He provided us with references to the many 'hidden' and occasionally obscure studies, and patiently answered questions.

68 We owe this information to Elio Corona, professor for dendrotechnology at the Università della Tuscia in Viterbo, who first presented it to the participants of a symposium in Rome, '*Dalla Passione alla Resurrezione: 2000 anni di silenziosa testimonianza*', 6–8 May 1999. Interestingly, the Pilgrim of Piacenza claimed that the wood of the Cross itself was walnut ('Antonini Placentini Itinerarium' 20,5); this, however, has been shown to be unlikely: the wood of the cross of Yehohanan from Givat ha-Mivtar, in any case, partly preserved under the nail which went through his heel bone, was acacia. The pilgrim's thoughts may have been inspired by a 'prophecy' vaguely derived from Song of Songs 6:11 (cf. the exegesis by Cyril of Jerusalem, 'Cathechetical Lectures' 14,5).

69 Hypothetically, it might be argued that the *Titulus* was produced at some stage after the fifth century and that the argument could be turned round: at a time when the sequence Hebrew, Greek, Latin had been introduced into a growing number of manuscripts throughout the Empire, the forger would have followed the new norm. Against this hypothetical attempt at turning the tables, there is a decisive philological reason, which we shall encounter further down. And

there also is an historical argument: our sources are credibly adamant that the *Titulus*, or *a titulus* or a fragment of it, reached Rome thanks to Helena. Helena's *Titulus* either had the sequence Hebrew, Greek, Latin, as we can see it today, or Hebrew, Latin, Greek, as in the older manuscripts of St John's Gospel. If we suppose for a moment that it was Hebrew, Latin, Greek, a new forger, in whosoever's employment, would have had to manipulate an inscription, which many people had seen and had of course seen with a different order of languages. This could plainly not be risked if the claim to venerable authenticity was the aim. Thus, even if some might still want to assume that the Santa Croce *Titulus* is at best an early medieval copy, it would have to be a copy of a known original with the sequence Hebrew, Greek, Latin. But as we shall see in a moment, the decisive argument against such hypotheses is philological.

We may add a further observation: the Codex Alexandrinus was written, as far as we know, in Alexandria, which belonged (since AD 395) to the eastern Roman Empire, the later Byzantine Empire. Throughout the fifth century the other, bigger part of the *Titulus* was still in Jerusalem, which also belonged to the eastern Empire and its ecclesiastical structure. Since the Jerusalem fragment clearly presented the sequence Hebrew, Greek, Latin, the influence on a new and growing generation of codices could have come straight from Jerusalem. In fact, the Pilgrim of Piacenza, who visited Jerusalem in *c.*570, still saw it there ('Antonini Placentini Itinerarium' 20). That pilgrim gave a brief description and referred to a text which looks like a Latin version of St Luke's '*Hic est rex Iudaeorum*'. In any case, following our reconstruction of the Roman fragment (see below), the Jerusalem piece would indeed have preserved the words IESUS[...]XIUDAEORUM – the part with [NAZARENUS RE] was in Rome. The pilgrim from Piacenza could therefore easily recall the text the way he did. A separate manuscript of his report, version B, even follows the text from St John, but this is a later western 'recension', apparently on the basis of the actual fragment in Rome.

70 E.g., Mark 1:24; 10:47; 14:67; 16:6; Luke 4:34; 24:19.

71 Conversely, unlike in the case of the order of languages, later manuscripts would not have had to 'correct' the text, as there was sufficient Gospel evidence for the legitimate co-existence of both forms.

72 P. L. Maier, 'The Inscription on the Cross of Jesus of Nazareth', *Hermes* 124, 1996, pp. 58–75, here p. 73.

73 See F. C. Kenyon, *The Palaeography of Greek Papyri*, London, 1899, 2nd ed. Chicago, 1998, p. 161; W. Wattenbach, *Anleitung zur griechischen Paläographie*, Leipzig, 1895, 2nd ed. Hildesheim, 1971, pp. 97–8.

74 Cf.: Inscriptions Reveal. Documents from the time of the Bible, the
   Mishna and the Talmud, Israel Museum Jerusalem, Cat. No. 100,
   Jerusalem 1973, pp. 48–9.

75 Ibid., p. 48.

76 *Inscriptiones Graecae Editio Maior XII* (1) Berlin, 1895, inset 4,
   column 3; cf. M. Avi-Yonah, *Abbreviations in Greek Inscriptions*
   Jerusalem/London, 1940 (Suppl. of the *Quarterly of the Dept of
   Antiquities in Palestine*, vol. 9, p. 119). We owe this information to
   Dr Leah Di Segni, The Hebrew University of Jerusalem, and to Dr
   Ulrich Victor Humboldt, University of Berlin. The inscription refers
   to an unnamed Flavian emperor and must therefore be dated to AD
   69–96.

77 See C. P. Thiede & M. d'Ancona, op. cit., pp. 123–9. Only much later,
   during the sixth and seventh centuries, the γ for 'Y/OY' suddenly
   became fashionable; it is well known even to non-papyrologists from
   illuminated manuscripts. Very tentatively, we might suggest that the
   sudden re-emergence of this first-century (and older) symbol, letter
   and abbreviation could have been due to the same influence which
   occasioned the revised order of the languages in later manuscripts of
   St John's Gospel (see pp. 83–4 and note 71 above).

78 See L. Boffo. *Iscrizioni greche e latine per lo studio della bibbia*,
   Brescia, 1994, e.g., no. 30.

79 There is not enough specific material left for tree-ring dating etc.; cf.,
   among others, P. Phillips (ed.), 'The Archaeologist and the Laboratory',
   CBA Research Report No. 58, London, 1985.

80 On the problems of radiocarbon analysis in dating damaged organic
   material and in particular, ancient handwriting, see C. P. Thiede,
   'Radiocarbon Dating and Papyrus P64 at Oxford', in *id.*, *Rekindling
   the Word*, Leominster, 1995, pp. 33–6.

5   JEWS AND ROMANS IN JERUSALEM: THE *TITULUS*, GOD, THE LORD
    AND THE SAVIOUR

1 Ch. Rohault de Fleury, *Mémoire sur les instruments de la passion de
   N.-S. J.-C.*, Paris, 1870, p. 196.

2 Ibid., pp. 196–7.

3 B. Drach, 'Explication du titre hébreu de la Ste-Croix, et dissertation
   sur la langue dans laquelle il fut écrit', in *Annales de philosophie
   chrétienne* 9/18, 1839, pp. 291–308, 341–52.

4 The oldest surviving manuscripts of the Hebrew Bible. Papyrus Nash
   was discovered in Egypt in 1902 and can be dated to the second/first
   century BC. The Dead Sea Scrolls were discovered between 1947 and

1956; they date from the second century BC (Hebrew and Aramaic finds) to the mid-first century AD (Greek papyri).

5 B. Drach, as in note 3, pp. 294–5.

6 Text in Cod. Vaticanus lat. 3912. Other contemporary references can be found in G. Bosio, *La trionfante e gloriosa Croce*, Rome, 1610.

7 D. Balduino Bedini O. Cist., *Le Reliquie della Passione del Signore*, Rome, 3rd ed., 1997, p. 50, erroneously states that the Latin line reads JS NAZARENUS RE. For the Greek line, he has NAZAPENYC B (i.e. at least no imaginary IC at the beginning!). Apart from the obvious fact that the Latin line reads NAZARINUS, with an 'I', there is no trace whatsoever of JS (and if there were it would of course be IS). See chapter 4 above. Bedini's reading of the – inexistant – JS/IS could lead to speculations about an early example of a 'Nomen sacrum' abbreviation of Jesus's name. And this error is further encouraged by the engraving of a reconstruction above the *Titulus* in Rome, which invents an IC for the Greek line and an I for the Latin line. The engraver mistook a small and low, curved indentation in the wood for a) (the inverted C), and added a preceding I, to produce a clearly fictitious IC 'abbreviation'.

8 G. Kroll, *Auf den Spuren Jesu*, Stuttgart/Leipzig, 11th ed., 1990, here p. 361.

9 For a photo and a reconstruction of the inscription, see G. Kroll, as in note 8 above, p. 83, plate 62.

10 Cf. B. Pixner, *Wege des Messias und Stätten der Urkirche*, Giessen/Basel, 4th ed., 1996, pp. 23–4, 47–8, 164.

11 For this spelling of *Nozri* (the simple noun, without the definite article), see also B. Pixner, as in note 10 above, p. 70. The *Holem*, later written with a tiny dot above or slightly to the left, to distinguish it from the consonant, is the name of the *Vahv* if spoken as a vocalized letter (o).

12 Leaving such gaps between words is a characteristic of Hebrew writing, well established in the Dead Sea Scrolls. Greek and Latin, however, were commonly written in *scriptio continua*, i.e., in continuous writing without spacing between words or sentences.

13 The fragment is displayed in a nineteenth-century silver reliquary; on top of the rectangular frame there is a small engraving with reconstructions of the fragmentary Hebrew, Greek and Latin lines, which differ, all three, from the faulty reconstruction of the complete *Titulus* that is on display at a wall of the side chapel. We referred to the engraving in chapter 4 and have to do so again, in the context of the Hebrew text, to alert readers once more to the erroneous and fanciful nature of this reconstruction. If we suppose that the extant part of the line began with the legible name of Jesus, written without

the final 'A' (ע), i.e. Yeshu, not Yeshua, and if we allow for a rare form of the *Shin* (שׁ) and a missing/lost initial *Yod* (י), we should read שִׁ, followed by נוצרי or (without the *Vahv-Holem*) נצרי (both Hebrew) or נעיא (Aramaic, in Kroll's reconstruction), or something very similar if we accept – against all the circumstantial evidence – an Aramaic dialect. Transferring this into cursive Hebrew or Aramaic – which would not have been used on a formal inscription to begin with – we may just about accept the writing of 'Yeshu' and a *Nun*, which follows, and we could even accept the following *Tsadeh* of the shorter Hebrew and Aramaic versions, in very cursive Hebrew. Then we need a *Resh* (Hebrew) or *Yod* (Aramaic) after it. The *Resh*, indeed, is conceivable. What next? There are no visible traces left on the fragment. Pure fancy takes over. The real problem with all this, of course, is the fact that there are no traces of letters before the twin elongations – nothing even remotely resembling a *Shin*, as the engraving demands it. Only if we suppose that the original part of the extant text did not begin with the definite article *Ha* (ה, *Heh*), but with a *Vahv-Shureq* (the last letter of Yeshu), followed by an identical-looking (!) *Nun*, a *Tsadeh* and a *Resh*, would we have the sequence of two parallel lower elongations (*Vahv-Shureq* + *Nun*), a rounded *Tsadeh* and a *Resh*. However this yields only four letters before the end of the visible line – and the fact remains that there are traces of five or theoretically six, with the first two elongations so close to each other that they belong to *one* letter (as we demonstrated above), which can only be a *Heh* (ה). Thus, interesting as the speculative approach presented in the engraving is – concocted by someone with some knowledge of Hebrew – it fails decisively and must be discounted.

14 Schalom Ben-Chorin, *Bruder Jesus. Der Nazarener in jüdischer Sicht*, Munich, 1977, p. 180. In his German transliteration, Ben-Chorin had written '*Jeschu Hanozri W(u)melech Hajehudim*'.

15 John 10:30; and see the credibly violent reaction of those Jews who regarded this statement as lethally blasphemous, 10:31–9. It is difficult to understand how some scholars can doubt the authenticity of this pericope.

16 Here we have the definite article in the first part of the sentence and no article in the second half ('This man said, "I am (a) king of the Jews"'). The official text in Latin, i.e. in a language without the definite article, left both options open. It would therefore be risky, philologically speaking, to read too much into the change from 'the' to its omission in consecutive parts of the same statement. After all, even 'a' king of the Jews would still have been as blasphemous to the hierarchy as 'the' king – there was only *one*, as they put it themselves, who was their king: the Emperor (John 19:15). See also the discussion

of the missing '*ho*' ('the') in the Greek line of the *Titulus* in chapter 4.

17 A point made forcefully by F. Bovon, *Les dernières jours de Jésus. Textes et événements*, Neuchâtel, 1974, p. 37.

18 The latest analysis of the sources calculates one million pilgrims for the three major festivals: W. Reinhardt, 'The Population Size of Jerusalem and the Numerical Growth of the Jerusalem Church', in R. Bauckham (ed.), *The Book of Acts in its First Century Setting*, vol. 4: *Palestinian Setting*, Grand Rapids/Carlisle, 1995, pp. 237–65, here pp. 262–5.

19 And for the same reason St Luke could not have invented such a statement, regardless of where and when he wrote.

20 1 Corinthians 15:1–8.

21 Cf. J. Zias, 'Ossuario col nome di Alessandro, figlio di Simone di Cirene', in A. Donati ed., *Dalla Terra alle Genti – La diffusione del cristianesimo nei primi secoli*, Milan, 1996, p. 167 (with plate); N. Avigad, 'A Depository of Inscribed Ossuaries in the Kidron Valley', in *Israel Exploration Journal* 12, 1962, pp. 1–12, plate 4.

22 St Peter does not call *the Jews* 'men outside the Law'. The Greek term used here, $\alpha\nu o\mu\omega\nu$, is a reference to the Romans who carried out the death sentence and who could be called lawless (distant from the Jewish Law); a Hebrew synonym, '*Resha-yim*' (lawless in the sense of 'wicked'), occurs in Jewish literature and often directly refers to the Romans. But even so, the apostle insists that his fellow Jews were not blameless – they 'took' Jesus and handed him over to the Romans. St Luke, who dedicated his Gospel and the Book of Acts to a high-ranking Roman official, 'His Excellency' Theophilus, would not have included this criticism of the Romans if it had not been an authentic and central element of St Peter's speech.

23 From c.AD 66 to c.AD 73 at Pella, see chapter 4.

24 S. Safrai, *Die Wallfahrt im Zeitalter des Zweiten Tempels*, Neu-kirchen-Vluyn, 1981, pp. 161, 259.

25 Acts 1:21–3.

26 Cf. Josephus, *Jewish Antiquities* 13,4,9; Eusebius, *Onomasticon* 144,28.

27 Cf. 1 Samuel 1:1 and 1 Samuel 1:19.

28 Mark 15:43; Luke 23:50.

29 Scholars differ as to the exact composition of the Great Court and the Small Sanhedrins, but the above combines the essence of the extant sources and assessments.

30 Cf. T. Elgvin, 'The Messiah Who Was Cursed on the Tree', in *Themelios* 22/3, 1997, pp. 14–21.

31 Cf. Josephus, *Jewish War*, pp. 361–3.

32 *Mishna Sanhedrin* 6,5; *Jewish Antiquities*, p. 44.

33 John 19:41. This excludes even the remotest possibility of the so-called Garden Tomb being the authentic site, as the tomb shown there is pre-exilic, i.e. *c.* seventh century BC.

34 Some scholars have doubted that someone like Nicodemus ever existed and have regarded the weight of spices brought to the tomb as proof for John's symbolic exaggerations. The credibility of person and action was, however, conclusively argued by J. A. T. Robinson, *The Priority of John*, London, 1985, pp. 281–7. Cf. also C. H. Dodd, *Historical Tradition in the Fourth Gospel*, Cambridge/New York, 1963, pp. 138–9.

35 Robinson, as in note 34 above, found four in Jewish sources, one in the first century BC, another post AD 70.

36 The so-called 'Acts of Pilate' were renamed 'Gospel of Nicodemus' in the fourteenth century.

37 Even in the centuries before its dedication to Pan it had been known as a site of Baal – cf. Joshua 11:17; Judges 3:3; 1 Chronicles 5:23.

38 Matthew 16:13–20.

39 A linguistic link first made in the Homeric 'Hymn to Pan', 47.

40 E. L. Sukenik, 'The Earliest Records of Christianity', in *American Journal of Archaeology* 51, 1947, pp. 351–65. In a later article, the epigrapher B. Gustafsson corrected details of Sukenik's readings and concluded that his Israeli colleague had indeed found the two oldest invocations of Jesus as helper. 'Jesus-help' is the text on the first ossuary, 'Jesus let [him who rests here] arise' is the meaning of the second. (B. Gustafsson, 'The Oldest Graffiti in the History of the Church?', in *New Testament Studies* 3, 1956–7, pp. 65–9, with plate. (For the cross marks on the second ossuary, see chapter 6.) In spite of recent critiques, these conclusions stand as philologically and archaeologically substantiated.

41 M. Biddle, *The Tomb of Christ*, Stroud, 1999, chapter XII, p. 9.

42 1 Kings 2:10.

43 It has occasionally been doubted that such a niche could have existed in a first-century synagogue. But recent excavations have produced two comparable cases, at Gamla (near the Sea of Galilee) and in Shuafat north of Jerusalem: cf. Z. Maoz, 'The Synagogue of Gamla and the Typology of Second-Temple Synagogues', in L. Levine, *Ancient Synagogues Revealed*, Jerusalem, 1981, pp. 35–41; A. Rabinovich, 'Oldest Jewish Prayer Room discovered in Shuafat Ridge' in *Jerusalem Post* (International Edition), 17 August 1991, p. 7.

44 B. Pixner, *Wege des Messias und Stätten der Urkirche*, Giessen/Basel, 3rd ed., 1996, pp. 297–311; *id.*, 'Church of the Apostles found on Mount Sion, in *Biblical Archaeology Review* 16.3, 1990, pp. 16–35,60;

see also E. Puech, 'La synagogue judéo-chrétienne du Mont Sion', in *Le Monde de la Bible* 57, 1989, pp. 18–19; C. Mimouni, 'La synagogue "judéo-chrétienne" de Jérusalem au Mont Zion' in *Proche-Orient chrétien* 40, 1990, pp. 215–34; J. Finegan, *The Archaeology of the New Testament*, Princeton, 2nd ed., 1992, pp. 236–42; R. Riesner, 'Das Jerusalemer Essenerviertel und die Urgemeinde', in W. Haase ed., *Aufstieg und Niedergang der Römischen Welt* II 26/2, Berlin/New York, 1995, pp. 1175–922, here pp. 1834–48; id., *Essener und Urgemeinde in Jerusalem, Neue Wege und Quellen*, Giessen/Basel, 2nd ed., 1998, pp. 58–72, 138–43. The latter includes a detailed discussion of opposing views.

45 J. Pinkerfeld, ' "David's Tomb": Notes on the History of the Building', in *Bulletin of the Louis Rabinovitz Fund for the Exploration of Ancient Synagogues* 3, 1960, pp. 41–3. The report was published posthumously; Pinkerfeld was murdered in a terrorist attack on an archaeological congress in Ramat Rahel in 1956.

46 E. Testa, *Il simbolismo dei giudeo-cristiani*, Jerusalem, 1962, p. 492.

47 The Caiaphas ossuaries from Talpiot are good, near-contemporary examples. In one case the inscription was added when the ossuary was already in place – the writing 'forks' downwards, as the scribe had no room for his arm and hand to continue a straight line. A similar case is the famous 'Petros eni' ('Peter is in here') inscription in the necropolis underneath the Vatican hill.

48 B. Bagatti, *The Church from the Circumcision*, Jerusalem, 1971, p. 121. These readings may remain controversial and there is an interesting survey, which does justice also to the most vociferous critic of a Judaeo-Christian interpretation, Joan E. Taylor: S. C. Mimouni, *Le judéo-christianisme ancien. Essais historiques*, Paris, 1998, pp. 366–87. In spite of doubts raised, Mimouni in the end accepts that the advocates of the Judaeo-Christian readings have a case.

49 In an abstract sense, describing (e.g.) religion and reasoning as 'the *master* of passions', 4 Maccabees 1:7; 1:30.

50 See C. P. Thiede, *Ein Fisch für den römischen Kaiser* ... pp. 216–46.

51 See C. P. Thiede, *Heritage of the First Christians* ... pp. 141–3, with plates. Cf. also the report and the analysis by one of the Israeli scholars involved in the investigation, the long-time director of the Israel Museum, Magen Broshi: M. Broshi, 'Evidence of Earliest Christian Pilgrimage Comes to Light in Holy Sepulchre Church', in *Biblical Archaeology Review* 3, 1977, pp. 42–4; id., 'Excavations in the Chapel of St Vartan in the Holy Sepulchre', in *Israel Exploration Journal*, 35, 1985, pp. 108–28, both with plates.

52 The 'SATOR-AREPO' inscription found at Pompeii, which most scholars now accept as Christian (cf. chapter 6) must predate the

destruction of the town by the eruption of the Vesuvius volcano in AD 79; it would therefore be the oldest known Christian text in Latin. The first extant classic of Latin Christian literature is the 'Octavius' of Minucius Felix, written between AD 143 and 161 at the latest (for a discussion of the date, see C. P. Thiede, 'A Pagan Reader of 2 Peter: Cosmic Conflagration in 2 Peter 3 and the "Octavius" of Minucius Felix', in *Journal for the Study of the New Testament* 26, 1986, pp. 79–96). Latin 'loan words' or Latinisms in the Gospels are a different matter; cf. A. Millard, 'Latin in First-Century Palestine', in Z. Zevit, S. Gitin, M. Sokoloff eds., *Solving Riddles and Untying Knots: Biblical Epigraphic and Semitic Studies in Honor of Jonas C. Greenfield*, Winona Lake, 1995, pp. 451–8. There was a time when some scholars supposed that St Mark, writing in Rome and for a Roman audience, chose Latin rather than Greek for the original version of his Gospel; see P.-L. Couchoud, 'L'Évangile de Marc, a-t-il été écrit en Latin?', in *Revue de l'Histoire des Religions* 47, 1926, pp. 161–92.

53 M. Sordi, *The Christians and the Roman Empire*, London/New York, 1994, pp. 85–95.

54 See M. Sordi, as in note 53 above, pp. 96–107 ('Philip the Arab and Decius: The First Christian Emperor and the "Pagan Restoration" ').

55 Cf. for example, how the Procurator Festus uses it when he talks about Nero to King Herod Agrippa, Acts 25:26 (not all translations are accurate in this verse).

56 The surprise is noted by Eusebius, *Vita Constanti* 3,28. Martin Biddle, who discusses and refutes the arguments for alternative sites suggested by J. E. Taylor and A. J. Wharton, draws a modern analogy: 'In exactly the same way, government officials faced with the discovery of the Rose Theatre in London in 1989, demolished three centuries earlier, admitted that they had not expected to find anything, although they knew that it was the right site. Makarios [the bishop of Jerusalem] dug more in hope than expectation and was, to Eusebius' surprise, proved "right" '. (M. Biddle, *The Tomb of Christ*, p. 65.) For the assessment of a leading Israeli archaeologist, Dan Bahat, in favour of authenticity, see D. Bahat, 'Does the Holy Sepulchre church mark the burial of Jesus?', in *Biblical Archaeology Review* 12/3, pp. 26–45. See also on the nature of the surviving archaeological and literary evidence, N. Belayche, 'Du Mont du Temple au Golgotha: le Capitole de la Colonie d'*Aelia Capitolina*' in *Revue de l'Histoire des religions* 214/1, pp. 387–413.

57 See M. Biddle, op. cit., pp. 72–6. Biddle assumes that the destruction was not complete; much of the tomb chamber may still survive inside the Edicule. 'In part it may even stand to more than the height of a man. Nor has the east wall been entirely destroyed.' And he con-

cludes, 'that there is much to be discovered when the time comes for restoration' (p. 119).

6   THE EARLIEST CHRISTIAN SYMBOL: BELIEVERS UNDER THE CROSS

1   The sheer number of Constantinian and post-Constantinian examples is almost staggering, not least in Britain, where the silver treasures of Water Newton, Mildenhall, Hoxne and other sites document altar hangings, spoons and other objects beautifully decorated with the Chi-Rho monogram. Wealthy Christian individuals and communities also decorated a living room at Hinton St Mary with a magnificent floor mosaic, showing Christ with the Chi-Rho behind his head.

2   In his treatise 'On the Deaths of the Persecutors', *De mortibus persecutorum*, Lactantius states that the great persecution of Diocletian was not fully implemented by Constantius Chlorus, the Caesar of the West: 'Constantius, to avoid appearing to disagree with the instructions of his superiors, allowed the churches – that is the walls which could be restored – to be destroyed, but the true temple, which is inside men, he left unharmed' (*D.m.p.* 15:7). The Latin terminology is unequivocal: Lactantius uses *conventicula* to describe the buildings, and *parietes* for their walls (probably made of wood), and he is therefore talking about separate, identifiable buildings with their own walls. Since Constantius's limited action took place in AD 304, these buildings could have existed at the turn of the century or before. Interestingly, the same term *conventicula*, is used in the so-called edict of Milan of 313, when Licinius and Constantine gave permission for Christians to assemble in public and to build churches: 'so that once more they may be Christians and put together (*componant*) their churches (*conventicula*) [*D.m.p.* 34:4]. We cannot escape the conclusion that separate church buildings, known as such, existed prior to Constantine and that Constantine, too, was aware of this fact.

3   See C. P. Thiede, *Heritage of the First Christians* ... pp. 79–86, with plates.

4   Cf. Ch. Thomas, *Christianity in Roman Britain to AD 500*, London, 2nd ed. 1985, pp. 218, 220–7. Examples of such movable lead tanks were found at Icklingham in Suffolk, at Lickford in Sussex and elsewhere. 'At least fourteen of these lead tanks are now known, half with the Christian monogram, and a role in the baptismal rite seems plausible enough.' (T. W. Potter & C. Jones, *Roman Britain*, London, 1992, p. 207).

5   The German New Testament scholar Klaus Berger, Heidelberg University, demonstrated that AD 68–9 is the most plausible date for

Revelation: K. Berger, *Theologiegeschichte des Urchristentums*, Tübingen/Basel, 1994, pp. 568–71. John A. T. Robinson before him had suggested AD 68–70 (J. A. T. Robinson, *Redating the New Testament*, London, 1976, pp. 221–3). Cf. C. P. Thiede, *Bibelcode und Bibelwort. Die Suche nach verschlüsselten Botschaften in der Heiligen Schrift*, Basel, 1998, pp. 86–7: after AD 65, and before the death of Nero on 9th June 68.

6 Cf. C. P. Thiede & M. d'Ancona, *The Jesus Papyrus*, pp. 123–9.

7 J. O'Callaghan, *'Nomina Sacra' in papyris graecis saeculi III neo-testamentariis*, Rome, 1970, p. 69. For the date of P18, see, among others, Ph.W. Comfort, *Early Manuscripts & Modern Translations of the Bible*, Grand Rapids, 1990, p. 39; *id.*, *The Quest for the Original Text of the New Testament*, Grand Rapids, 1992, p. 118.

8 Lactantius, *De mortibus persecutorum*, 44:5. Eusebius, in his later account, confirms that it was a cross, not an X (*Vita Constantini* 1, 28–30).

9 This translation follows J. L. Creed ed., Lactantius, *De Mortibus Persecutorum*, Oxford 1984, pp. 62–3.

10 A. Alföldi, *The Conversion of Constantine and Pagan Rome*, Oxford, 2nd ed., 1998, p. 18.

11 Eusebius, *Vita Constantini* 31, 1–2.

12 A papyrus of 'Hypomnema on Homer's *Iliad*', British Museum Pap 2055, in the left margin of line 17 (e.g.).

13 '*Christos*' means 'the anointed one', from '*chrio*', to rub with oint-ment, and is a translation of the Hebrew 'Messiah', but in early Christian literature, the itacistic association with '*chrestos*' was often used as a play on words: Christ was 'the Good One', the 'Helpful One'.

14 P. Styger, *Die römischen Katakomben*, Berlin, 1933, pp. 104–5.

15 Burials were not allowed to take place within the city walls. The area of discovery was inside the walls after the construction of the (in parts) still visible Aurelian Wall, built between AD 270 and 275.

16 M. Guarducci, *I graffiti sotto la Confessione di San Pietro in Vaticano*, II, Città del Vaticano, 1958, p. 443; cf. *ead.*, *Misteri dell'Alfabeto. Enigmistica degli antichi Cristiani*, Milan, 1993, pp. 54–60, with plates.

17 Cf. Ph. W. Comfort, *The Quest for the Original Text of the New Testament*, pp. 92–5, 109–10, with references to Herbert Hunger who was the first to recognize its early date.

18 V. Martin & J. W. B. Barns eds., *Papyrus Bodmer II, Nouvelle édition augmentée et corrigée, supplément, Évangile de Jean*, chapts. 14–21, Cologny, 1962, with plates of the complete codex.

19 Perhaps to be identified with the wider region of Gadara mentioned as the site of a miracle of Jesus, Matthew 8:28–34.

20 Cf., also generally on abbreviations, W. Wattenbach, *Anleitung zur griechischen Palaeographie*, Hildesheim, repr. 1971, p. 106. Χρονος, like Χριστος, begins with the two letters *Chi* and *Rho*.

21 For a photo and transcription, see J. Finegan, *The Archaeology of the New Testament: The Life of Jesus and the Beginning of the Early Church*, 2nd rev. ed., Princeton, 1992, p. 386.

22 P. Benoit, J. T. Milik, R. de Vaux eds., *Les grottes de Murabba'at*, DJD II, Oxford, 1961, pp. 275–7, figures 30 and 31, planches 164a and 164b.

23 As in note 22.

24 For general surveys, H. J. M. Milne, *Greek Shorthand Manuals: Syllabary and Commentary*, London, 1934, and, among others, A. Mentz, 'Geschichte und System der griechischen Tachygraphie', in *Archiv für Stenographie* 58/3, 1907, pp. 98–107, 129–45, 161–71, 204–6, 225–39; H. Boge, *Die Entzifferung griechischer Tachygraphie auf Papyri und Wachstafeln*, Giessen, 1976; C. P. Thiede, 'Schrift VII. Tachygraphie/Kurzschrift', in *Das Grosse Bibellexikon*, vol. 3, Wuppertal/Giessen, 2nd ed., 1990, pp. 1401–03; E. R. Richards, *The Secretary in the Letters of Paul*, Tübingen, 1991, pp. 26–41; C. P. Thiede., 'Shorthand Writing and the New Testament', in *id.*, *Rekindling the Word: In Search of Gospel Truth*, pp. 80–3.

25 See also G. Menci, 'Per una schedatura computerizzata dei sillabari tachigrafici', in A. Bülow-Jacobsen ed., *Proceedings of the 20th International Congress of Papyrologists*, Copenhagen, 1994, pp. 621–3.

26 Suetonius, *De vita Caesarum*, 8,3,2.

27 Tertius, who wrote St Paul's letter to the Romans (see Romans 16:22) is an obvious candidate. See, e.g., E. R. Richards, pp. 169–72. The other one is the customs official and disciple Levi-Matthew, traditionally (and again in recent scholarly literature) associated with St Matthew's Gospel. On St Matthew and shorthand, cf. among others, E. J. Goodspeed, *Matthew, Apostle and Evangelist*, Philadelphia 1959, pp. 16–17; R. H. Gundry, *The Use of the Old Testament in St Matthew's Gospel*, Leiden, 1967, pp. 182–4; B. Orchard & H. Riley, *The Order of the Synoptics*, Macon, 1987, pp. 269–73; C. P. Thiede & M. d'Ancona, op. cit. pp. 158–60.

28 Cf., among others, Ph. W. Comfort, *The Quest for the Original Text of the New Testament*, p. 111. More recently, Comfort has suggested that P2G and P2J should be dated to 'late second or third century': Ph. W. Comfort and D. P. Barrett, *The Complete Text of the Earliest New Testament Manuscripts*, Grand Rapids, 1998, p. 115.

29 B. P. Grenfell & A. S. Hunt eds., *The Oxyrhynchus Papyri Part XIII*, London, 1919, pp. 10–12, here p. 10, with plate I.

30 H. Sachs, E. Badstübner, H. Naumann, *Erklärendes Wörterbuch zur christlichen Kunst*, Leipzig/Berlin/Hanau, 1975, p. 102.

31 In '*Contra Faustum Manichaeum*', 20,6.

32 'On the Mysteries of Greek Letters'. It has survived in a Coptic manuscript, which means it must have been read among the Egyptian Christians, where, it seems, the trinitarian triangle had been particularly popular for a long time. As a matter of fact, papyrus P29 was found at the Egyptian site of Oxyrhynchus.

33 '*De Iside et Osiride*', 56.

34 Acts 17:28, a verbatim quote from Aratus, 'Phainomena' 5. Even if we should allow, for the sake of argument and against all intrinsic evidence, that St Luke invented this speech and that the book of Acts was not written before AD 62, which is its obvious date, but in the Eighties of the first century, as many scholars still maintain, the fact remains that there is a first-century Christian writing, of enormous influence wherever Christian texts were read, which quotes a Greek philosopher. The same, needless to say, applies to St Paul's quote from Callimachus, 'Eis Dia' 8, and (Pseudo-)Epimenides, 'De oraculis', in Titus 1:12 (cf. C. P. Thiede, *Ein Fisch für den römischen Kaiser ...* pp. 52–6, 224).

35 And Romans is undoubtedly a letter inspired by trinitarian thinking: cf., for example, 8:11.

36 2 Corinthians 13:13. The other one is St Matthew 28:19.

37 See plate 12.

38 Minucius Felix, 'Octavius', 9,3; 28,7; Tertullian, 'Apologia', 16,1–5.

39 Cf. Josephus, '*Contra Apionem*' 2,7:80–1; Tacitus, *Historiae* 5,3:2; 5,4:2.

40 There is a much disputed fresco in the Callisto Catacombs, from the second quarter of the third century, which some have interpreted as the crowning of Jesus with the crown of thorns. But, for that, the crowned man is too well clad – he wears the same tunic and pallium as the two other men in the scene. It looks as though he is wearing a laurel wreath and one of the men distinguishes him by holding a long staff over his head. A dove is approaching from the right. Shall we think of John the Baptist who 'marks' Jesus (Matthew 3:13–17)?

41 'Octavius', 29,6.

42 'Octavius', 29,8.

43 The shape is that of a Latin cross, 43 centimetres high, and the holes for the fastening can still be seen. Some scholars doubt that the mark was caused by a cross and suggest traces of a wall cabinet; however, the most detailed study of the case has shown that it was a cross: L. W. Barnard, 'The Cross of Herculaneum Reconsidered', in W. C. Weinreich ed., *The New Testament Age: Essays in Honor of Bo*

Reicke, vol. 1, Macon, 1984. See also G. Kroll, *Auf den Spuren Jesu*, Leipzig/Stuttgart, 11th ed., 1990, pp. 367–8.

44 Text and photos: C. P. Thiede, *Heritage of the First Christians*, pp. 93–4. It has been objected that there cannot have been such Christian palindromes at such an early date in Britain. However, the second century is of course anything but an early date. Christianity could easily have come to Britain with the first merchants after the Claudian conquest in AD 43, and it must have been a recognizable presence at the time of St Alban's martyrdom in c.AD 209 (cf. C. P. Thiede, *Religion in England*, Gütersloh, 1994, pp. 12–18). Pre-Constantinian Christian artefacts in Britain may be recognized increasingly: a challenging example is the recent discovery of the so-called 'Arthur Stone' near Tintagel. Between the first and second lines, there is a cross on the stone, and, underneath it, the letters PATERN[OSTER], 'our father', the beginning of the Lord's prayer in Latin. The three surviving letters of the first line, [AXE], have been reconstructed to read M[AX-E]NTIUS. (R. Little, 'The Arthur Stone' in: *Current Archaeology* 163 (1999), p. 278.) Maxentius was an embattled 'Augustus' of the Western Empire between 306 and 312, and he has had a bad press as the man who was defeated by Constantine at the Milvian Bridge, but he was the first of the Tertrarchs after Diocletian who stopped the persecution of the Christians. A stone erected in his honour, in south-west Britannia, would not be surprising at all. A stone dedicated to the (eastern) co-ruler Licinius was discovered only 450 yards away from the excavation site of the Arthur Stone.

45 *'occultis se notis et insignibus noscunt'*, 'Octavius', 9,2. On other supposedly secret signs and symbols, like the fish, see C. P. Thiede, *Ein Fisch für den römischen Kaiser* ... pp. 72–8.

46 Cf., among others, J. Finegan op. cit. pp. 346–8.

47 For an illustrated survey, see J. Finegan, as in note 21 above, pp. 355–74. He discusses, among other things, the controversial Talpiot and Dominus Flevit ossuaries. The X or *Chi* on its own has occasionally led scholars astray in other, non-Jewish contexts: in J. Foster's *The First Advance. Christian History I: AD 29–500*, rev. ed. by W. H. C. Friend, London, 3rd ed., 1997, p. 30, there are three photos. One of them shows a ceremonial bowl. In its middle, we see the following letters: SIC X

     SIC XX

The caption explains that 'Christians in the early centuries also liked to acknowledge their faith by putting Christian symbols on everyday objects, as here on a ring, seal, and ceremonial bowl.' However, the bowl is a so-called *'largitio'* (present) plate, dedicated to Constantine's temporary co-ruler Licinius and has no Christian connotations whatsoever. It celebrates Licinius's ten years in office, in AD 317. The 'X' signifies 'ten', the XX 'twenty', and the meaning is: 'As your [sic] first ten [X] years in office, so [sic] may be your twenty [XX] years in office'. And around the rim, we read the wish: 'O Licinius, may you always be victorious'. Cf. C. P. Thiede, *Heritage of the First Christians*, p. 118.

48 F. Strickert, *Bethsaida. Home of the Apostles*, Collegeville, 1998, pp. 149–50, with photo on p. 151.

49 Admittedly, the Herculaneum cross could be much older – AD 79 is the latest possible date. Equally, the Bethsaida cross could of course be older than AD 70.

50 As in note 48 above, p. 152.

51 B. Pixner, *Wege des Messias und Stätten der Urkirche*, Giessen/Basel, 3rd ed., 1996, p. 132.

52 B. Pixner, as in note 51 above, p. 423. Concerning the 'invincible sun', we could add that the cult of the 'Sol Invictus', succeeding to that of 'Sol Indiges' originated in Syria, not far from Bethsaida. Cf. C. P. Thiede, *Ein Fisch für den römischen Kaiser. Juden, Griechen, Römer: Die Welt des Jesus Christus*, Munich, 1998, pp. 88–9.

7   THE LASTING QUEST

1 See Selina Hastings, *Evelyn Waugh: A Biography*, paperback edition, London, 1995, pp. 538–41.

2 See chapter 1, note 26.

3 Ruth Harris, *Lourdes: Body and Spirit in the Secular Age*, London, 1999, p. 57.

4 Quoted in Adam Nicolson, *Regeneration: the Story of the Dome*, London, 1999, p. 51.

5 London, Weidenfeld & Nicolson, 1996; paperback, with new afterword: London, Orion, 1997, p. 195.

6 See Stephen Neill and Tom Wright, *The Interpretation of the New Testament 1861–1986*, 2nd ed., Oxford, 1988.

7 Ian Wilson, *The Blood and the Shroud*, London, 1998.

8 Wilson, op. cit., p. 239.

9 U. Victor, 'Was ein Texthistoriker zur Entstehung der Evangelien sagen kann', in *Biblica* 79, 1998, pp. 499–513. See also Thiede & d'Ancona, op. cit., p. 140 ff.

10 See K. K. Ruthven, *Myth*, London, 1976, p. 5 ff.

11 See I. Ramelli, 'Petronio e i Cristiani', in *Aevum* 70, 1996, pp. 75–80; C. P. Thiede, *Ein Fisch für den römischen Kaiser* ... pp. 110–34, also on the Greek author Chariton of Aphrodisias and his borrowing from Matthew's Gospel.

12 So again during a panel discussion on Qumran Cave 7 at the Notre Dame Centre Jerusalem on 3 January 1999.

13 H. Koskenniemi, 'Uutta tietoa evankeliumien syntyajoista' in *Sanansaattaja* 23, 1996, p. 4; *id.*, 'Vielä Matteusken evankeliumin syntyajasta', in *Sanansaattaja* 32, 1996, p. 8.

14 J. M. Vernet, 'Si riafferma il papiro 7Q5 come Mc 6, 52–53?' in *Rivista Biblica* 46, 1998, pp. 43–60.

15 For a recent survey, see H.-J. Schulz, *Die apostolische Herkunft der Evangelien*, Freiburg/Basel/Wien, 2nd rev. ed., 1997. The scene was set, of course, without reference to papyri, by J. A. T. Robinson, op. cit. and the magisterial commentary on St Matthew's Gospel by Robert Gundry: R. H. Gundry, *Matthew: A Commentary on his Handbook for a Mixed Church under Persecution*, Grand Rapids, 2nd rev. ed., 1994, pp. 609–23.

16 In a recent article on P64, T. C. Skeat ignored the evidence, stuck to the old Greek reading and claimed that he had discovered that P64, P67 and the Paris codex of St Luke's Gospel, P4, once belonged to a second–third century 'four Gospel codex' (T. C. Skeat, 'The Oldest Manuscript of the Four Gospels', in *New Testament Studies* 43, 1997, pp. 1–34). This interpretation was followed by Graham Stanton ('The Fourfold Gospel', in *New Testament Studies* 43, 1997, pp. 320–51). These theories are ruled out by the obvious fact that P4 (Luke) on the one hand and P64/P67 (Matthew) on the other were written on a different type of papyrus and according to different scribal rules, even if perhaps by the same scribe. And if we assume, against the evidence and for the sake of argument, that these papyri did once form one codex, where is any evidence for a *four* Gospel codex? There is no trace whatsoever of a similar-looking papyrus of St Mark's and St John's Gospel anywhere in the vicinity of P4 and P64/P67. As for the new, improved reading of St Matthew 26:22 in P64, the decisive evidence was produced – against Skeat et al., under a confocal laser-scanning microscope, and the publication of this analysis has met with universal approval: C. P. Thiede & G. Masuch, 'Neue mikroskopische Verfahren zum Lesen und zur Schadensbestimmung von Papyrushandschriften', in B. Kramer, W. Luppe, H. Maehler, G. Poethke eds., *Akten des 21. Internationalen Papyrologenkongresses*, Berlin, 1995, Stuttgart/Leipzig, 1997, pp. 1102–12, with plates 5–7.

17 Quoted in Ben Rogers, *A. J. Ayer: A Life*, London, 1999, p. 45.

18 Quoted in John Wilkinson, *Jerusalem as Jesus Knew It: Archaeology as Evidence*, London, 1978, p. 199.

INDEX